The Keynesian Fallout

The Keynesian Fallout

Narindar Singh

Sage Publications
New Delhi/Thousand Oaks/London

Copyright © Narindar Singh, 1996

First published in 1996 by

Sage Publications India Pvt Ltd
M–32, Greater Kailash Market–I
New Delhi 110 048

Sage Publications Inc
2455 Teller Road
Thousand Oaks, California 91320

Sage Publications Ltd
6 Bonhill Street
London EC2A 4PU

Published by Tejeshwar Singh for Sage Publications India Pvt Ltd, Phototypeset by Line Arts Phototypesetters, Pondicherry and printed at Chaman Enterprises, Delhi.

Library of Congress Cataloging-in-Publication Data

Narindar Singh.
   The Keynesian fallout/Narindar Singh.
     p. cm.
   Includes bibliographical references and index.
    1. Keynesian economics. 2. Employment (Economic theory) 3. Public works.
    4. Totalitarianism. 5. Economics—Moral and ethical aspects. I. Title.
   HB99.7.N37   330. 15′6—dc20   1996   95–25765

ISBN: 0–8039–9277–7 (US–hb)   81–7036–511–2 (India–hb)
        0–8039–9278–5 (US–pb)   81–7036–512–0 (India–pb)

Sage Production Editors: Khorshed Chandra and Evellyn George

To
Beant
My wife
For sustaining me through the decades
And to our children
As also to our grandchildren
Kavindar, Avanindar and Amitoj

No more than one or a few decades remain before the chance to avert the threats we now confront will be lost and the prospects for humanity immeasurably diminished.*

* From the 'World Scientists' Warning to Humanity' released by the Union of Concerned Scientists on 17 November 1992.

We are all in the gutter, but some of us are looking at the stars.

Oscar Wilde (1970: 54)

My conscience is the genuine pulpit article: it annoys me to see people comfortable when they ought to be uncomfortable; and I insist on making them think in order to bring them to conviction of sin. If you dont like my preaching you must lump it. I really cannot help it.

George Bernard Shaw (1962b: 486)

I *want*, so to speak, to raise a dust; because it is only out of the controversy that will arise that what I am saying will get understood.

John Maynard Keynes (K-XIII: 548)*

The test of a man's Liberalism today must not be his attitude towards the questions which were important a generation ago, but to those which are most important to the generation coming.

John Maynard Keynes (K-XIX: 648)

* Page 548 of Volume XIII of *The Collected Writings of John Maynard Keynes*, Macmillan, London. Except once on page 165 this is the way that Keynes is cited throughout this essay.

Contents

Foreword

In the early 1970s, the late Joan Robinson tried to alert the economics profession to what she described as 'the second crisis' facing economic theory. The first crisis she identified was the one that formed the backdrop to the Keynesian revolution, 'the breakdown of a theory which could not account for the *level* of employment.' 'The second crisis', she said, 'arises from a theory that cannot account for the *content* of employment.'

In this book, Professor Narindar Singh, taking the cue from Joan Robinson, deals with the third crisis in the series—the problem of 'misemployment' which arises when state spending, on the basis of the Keynesian doctrine, attempts to raise the level of employment but remains indifferent to the content of employment. He cites as examples employment in the armaments industry and in a wide range of industries that produce goods of doubtful usefulness or that result in the generation of pollution. Since both arms and pollution threaten human lives and pose serious threats to the very survival of the human species on the planet Earth, they must be considered as 'bads' instead of 'goods.' Misemployment, thus, is also the misdirection of the finite resources of the planet, and that too on a massive scale. Unknown to most human beings, but thanks to the profit-seeking producers, the constantly persuading and pressurizing advertisers, the high profile policy makers and the prestigious intellectual support of the economists, humanity is being rapidly driven to perdition. It is this unprecedented crisis, or this serious crime, that Narindar Singh holds Keynes responsible for. In *The Keynesian Fallout*, therefore, the author tries 'to make Maynard Keynes face a kind of critique the like of which he may not have faced before' as he puts it.

The work is addressed primarily to economists, though the author is eager that others too should listen to him because of 'the sheer

globality and gravity of the issues involved.' He has, therefore, tried
to use a jargon-free idiom. True, he avoids much of the professional
jargon of economists, but the idiom he uses is highly personalized
and his style is allusive though evocative. In order therefore not to
miss the thrust of his presentation, readers may find it helpful to think
of what lies before them as the proceedings of a trial of war criminals,
some dead, some alive. Imagine that Narindar Singh is the prosecution
attorney in this public interest case and is addressing himself to the
jury. Fortunately, he begins with his concluding statement which is
presented in the Preface. Hence, I recommend a careful reading of it
to readers, specially those who usually dismiss the preface to a book
as a bit of a private chat on the part of the author before he enters
into serious stuff. In this case, the Preface *is* the stuff, the rest being
a record of the examination of the accused and of the evidence
presented. The polemics of the text is often impatient and trenchant
in tone. But, as the author says, 'it is the nature of the message which
informs the tone and not the tone the message.'

Though the crime is against the whole of humanity, of the present
and of the future, the court scene is set firmly and almost exclusively
in the United States of America, with evidence drawn from its rulers
and government, from its cities and slums, its clubs and universities,
its publications and TV shows. Readers must be prepared to orient
themselves to such a scene.

Keynes, of course, is Accused Number One. The accusation begins
on a low key, finding fault with Keynes for 'two schoolboy bloomers'
in his understanding of Voltaire. But soon he is accused of being
fixated on the short run to the point of being actually contemptuous
of long-term concerns; of being superficial without any concern at all
with the deeper problems of existence; of failing to note that exponential growth of output would lead to an equally exponential exhaustion of the mineral reserves of the Earth and the erosion of its
life-support systems; of being a self-proclaimed immoralist who refused to recognize any moral obligation or to obey any inner sanction;
of not having or developing a critical consciousness that enables one
to perceive the true meaning of the counter-existential pursuits and
propensities of the managers of the status quo. He is accused, most
of all, of generating the third crisis as a direct consequence of the
remedies he had proposed for the first.

The second accused is Adolf Hitler. And why? Well, didn't Hitler
start a programme of 'public works,' including preparations for war,

as the way out of an economic depression even *before* Keynes started preaching it? And, didn't he also get his men to dig holes of a sort, and fill them up somewhere along the line? And didn't Keynes himself say in the Preface to the German edition of *The General Theory* that 'in offering a theory of employment and output as a whole, which departs in important respects from the orthodox tradition' he might expect 'less resistance from German, than from English readers' and that his theory was 'much more easily adapted to the conditions of a totalitarian state'? The Nazis made death and destruction into a veritable industry. But 'it turns into no more than a muffled whisper in comparison with the orgy of death, destruction and waste unleashed by their liberal superseders everywhere.' Much of the world, the United States particularly, is now governed by those who owe allegiance to Keynes, the adviser and Hitler, the practitioner. The liberal vanquishers of the totalitarian Hitler have brought the human race to a point where its very existence has become threatened with termination, concludes the attorney.

In turning to the third accused, Narindar Singh says: 'If someone were to ask me to choose one, just one, legatee of what I like to call the Keynes–Hitler sodality, I would without a moment's hesitation choose Professor Paul Anthony Samuelson of the MIT.' Since he is the only living one among the three main accused, our attorney has taken up issues directly with him. The trial documents deal with these person-to-person encounters where the attorney begins with some of the minor crimes, a couple of distorted quotations in Samuelson's *Economics* and even in one of his scientific papers which assume significance because of his proclamation once that he dislikes being wrong. But more serious accusations are in store. Samuelson personifies the ideology of the Keynes–Hitler sodality and has succeeded, primarily through his widely used textbook, to put a thick and not easily penetrable gloss over it. He has done this by projecting the image of a mixed economy, of market spending by the people at large and of public spending by the State and thus sustaining without breakdown the elaborate economic processes of a highly complex economy such as that of the United States. In so doing he cleverly hides the fact that the mixed economy rapidly becomes one of private appropriation of benefits and the public assumption of costs, often of reckless costs generated by the rich and the powerful. Samuelson also glorifies the role of spending in the economy, forgetting that how it impacts the economy depends much on the specific instances of spending. Where a great deal of spending is incurred on weapons, on entitlements for the well-to-do, and on bailouts for unscrupulous financial operators, the mixed economy becomes a mixed-up economy. And, in any case, spending can be only by those who can afford to spend. What about the many who constitute America's domestic Third World—those who lie beyond the bounds of Samuelson's concern?

Samuelson is also guilty of callous indifference to the perils of military inexorability. To him the Vietnam War was only a form of public spending that America could well afford, a position that made him completely insensitive 'to the deliberately genocidal decimation of the Vietnamese as also to the process of the virtually open-ended weaponization of America.' And, wasn't it also Samuelson who took over the Hitler–Göring guns–butter duality ('Guns will make us powerful; butter will only make us fat') and converted it into the basic trade-off problem in economics? 'If we are willing to give up some butter, we can have some guns; if we are willing to give up still more butter, we can have still more guns.' This is the dictum that students of economics all over the world are made to believe as the basic premise of the science of economics.

Narindar Singh, attorney *pro bono publico* builds up his case step by step, point by point, using all the skills and techniques at his disposal. The experts he invokes are many; the evidence he presents is massive. He taunts and he teases. He is shrill and he is sharp. He appeals to the mind and appeals to the heart; he is convinced of the cause he is championing and of the gravity of the issues at stake.

Because Professor Narindar Singh has taken up this case on behalf of all of us, we must give him a patient hearing.

Madras Institute of Development Studies   **C.T. Kurien**
Madras

Preface

> I have painted the prospect in the blackest colours. What is there to be said on the other side? What elements of hope can we discern in the surrounding gloom? And what useful action does it still lie in our power to take?
>
> John Maynard Keynes (K-XXI: 54)

However, what Keynes took to have been the blackest colours appear *at least now* to have been no more than the greyest of grey. Instead, it is the *prospect itself* which has become the darkest conceivable. The reason? The historically unique threat of extinction which we as a race have come to confront. Therefore, the colours we need to paint the prospect *now* would have to be even blacker than those which Keynes thought were the blackest. For his problematic was no more serious than *cyclical unemployment*, ours no less daunting than *chronic misemployment*. Besides, while the former came never to spell the *possible* termination of human history, the latter does little else.

This is the reason why this essay seeks to change the very problematic of macroeconomic research from mere cyclical unemployment to chronic misemployment. Indeed, if the question of misemployment had been as inconsequential as Keynes claimed it was, we would not be facing such menacing problems as global warming, ozone depletion, deforestation, soil dissipation, garbage accumulation and so on. In other words, the crisis of global ecology is not cyclical but chronic in nature and can only get exacerbated by the Keynesian remedies. This calls for nothing less than a 'paradigm shift' in the sense in which Thomas Kuhn uses the term.

But given his well-known fixation on the short run and the concomitant disdain for the long, even a self-proclaimed Cassandra like

Keynes could not anticipate any serious long-run problem with the prevailing order, much less foresee the kind of existential predicament which defines our time. No wonder, he could not possibly avoid prescribing short-run solutions which would before long congeal into long-run problems. This indictment of Keynes cannot be emphasized too strongly and is indeed basic to my argument.

Be that as it may, since it is primarily concerned with the long-run catastrophe produced very largely by short-sighted Keynesianism, this essay is not intended to stop with John Maynard Keynes. It is intended instead to *begin* with him. Or, rather, with some of the more important ideas which, to the escalating applause of the Uncritical, he came to articulate over the years.

Standard economists could well dismiss this as an unpardonable overstatement. But, undaunted by his formidable reputation as the greatest economist of the twentieth century, I have decided to try to make Maynard Keynes face a kind of critique the like of which he may not have faced before. Audacious that it may well be, such a project still seems to me to be eminently in order and perfectly executable, too. Besides, the need for a critique of this kind inheres, to my mind, in the nature of the prevailing situation. Which happens to be too grim to permit any overstatement or exaggeration and to the precipitation and the gravity of which Keynesianism can be seen to have made no mean contribution.

Unlike Paul Baran and Paul Sweezy (1968: viii), therefore, one need not plead guilty to the charge of exaggeration. For given the threat of extinction which this essay is focused on, one cannot even indulge in the luxury of exaggeration, no matter how hard one tried. Besides, to paraphrase Lord Shackleton (1977: 16–17), in a situation as menacing as ours, what appear to be overstatements today have a strong tendency to become understatements tomorrow so that the question of an intellectual overkill can never arise.

It follows that in a situation like this, one can hardly avoid being a bit impatient and trenchant in tone. But given the inherent fundamentality of one's message, one need only ensure the cogency of one's argument; and *that*, hopefully, I have been able to do: with the result that it is the *message* of this essay which has come to inform its tone and not the tone the message. *That is, its tone is not just a matter of one's taste nor style, but is, above all, a manifestation of the gravity of the prevailing crisis.*

It annoys me no less than it annoyed George Bernard Shaw, for one, to see people contented and comfortable when they ought to be discontented and uncomfortable. In particular, because the Union of Concerned Scientists tells us that our race doesn't have more than a few decades left to mend its ways. By April 1993, as many as 104 Nobel Prize winners—a majority of the living laureates in the sciences—and some 1,570 other eminent scientists worldwide had signed this 'Warning to Humanity' which began as follows: 'Human beings and the natural world are on a collision course. Human activities inflict harsh and often irreversible damage on the environment and on critical resources. If not checked, many of our current practices put at serious risk the future that we wish for human society and the plant and animal kingdoms, and may so alter the living world that it will be unable to sustain life in the manner that we know. Fundamental changes are urgent if we are to avoid the collision our present course will bring about.' It seems quite in order, therefore, to undertake an in-depth examination of the prevailing situation as also of the reigning orthodoxies used to gloss it, prominent among which is Keynesianism broadly understood.

This explains why a major part of this essay would be concerned with some of the ominous consequences of John Maynard Keynes. It is these which I have designated as the Keynesian fallout. Which to my mind manifests itself in the reckless pursuits of the military-industrialism of our time. But recklessness and overreaching are nothing but two sides of the same semantic coin. And, as the evocative Greek myth of Icarus shows, overreaching can end only in the annihilation of the overreacher. This simply means that, if not stemmed in time, the Keynes-oriented pursuits of the military-industrialism now rampant in the world cannot but spell an inexorable paralysis of our habitat and therefore the extinction of our species, too.

The point of it all is that the contemporary Western civilization, which we in the East appear hell-bent on aping, is a perfect recipe for disaster and the sooner mankind made what Edward Goldsmith calls the Great U-Turn the better would it be.

I do like to believe that my argument would be of considerable interest even to people who are not economists. But still, it is addressed more directly to those who are. For it is intended largely to persuade *them* to re-examine the very axioms of what they take to be a science but which to me is anything but. Even so, given the sheer globality and the gravity of the issues involved, my essay, I hope, will find an audience far beyond the traditional confines of economics. In particular, because of the jargon-free idiom in which it has been couched.

It seems to me that a most effective way to dispel the illusions produced by mainline economics these days would be to examine the ominous fallout of the supposedly revolutionary economics of John Maynard Keynes. Central to this economics is the role assigned to the manipulation of a *quantity* called Effective Demand. I say 'quantity' because the quality or the precise composition of what is taken to be Effective Demand is not a concern of the Keynesians nor ever was of Keynes himself. Orgiastic consumption, orgiastic military spending and orgiastic investment in life-threatening industries would all be welcome if only they could raise Effective Demand to a level high enough to ensure what is known as Full Employment. Neither the economists nor the policy makers seem to stop for a moment to see that the employment in question could in fact be gross misemployment and also that frenzied spending, whether on consumption or on weapons, would perforce be doing exceeding damage to human ecology, both national and global.

This is the fallout, which literally means debris, produced by the so-called Keynesian revolution that this essay is primarily meant to examine. It is easy to see that the practitioners of Keynesianism share with Keynes himself their over-reduced perceptions. But these perceptions, no matter how reduced, produce ample material rewards for the privileged minorities at least, though only for the time being. The beneficiaries, therefore cannot but seek untold delight in taking part in what Nicholas Georgescu-Roegen (1974: 330) calls 'the Square Dance of Effective Demand.' And a Square Dance it is in the literal sense of the term, too. For those taking part in it are unwaveringly fixated on what lies within the ambit of their immediate concerns. In consequence, therefore, they are either not aware of or are not concerned with a rapidly precipitating planetary breakdown. What we are confronting, then, is a potential threat of the termination of our history itself: a kind of threat we have never faced before in all our evolutionary past. This is the alarming and unignorable crux of our existential situation today: a fundamental novelty, indeed, if ever there was one. Indifference towards this novelty could only spell little but a state of terminal smugness.

Besides, a very large part of at least the moral responsibility for the predicament we are in falls directly on the shoulders of the man called John Maynard Keynes. That is why I have given his name to the prevailing situation this essay is concerned with and why it is his work which I refer to far more extensively than anyone else's.

Needless to say, the cerebrations of a man like Paul Samuelson manifest a continuation of Keynesianism in our own time so that an analysis of the Keynesian fallout could not be complete without an examination of the Samuelsonian world-view. No wonder that Samuelson figures in this book more prominently than any other mainline economist after Keynes. But he figures in it not as Samuelson *per se*, but as an embodiment of a world-view which to my mind has lost its basic validity.

Besides, since this essay seeks quite explicitly and exclusively to examine the lethal fallout of military-industrialism, it is not even intended to provide an alternative to the prevailing order. And certainly, it would be beyond the power of any individual no matter how talented or even gifted, to provide the blueprint of such an alternative. To ask for it therefore would be to ask for the impossible. It could well mean tempting one to begin chasing a red herring, too. For the central task of our time is *not* the articulation of a viable vision of the future. The central task instead is to so stem the catastrophic *drift* of the present, to so impede it, that the future becomes possible. Indeed, once it becomes possible, the future will itself take care of its precise configuration. And if enough care is not taken to make it possible, anything done to prepare a blueprint of it would be an exercise in futility.

It is to avoid undertaking precisely such an exercise that we would do well to focus on the dangers inherent in what Georgescu-Roegen (1974: 329) calls 'the fallacy of the industrialization axiom.' We would do well also to focus on the nature of the perils involved in the fallacy of the security-through-weapons axiom. It is only when these two overarching fallacies of the present age come to be seen for what they are that a chain reaction of awareness, as Albert Einstein once termed it, could be expected to begin.

In a context like this, Keynes, in particular because of his pre-eminence in the economics profession, could only be a convenient peg to hang one's argument on. Which, thus hung, would seek to highlight the perils of shortsightedness—that of Keynes and of the economics profession as a whole and that of the contemporary pyramids of power as well.

Indeed, this immanent shortsightedness informs or rather deforms the contemporary civilization *per se*: a civilization which happens to be the very first 'now' civilization (Ornstein and Ehrlich 1989: 158) in history. That is, what we have is a civilization hooked irrevocably on the most immediate present, the *now*, and as such it can spare but little thought even for the immediate let alone a distant future. No wonder that the short-sightedness of the economics profession is not a latter-day phenomenon at all but has evolved instead with the now-civilization itself. Which also explains why it has long continued in the form of partial perceptions of reality which the economists in particular have taken care to cultivate and promote. For instance, Thomas Arnold, an early nineteenth-century historian [and Matthew Arnold's father], came to dismiss Ricardian economics as a whole as no more than a one-eyed endeavour (Georgescu-Roegen 1986: 253).

A specific instance of one-eyed intellection is what Professor Samuelson calls 'revealed preference.' According to him, consumers' preferences which happen to be entirely unobservable in themselves still get revealed by the choices they make. But no matter how enormously profound this insight, it fails altogether to reveal anything about the self-destructive momentum of a present-day consumer society like the United States. Nor does it reveal a thing about a society—again, like the United States—addicted to virtually open-ended weaponization. Therefore, it seems perfectly in order to dismiss this concept, if a bit impishly, as follows:

An eminent Don of MassTech
Has invented a thing called Revealed Pref.
But in the over-revealed Pref. for Arms
He sees no possible source of harm.
For in all the orgies of the Pentagon
He finds nothing but a relentless growth Amazon.

But, then, one-eyedery has become in our own time what it could not possibly have been in David Ricardo's: something exceedingly dangerous. The very ultimate perils which it now congeals are manifested in the single-minded concerns of the military and industrial managers alike. And it is in more or less completely ignoring these concerns and their catastrophic implications that the economists themselves come to cultivate one-eyedism as a metaphysical principle of over-arching importance. But while this principle entails an abstraction

from all the grim *essentials* of the prevailing situation, it also entails
a remorseless pursuit of *inessentials*, of distractions, of all sorts of
red herrings.

Evidently, an argument like this must by its very nature be exceedingly controversial. But one couldn't help it. In any case, Keynes was
no stranger to controversy. As he himself put it in the preface to *The
General Theory*: 'Those who are strongly wedded to what I shall call
"the classical theory," will fluctuate, I expect, between a belief that
I am quite wrong and a belief that I am saying nothing new. It is for
others to determine if either of these or the third alternative is right.
My controversial passages are aimed at providing some material for
an answer; and I must ask forgiveness if, in the pursuit of sharp
distinctions, my controversy is itself too keen.' And, then, he went
on to add the following: 'I myself held with conviction for many years
the theories which I now attack, and I am not, I think, ignorant of
their strong points' (K-VII: xxi).

But, alas, there is no such reservation with which *I* can qualify my
critique of Keynesianism, or for that matter of economysticism as a
whole. For economics happens to be conditioned by a world-view
which is not just reductionist but over-reductionist in nature and by
this token alone it is not just misleading but grossly misleading.
Indeed, as we shall see in Chapter 4, even mechanics, which is the
very ultimate exemplar of reduction in normal science, is not remotely
as reductionist as economics, Keynesianism included.

A particularly glaring instance of the kind of over-reductionism
practised by the economics profession is the economics of an illusion
called growth. Illusion, because in getting fixated on a one-
dimensional figure, the economists manage somehow not to see the
inexorable, escalating and unsustainable consumption of the terrestrial
capital taking place simultaneously with what they take to be growth.
Nor do they bother about many of the components of the 'growing'
output being inherently eco-disruptive. But a theory of growth to be
at all meaningful, could ill-afford to ignore the qualitative changes
taking place in the human habitat over time on account of a relentless
depletion of resources and a simultaneous release of a variety of
pollutants and toxic products into the environment: exactly what the
mainline growth theory does manage to ignore. No wonder that
Wilfred Beckerman (1972: 337–38), for instance, could insist that we
as a race should learn to do without such resources as keep disappearing. Besides, one day, according to him, it might become possible to

mine the Earth *to a depth of one mile at every point in its crust* so
that the actual reserves might turn out to be one million times as large
as those which are now known to be available. Therefore, and entirely
unbothered by the seismic and other consequences of such a literal
kind of an Earth-eating exercise, Beckerman claimed that by the time
we reach AD 100, 000, 000, 'we will think up something'.

Robert Solow's dismissal of the resources problem is equally ama-
zing: growth does not even need any resources, he says. Indeed,
growth to him seems to be no more than a mere word symbolized by
the letter 'g.' Which, undeterred by a deteriorating habitat, he can
manipulate the way he likes. And, believe it or not, that alone is the
reason why he can manage to assure us that given the substitutability
of what he calls 'other factors' for 'natural resources,' we do not 'in
principle' face any problem. Besides, without caring to specify what
these other factors could be, he makes the following declaration: 'The
world can, in effect, get along *without natural resources*, so exhaustion
is just an event, not a catastrophe' (Solow 1974: 11; emphasis mine).
In sum, Solow's isolation of growth from such 'extraneous' considerations as the unending consumption of the terrestrial capital, as
also from the depletion of the stratospheric ozone, is one of the more
deplorable instances of the wrong kind of mechanics deployed by
the economics profession these days. No wonder that a mere word
called growth is given precedence over the attenuation of the ozone
shield.

But neither Beckerman, nor Solow, nor to my knowledge anyone
else tells us what to substitute for the disappearing forests, topsoil,
ozone and, above all, biodiversity itself. Incidentally, the protective
ozone shield over the heavily populated latitudes of the northern
hemisphere is now known to be thinning twice as fast as scientists
thought it was just a few years ago (Postel 1992: 3).

But the economists manage to ignore such threats, no matter how
menacing, with the help of the *ceteris paribus* formula: a formula
which can play an indispensable role only in a study of situations
which can be *reduced* to mechanistic dimensions but must necessarily
play a counter-productive role in a study of those situations which do
not admit of such reduction. This is an adaptation of a point which
Georgescu-Roegen (1974: 203) once made. But its implications are
much starker than those of his. For the universe which economics
purports to deal with is *not*, contrary to what Georgescu-Roegen
presumes, undergoing any evolution at all, except in the very

superficial sense that with the passage of time, the economic process has continued to become ever more *complex*. But 'evolution' also signifies 'an opening out', 'an unfolding', 'an expansion'. Opposed to 'evolution' in this sense is 'involution' which signifies, among other things, 'a curling inwards', 'a contraction'. Ironically, carried away by economic evolution in the narrow, superficial and unsustainable sense, the economics profession manages to elide the stark and menacing reality of economic *involution*. Which an unending destruction of resources and an unprecedented extinction of species of different life forms cannot but entail.

Ours has come to be known as the Age of Extinction—biotic extinction, that is. Which happens to be one of the more serious existential problems of today. To give a round number guesstimate, species extinction *among birds and mammals* may already be taking place, or would soon be, at a rate 100 times the average level of the past 50 million years (Ehrlich 1986: 158). But taking life as a whole, a minimum of 140 plant and animal species are condemned to extinction every day (Postel 1992: 3). This argues a disastrous loss of biodiversity which, to put it extremely mildly, does not bode well for the future of our race. But I do not know of any professional economist having become concerned with what this could mean—concerned, that is, with the economic causes and perilous consequences of this phenomenon.

No wonder, then, that with Asia, Europe and the United States taken together continuing to lose more than 27, 000 *million* metric tons of topsoil every year through erosion (Myers 1985: 40): with the world as a whole continuing to extract some 50, 000 *million* metric tons of minerals every year from the Earth's crust (George 1990: 439): with tropical rainforests likely to disappear altogether by AD 2057 (Guppy 1984: 929): with remorseless destruction of biodiversity caused by the cutting and burning of forests (Ehrlich 1991: 31): with the greenhouse gases *already* injected into the atmosphere over the past two centuries likely to cause the world's average temperature to rise from one to four degrees Celsius over the next fifty to seventy years (Jones and Wigley 1990: 84): with ozone depletion threatening to cause nothing less than the very end of civilization itself (Edelson 1989: 63): even the possibility of economic evolution in any meaningful sense of the term is unthinkable. Instead, it is involution and involution *alone* which stares us menacingly in the face.

All things, *or rather the existential conditions of today*, continue to get *worse*. They cannot possibly be taken to remain unchanged. Besides, they belong to an unboundable universe to which we can assign nothing but *omnibus peioribus* as a name. And this Latin expression translates as 'all things getting worse'. It would be an act of extreme folly to try to force all things which are getting worse—*omnibus peioribus*—into what Alfred Marshall (1974: 304) thought to be 'a pound called *Coeteris Paribus*'. The folly would be macabre, too, because, to coin an Orwellian expression, it makes us 'unsee' some of the most critical problems that bedevil us today.

The *ceteris paribus* formula has been justified on the ground that 'any practicable theory must take for granted the stability and continuance of certain background circumstances' (Whitaker 1987: 396). Once in a while, though, even a mainline economist may come to admit that 'theorists can always resist facts' and also that *ceteris paribus* can be made to absorb a good deal of punishment'. None other than Paul Samuelson (1979: 893) has made this point which, nevertheless, he follows up with the following assertion: 'Inevitably, at the earliest opportunity, the mind slips back into the old grooves of thought since analysis is utterly impossible without a frame of reference, a way of thinking about things, or in short a theory'. Nevertheless, his reason for refusing to throw the old theory away simply won't wash in the new situation: facts may well be changing always; still such facts as define our historically unique predicament *today* are *not* that 'hard to establish'. Besides, it is their sheer novelty which renders utterly obsolete and irrelevant the *old* frame of reference, the *old* way of thinking about things, or in short the *old* theory. In other words, the existential crisis of today is so exceedingly grave that the stability and continuance of the background circumstances which Whitaker insists upon, and the immutability of the old frame of reference which Samuelson finds indispensable, can no longer be allowed to stand in the way of an examination of the *bona fides* of the prevailing order. For in refusing to let our habitual beliefs be shaken into doubt by existential novelty, 'we either do no thinking at all, or our thinking, such as it is, has a routine character' (Cohen and Nagel 1968: 199). Therefore, a decision to ignore the new conditions altogether or even consciously to impound them within the enclosure called *ceteris paribus* can only signify a kind of psychic timidity which Byron at least would be delighted to describe as 'intellectual eunuchery'. Little wonder that very richly endowed with this very special gift that they are:

> Throngs of economists, throughout the crisis,
> Have done nothing in particular,
> And've done it very well:
> *Yet* MIT sets the world ablaze
> In good Doctor Solow's glorious days!

I only hope that W.S. Gilbert won't start turning in his grave for the liberty I have taken with the famous lines he once composed:

> The House of Peers, throughout the war,
> Did nothing in particular,
> And did it very well:
> Yet Britain set the world ablaze
> In good King George's glorious days!

But good Doctor Solow's glory and the glory of many of those whom Joan Robinson once (1973: 92) described as 'superfluous economists' lies in soaring to a stratosphere of pure theory where they become completely desensitized to the problems of this tormented planet and of the hapless people who inhabit it.

But even when they are not entirely desensitized, they fail generally to comprehend the true gravity of these problems. Keynes, in any case. '[We] are in deep water' he once (K-VII: 183) affirmed. But then, the 'we' became a wild duck which had dived down to the bottom—as deep as she could get—and had 'bitten fast hold of the weed and tangle and all the rubbish' down there so that 'it would need an extraordinarily clever dog to dive after and fish her up again'. But having put the 'we' in deep water in the form of the wild duck: in other words, having identified mankind *as a whole* as 'the wild duck', Keynes failed to realize that there would not be any dog available, extraordinarily clever or only ordinarily so, to fish her up again. Or rather fish *us* up again. Besides, even if such a dog were in fact available, he would fish us up only in order to hand us over to the duck hunter. **In other words, even if some extraordinarily clever policy makers did tide us over a given crisis, they could not but create a far more tenacious fallout of long-run problems. This, I would be arguing, was to turn out to be the essential bane of Keynesianism.**

But worse still, Keynes, no matter how macrocosmic he took his concerns to be, did *not* have a comprehensive enough vision. No wonder that he failed to see the market economy tending towards 'complete collapse'. Rather, according to him, capitalism was 'subject to severe fluctuations in respect of output and employment' all right, but was not 'violently unstable'. Finally, he saw little more wrong with it than an inherent tendency to remain 'in a chronic condition of sub-normal activity for a considerable period' (K-VII: 249).

Per contra, I submit that, if anything, the 'system' does have a marked tendency towards complete collapse, not long-term stability. With the kind of inherently unsustainable resource-prodigality literally programmed into its basic structure, it could hardly be otherwise. And the situation now happens to be much, much worse than what Keynes could possibly have imagined. To cite a particularly egregious instance: Motor vehicles of the metropolitan San Francisco, according to the figures supplied to me by the Transport Commission of that region, consumed during the calendar year 1989 over three billion gallons of petrol and diesel. The roughly corresponding figure for the *whole of India* happens to be some two-and-a-half billion [American] gallons.

This is not to say that India is consuming too little of fossil oil but rather that San Francisco is consuming too much of it. With a public transport system virtually non-existent, it could hardly do otherwise. Or, perhaps, to encourage it to continue with its prodigality, a sturdy enough public transport system has not even been allowed to come into being. On 6 June 1992, a Bay Area newspaper, *San Ramon Valley Times*, reported that Michael Barkley of Manteca, who commutes daily to San Ramon, had filed a lawsuit against San Joaquin and Stanislaus counties, charging that they were spending money lavishly on widening the roads and fixing the potholes but nothing at all on buses. Counties of the Bay Area itself and indeed of the rest of the United States too could be accused of a similar hostility towards public transport. Nor is such hostility a very recent phenomenon. In fact, Ornstein and Ehrlich (1989: 77) cite an even more glaring instance of the deliberate crippling of public transport in the United States. Shortly before the Second World War began, they say, people with stake in the automobile industry decided to have the Los Angeles area's very effective public transport system *actually dismantled*. Los Angeles did become crowded with cars as a result and, in due course, it did also come to be known for its smog in order to produce which, as it were, it cannot but have made a major contribution to a relentless running down of a non-renewable source of energy.

It follows that with oil reserves bound to disappear sooner rather than later, an inexorably prodigal society like the United States is destined *only* to collapse. There is nothing that can make it last for a historically significant span of time. Nor is there anything which can sustain for much longer the military-industrial civilization itself of which the metropolitan San Francisco and Los Angeles are but the most telling exemplars.

In fact, even this side of that *ultimate* crisis of the military-industrial civilization, whatever—just whatever—its managers do to solve its immediate problems, happens only to be depletive of the planet's resources and disruptive of its biosphere as well. It can therefore spell nothing but unrelenting atrophy of the system. Which, therefore, cannot even be described as properly and inherently systematic and rational. In a paper on 'Land Warfare', which he wrote in 1971 but which having remained classified could not get published for many years, Norman Augustine (1986: 510) made the point that, as on 18 April 2036, the US Air Force would consist of precisely *one* airplane. Besides, he said, the continuing escalation of costs over time would oblige the US Air Force to share this plane with the US Navy for three days a week; and further, that all this economizing would enable it to get a duplicate copy of the machine only once in 15 years. Similarly, according to Augustine, the US armoured forces would have been reduced to possessing just one tank by the year 2027. He is now reported to have said that because of a further acceleration of the cost-escalation process, the one-plane situation would come to precipitate by the year 2020 itself (Romm 1992: 15).

Augustine should know. For he has spent a lifetime in the arms business and is now going to be the president of the recently merged company called Lockheed Martin—the largest military contractor the world has ever known. True that his calculations are based on the rather wild assumption that the Pentagon budget would be held constant at the 1971 level. But the point involved here is *not* that the US military spending would or even could be held constant at the 1971 or the 1995 level. To my mind, involved here is the implication, which must have been far from Augustine's mind, that decisions to acquire more and more of weapons in future would spell far more than proportional increases in the burdens imposed on what Noam Chomsky (1993: 275) calls America's 'Third World at Home'. This only means that the intensifying military mania, particularly in view of the accompanying technological sophistication, would not only fail to generate new jobs directly but would also cause an indiscriminate destruction of jobs indirectly, particularly in America's domestic Third World and perhaps even in the First. After all, in Norman Augustine's example, how many people would be needed to produce one plane every fifteen years?

Besides, what goes for the fabrication of expensive or what in the jargon of the gun-pushers are known as gold-plated weapons would also go for the fat-city consumerist contraptions of a military-industrial society like the United States. Which only means that the production of gold-plated weapons and gold-plated consumerist gadgetry together must spell mounting burdens for the vast underlying multitudes by way of inflation, unemployment, homelessness, uncared for health and so on.

It follows that in the process, the ever overreaching military industrialists cannot but create a situation in which the very existence of the race comes under threat either through stockpiles of weapons or through a paralysed ecology. But the choice between the Nuclear Bang and the Ecological Whimper can hardly be taken to be a very enviable one. For either of the two threatens our race with little less than extinction.

Indeed, every tycoon and every pauper, every sage and every smuggler, every priest and every jester must perish in a world-systemic collapse brought about by either the Bang or the Whimper. This is the fundamental and overriding 'equality' of our time—macabre though it may well be. Or, this is the 'new equality of insecurity, ' which, according to C.B. Macpherson (1988: 277), has changed the very terms of the political problem and according to me the very terms of human existence itself. But the *cognoscenti* and their concerns remain entirely undisturbed by the deathly culmination of the crazed drive for security which George Bernard Shaw once (1962a: 305) described as 'the chief pretence of civilization'. But I hope he would have readily agreed that, given the ascendancy of consumerism today, 'prosperity' has replaced 'security' as the chief pretence of civilization. It stands to reason, therefore, that if Shakespeare were to write *Macbeth* once again, he might come to speak not of security but of prosperity as the 'chiefest enemy' of the human race.

Be that as it may, the sheer lethality of exotic weaponry apart, the costs involved, even if only a fraction of the costs of consumerist orgies, would destroy whatever value 'defence' spending might ever have had as a source of economic stimulation and job generation.

Even the economists perhaps would find this to be of some interest if not concern.

What all this means is that with the passage of time, the military-industrial civilization is becoming *increasingly* chaotic and, in a world-historical context, increasingly unsystematic. In fact, the one thing it seems unconcerned with is its own inherent and easily perceivable unsustainability. 'What's New in the New World Order?' Paul Sweezy (1991: 1) asked some time ago and then answered this question as follows: 'One is tempted to respond that there's nothing new in the New World Order. There isn't even a new world order. And for that matter there isn't any world order at all'. This is very strongly reminiscent of Voltaire's caustic remark that 'The Holy Roman Empire was neither holy, nor Roman, nor an empire'.

Needless to say, the focus of my critique is the military-industrial civilization of our time, and entirely incidental to this exercise is my critique of John Maynard Keynes who is, after all, the twentieth-century ideologue 'par unexcellence' of military-industrialism. This deliberately Orwellian coinage appears to me to be fairly intelligible and at least to some may appear to be even witty—particularly in the polemical context in which it has been used.

Be that as it may, I have used all my wits, no matter how limited, to compose a self-consciously *polemical* argument against Keynes. Besides, there is a good reason why my polemics against Keynes has to be much sharper than his against the 'classical economists' of his time could have been. For he, like them, took the basic validity and legitimacy of military-industrialism for granted. It is this validity which I question. *Therefore, while his debate with them could only be over the mere management of the system, mine with him is over the basic credentials thereof.*

Indeed, we have it on high authority that the 'current economic theory is almost wholly a theory of the administration of a given industrial apparatus' (Schumpeter 1961: x). But in view of its extreme and irredeemable ecological untenability, the industrial apparatus of our time cannot be taken as 'given' any more. In fact, Schumpeter (*ibid.*: 61) had himself asked, 'Can capitalism survive?' and replied, 'No. I do not think it can'. For, according to him, the very success of capitalism 'undermines the social institutions which protect it'. But what he failed to see, and what we shall see later in this essay, is that capitalism does not just undermine itself by undermining the institutions which protect it. Rather, it also undermines itself by *creating* institutions which would ultimately and necessarily come to undermine it.

The one I have in mind is the system of social security which American capitalism, for instance, created in 1935 but which by now has grown into an albatross around its neck: that is, something which it can neither cut to reasonable size nor afford to carry much longer. But, for the present, let us just remember that the very success of contemporary capitalism in unleashing what C. Wright Mills (1972: 25) once described as 'the new American celebration' cannot but undermine or rather destroy its ecological base and thus doom it so thoroughly as to give it 'neither choice nor chance'. Which only means that economic theory, to be at all pertinent, must cease to be a theory of the administration of the given industrial apparatus and become instead a theory which puts it under relentless examination.

But ideologically committed to the status quo as he was, Keynes did not and could not undertake an exercise in genuine intellectual liberation: no matter how sustained his 'struggle of escape from habitual modes of thought and expression' (K-VII: xxiii). In contrast, it is nothing less than the validity and legitimacy of the prevailing *system* which I question. Therefore, my essay has to be and is unmitigably polemical. In any case, it is a critique not an apology and therefore cannot help being what it is: a relentless exercise in polemics.

But this polemics is specifically and self-consciously intended to defy and dispel 'the current atmosphere of Western triumphalism' which, as Noam Chomsky reminds me in personal communication, has come to subjugate 'a good part of the Indian intelligentsia as well'. As I see it, therefore, a Third World academic can do little better today than to refuse to be so subjugated. In other words, one can do little more pertinent than to show that the triumphalist euphoria now dizzying the Western, and in particular the American, powers that be and their ideologues is nothing but a confounding illusion.

Hopefully, out of a demystifying exercise like this would be born the possibility of a future both viable and humane. For it is only when one has dispelled the reigning mystifications that one can begin to gather one's resources for what the late Raymond Williams (1985: 268) once called 'a journey of hope'.

Jawaharlal Nehru University   **Narindar Singh**
New Delhi
May 1995

Acknowledgements

Paul Sweezy, Noam Chomsky, H. K. Manmohan Singh, Tapas Majumdar, Christopher Thomas Kurien and Harsh Sethi have read earlier versions of various chapters of this essay which I have revised in the light of their comments. To them, my thanks. As also to my old teacher and friend Amrik Singh and a number of young friends like Krishna Kumar, Bhupinder Singh Chimni and Rakesh Kapoor who took keen interest in the progress of *The Keynesian Fallout*. Besides, Father George Gispert of Vidya Jyoti, Delhi helped me coin each one of the Latin neologisms I have used.

My sons, Tejindar and Munindar kept me under relentless pressure, as only sons could and would, with the result that I have been able to complete this book much sooner than I would otherwise have been able to. Munindar, in addition, word-processed several drafts of *The Fallout*. But with the demands of his own academic work continuing to increase, I persuaded him to let me ask someone else do the job: Suraj Sharma and then S. Raju Aiyer, both of the Jawaharlal Nehru University. The final version is the product of Raju Aiyer's truly exceptional skills as a computer-typist.

Part One: Hitler — Alive and Kicking

It may prove possible for more radical views to prevail. But it is necessary for these radical views to be publicized, to be strong and clear statements based on trustworthy information. This is a slender hope, but it is all that the present world can justify.

Bertrand Russell (1967: 74)

Turn your ears to the wind of death,
Your eyes to the derricks of death!
Shout BEWARE! BEWARE! as if Ezekiel
Stood again on his street corner in Jerusalem.

Aaron Kramer (1984: 77)

Keynes and Hitler*

Words ought to be a little wild, for they are the assault of thoughts upon the unthinking.

John Maynard Keynes (K-XXI: 244)

The Führer and the Führungen

John Maynard Keynes once (K-VII: xxvi) remarked that 'in offering a theory of employment and output as a whole, which departs in important respects from the orthodox tradition', he might expect 'less resistance from German, than from English, readers'. For, his theory of output as a whole, he said, was 'much more easily adapted to the conditions of a totalitarian state' than was the then reigning economics of *laissez-faire*. This disarming sentiment appears towards the end of the preface to the German edition of *The General Theory* and could well have been intended to appease the unappeasable ego of the Nazis. In fact, in his own words, Keynes was trying only to 'contribute some stray *morsels* towards the preparation by German economists of a full repast of theory designed to meet specifically German conditions' [emphasis mine].

What we have in John Maynard Keynes, then, seems only to be an academic version of Arthur Neville Chamberlain. But while the latter has been derided more or less universally, Keynes has only been applauded no end.

That apart, we are told (Schefold 1983: 416–17) that the text of the preface to the German edition of *The General Theory*, as it appears

* An earlier version of this chapter appeared in the *Economic and Political Weekly* of 15 October 1994.

in Volume VII of *The Collected Writings of John Maynard Keynes*, is not exactly the same as the text of the preface which appears in the German version of the book itself. For the latter incorporates the last-minute alterations which Keynes made and conveyed to his translator and the German publishers. The editors of *The Collected Writings*, it seems, failed to compare the two versions and simply used the one found in the Keynes papers at Cambridge. Anyway, the alterations which Keynes made in this preface are worth noting: On the one hand, he says that the relevance of his theory to conditions under a totalitarian state is yet another reason why he calls his theory *a general theory*; and on the other, he comes to define a totalitarian state as one in which the state leadership or the *staatliche Führung* 'is more pronounced'.

Keynes signed the preface to the German edition late in 1936 when Nazism in its original incarnation was still in the ascendant. Therefore, his distressing entreaties about the relevance of his theory to Germany under the Nazis speak volumes for the revolutionary character of the so-called Keynesian revolution. In particular, because we know and Keynes also must have known what the Nazi *Führung* was doing in Germany at the time. Besides, given the reckless rampancy of that *Führung*, an expression like Keynes's 'more pronounced' could only be a tendentious euphemism. For Nazism did not just mean a kind of state authority which was somewhat more pronounced than the one relatively liberal in orientation. Above all, it meant concentration camps and the rest of the brutalities unleashed by Hitler and his hordes. What the Nazis were doing therefore merited a relentlessly withering treatment for which Keynes certainly had the necessary vocabulary if not the will. Consider, for instance, his dismissal of a mere paper by Michal Kalecki as one which was full of 'high, almost delirious nonsense' (K-XII: 829).

Imagine someone who could be so mild as to try, with the help of a phrase like 'more pronounced', to ignore the misdoings of one of the most virulent dictatorships known to history and at the same time react so violently to a mere paper which had been written by a scholar of stature and supported by none other than Joan Robinson.

This only means that 'for all the extraordinary speed of his brain [and] the lightning rapidity with which he sucked in and devoured information' (Holroyd 1971: 242), Keynes did manage not to see the essential gravity of the Nazi menace. No wonder that Bertrand Russell who according to Holroyd found Keynes's intellect to be the sharpest and clearest he had ever known could not help wondering sometimes that such sharpness and clarity might well conceal a lack of depth. Verily, only a woeful lack of depth or what I shall later describe as lack of empathy could explain why even a liberal like Keynes could be so polite towards the Nazis.

It follows that, in examining Keynes, it would be impossible to overemphasize the significance of the 'totalitarian connection'. Indeed, as Joan Robinson put it once (1973: 102), 'Hitler had already found how to cure unemployment before Keynes had finished explaining why it occurred'. As she saw it, then, the Keynesian revolution was not a great intellectual triumph. On the contrary, it was a tragedy because it came so late. This she said during the course of her famous Richard T. Ely lecture entitled 'The Second Crisis of Economic Theory' which she gave in 1971. A little later, she gave another provocative lecture entitled 'What has become of the Keynesian Revolution?' This was meant to suggest, among other things, a parallel between the role which Keynes had assigned to hole-digging and what the Nazis also could do. That is to say, if Keynes could expect 'not only employment, but the real national dividend of useful goods and services' as well (K-VII: 220) to increase as a result of sheer hole-digging, the Nazis too could conjure up equally weird schemes to boost the level of employment. Besides, they did not have to wait for Keynes to be told to do the conjuration. 'It was a joke in Germany', Joan Robinson said, 'that Hitler was planning to give employment in straightening the Crooked Lake, painting the Black Forest white and putting down linoleum in the Polish Corridor' (Robinson 1979: 170). But that kind of a joke apart, military spending was in fact a most important programme of hole-digging which the Nazis had launched. *Which only means that having been preceded by the employment generating measures of the redoubtable Adolf Hitler himself, Keynes's remedies have been grossly overrated.*

One may cite here a statement which Professor Samuelson (1986: 279) has made: 'Lord Keynes was not the first, nor the last, to advocate public works in times of slump. Adolf Hitler knew as little of economics as he knew of morality. Still, his sprint to rearm Germany and mount a campaign of revenge and conquest did succeed in bringing Germany to a state of full employment from the situation in 1932, when one in four Germans, like one in four Americans, was without hope of finding a job'. But many scholars, and Professor Samuelson not excluded, who, unlike Adolf Hitler, happen to know as *much* of

economics as they know of morality, have managed nevertheless to
continue to endorse the Pentagon's sustained sprint to acquire ever
more of weapons. Nor have they failed to support such of its activities
as were *not* in revenge for anything which, say, the Vietnamese might
have done to the United States for the simple reason that they had
done nothing. Besides, the Pentagon has failed altogether to match
Hitler's record, whatever it was worth, on the employment front. Still,
the scholars have not thought it necessary even to refer to, much less
emphasize, the Pentagon's role in the *actual promotion* of unemployment in the United States. But one would do well to remember that
military spending and fat-city consumption together happen to pre-
empt the resources which could otherwise be used to promote genuine
economic construction and employment generation. No wonder, average
unemployment in the United States has continued only to mount from
4.5 per cent in the 1950s to 4.7 per cent in the 1960s, 6.1 per cent in
the 1970s and 7.2 per cent in the 1980s. Nor do the prospects look
much better during the 1990s (Cloward and Piven 1993: 693). More
important, the scholars have failed to focus on the Pentagon's contribution to the relentless brutalization of the *pan-human* situation.

Unabating Brutalization

Indeed, the explosive escalation of military spending worldwide, and
not in the United States alone, since the end of the Second World War
signifies the continued virulence, not the demise, of Hitlerism: in the
substantive though not in the formal sense. This alone should explain
why soon after the war, the four principal Allies began a nauseating
scramble to recruit German scientists—'a hunt pursued with much
greater energy than the search for war criminals and Nazi plunder'
(Van der Vat 1987: 21). Even more serious, and according to Bertrand
Russell (1967: 110), films showing Nazi tortures were used for the
instruction of American servicemen fighting in Vietnam. It follows,
therefore, that one must take all the care to focus upon the menace
of Hitlerism *de facto*. For, thus alone can one dispel all the guiles of
liberalism *de jure*.

**Indeed, reckless military spending spells above all a brutaliza-
tion of the human situation no less deadly than the pathology
which Hitler embodied and promoted. It is in this vital sense that
Hitlerism, though not Hitler himself, can be taken to have won**

the War. The reappearance of swastikas in Poland and of skinheads in the former East Germany which Robert Heilbroner (1993: 14), for instance, has referred to are a much milder manifestation of Hitlerism than the consolidation and intensification of the cult of brutality which I am talking about. But then Hitlerism, understood essentially as the ugliest ever manifestation of militarism with its unabashed obsession with military spending, can only spell illimitable deprivations and explosive poverty. One may refer here to a point which President Eisenhower or rather his speech writer at the time, Emmett Hughes, made early in 1953:

> Every gun that is made, every warship launched, every rocket fired signifies, in the final sense, a theft from those who hunger and are not fed, those who are cold and are not clothed.
>   This world in arms is not spending money alone. It is spending the sweat of its labourers, the genius of its scientists, the hopes of its children (Eisenhower 1988a: 570).

In sum, as Eisenhower could well have added, it is a world brutalized through and through.

Paradoxically, it is *only* when this quotation is taken out of context, as it generally is, that it comes to serve as a most evocative insight into the nature of the prevailing social reality. But kept firmly within the context of Eisenhower's 1953 speech, and in the context of his world-view, it is no more than a flourish of misleading and even hypocritical rhetoric. No wonder that the speech entitled 'The Chance for Peace' did not persuade him 'to take any meaningful chance for peace' nor did it have any effect whatsoever on American policy (Brands 1993 : 43). For he was trying *essentially* to argue that the American arms build-up was no more than a response to the Soviet threat. If so, what role would he assign to what he or rather another speech writer of his, Malcolm Moos, would come before long to call 'the military-industrial complex'? (Eisenhower 1988b: 595). This complex exercised a great deal of 'unwarranted influence' in the councils of government as he affirmed and could certainly not have begun to do so in less than eight years of his 1953 speech. Eisenhower should have known, if anyone could have, that the so-called Soviet threat was little more than a most tendentious invention of the American military-industrial complex itself—a threat which, as Voltaire would have said, had to be invented simply because it did not exist.

Indeed, already, when the Soviet Union was cracking up, Dick Cheney, the Pentagon chief at the time, began to feel 'uneasy' about cuts in the military budget which could well be demanded in the new situation (Beschloss and Talbott 1993: 445). But now that the Soviet Union has disappeared altogether, the American powers that be find themselves in a bit of a fix. Thus, for instance, Senator John McCain, who is an opponent of the B-2 bomber all right but— naturally—not of weaponization *per se*, has had company 'representative after representative' come to him to press for the maintenance of the bomber industrial base, the fighter industrial base, the missile industrial base. Which pleadings make him see the end of the 'Cold War' as 'the harsh reality' America is now facing (Isaacs 1994: 15).

Some such realization seems already in 1992 to have pushed the US General Colin Powell into a state of discomfort. In support of this view, one may cite a most revealing quote from him: 'We no longer have the luxury of having a threat to prepare for'. It would be hard to specify a concrete threat now, the General added, 'without straining credulity'. In his view, therefore, America must continue to arm itself against the *abstract* threat of 'being unprepared'. For: 'The real [*sic*] threat we now face is the threat of the unknown, the uncertain' (Borosage 1992a: 292). More recently, the General, a former Chairman of the Joint Chiefs of Staff, has said that the USA is 'running out of demons' and has suggested that North Korea be projected as one (Borosage 1993: 347). In fact, a series of 'crisis meetings' are reported to have already been held to consider contingency plans for a 'limited' missile attack on that country. This suggests the consolidation of a system which remains forever impelled to conjure up some crisis or other and thus to exaggerate some threat or other to American security. Evidently, it must perforce remain entirely unconcerned with the waste or even the destruction of resources which the continuation of such conjurations cannot but cause. No wonder that a Senate committee has recently found that 'by purposely exaggerating the nuclear threat, the Pentagon persuaded the Congress to spend $350 billion on nuclear hardware in the 1980s (O'Connor 1993: 350). Economists have long worried *only* about the *allocation of resources* in the abstract. They would obviously do well to begin worrying about the *misallocation of resources in the concrete*. For the foregoing bespeaks a system which, from the point of view of resources, and, therefore, from the point of view of economics itself, has become irrational *de profundis*.

But, then, those who hunger and are not fed must die sooner, rather than later of starvation and other poverty-produced diseases. No wonder that a world which spends $1 million per minute on arms (Sivard 1993: 8) also lets during the same minute some fifty-seven people die of hunger and hunger-related diseases. I have explained the basis of this computation elsewhere (Singh 1989: 201n). But let us note here only that fifty-seven people dying every minute means 82,000 people dying every twenty-four hours of plain hunger. And this in turn means that the world is experiencing one Hiroshima a day. This, in a word, is what Johan Galtung describes as the 'Silent Holocaust' of our time. Mankind is not just hanging from what Eisenhower called 'a cross of iron'. Rather, vast numbers of it are simply being crushed under a cross—of gold—which is getting heavier and heavier with more and more money going into the fabrication of gold-plated weapons.

This is the brutal modernity of which Hitler was but an early embodiment.

Impelled by their crazed minds, the rulers of the Thousand-Year Reich came to make death and destruction into a veritable industry. *Even so, 'the blood-curdling paeun of universal destruction' (Trevor-Roper 1975: 118) orchestrated by the Nazis turns into no more than a muffled whisper in comparison with the orgy of death, destruction and waste unleashed by their liberal superseders everywhere*. In fact, on account of their reckless profligacy alone, the formally democratic Reiche of today will not last for even a fraction of the millennium that the Nazis allotted to their totalitarian version. For even if they manage to escape a violent nuclear convulsion, they, the liberal Reiche of our own time, will be destroyed by sheer gluttony and effluence.

According to Lord Tedder (1975: 14): 'Although Hitler is dead, the agonies he brought on mankind are still alive.' But to my mind, these agonies have not just continued to be alive but to multiply. No wonder that the supposedly liberal vanquishers of the totalitarian Hitler have brought our race to a point where its very existence has become threatened with termination. Nor are their imperial goals kept far in the background. Thus, about the time that he defined guns as theft from those who hunger, Eisenhower also made the following point: 'Now let us assume we lost Indo-China. If Indo-China goes, the tin and tungsten we so greatly value would cease coming. We are after the cheapest way to prevent the occurrence of something terrible—the loss of our ability to get what we want from the riches of the Indo-Chinese territory and from South-East Asia' (Russell 1967: 117). Is it very different from the Nazi demand for *Lebensraum*?

This, then, should explain the extremely pervasive and virulent reign of Death in our own time. Indeed, and slightly to alter a point which Robert Lifton once made (Garrison 1980: 36), upon the natural order of living and dying has been superimposed an unnatural order of death-dominated life. In other words, *Homo sapiens* has quite evidently degenerated into *Homo insipiens*: certainly the rulers and the ruiners of it. A situation like this bespeaks a kind of obtuseness, a kind of unreason, *which even the Nazis had not yet come to cultivate*.

Symbolizing this continuing ascendancy of Unreason in our time is Ronald Reagan. After the end of his presidency, no one would dream of asking him for his thoughts about any topic, 'because it is understood, as it always was, that he has none' (Chomsky 1991: 375). A few years earlier, when Reagan was still in power, William Thompson (1987: 174) found him to be 'the archetypal leader of our post-industrial unconscious polity precisely because he is not a thinker'. Reagan, he said, 'is almost entirely unconscious. He is indeed Walt Disney's *Homo ludens* and not Luther's, Calvin's nor Marx's *Homo faber*'. And the polity is unconscious simply because those who happen to manage it are insensitive to the existential perils and contradictions which can only spell our extinction as a species. Therefore, it is not just Ronald Reagan who is Walt Disney's *Homo ludens* that is, an animated cartoon in human form. Rather, it is the whole lot of our rulers who can be designated as *Homo ludens*, big and small, whom our species is condemned to suffer: in the First World in particular, but in the Third World and what till only the other day used to be the Second World as well. Still, Reagan's dubious pre-eminence as a Disneyesque biped does merit special attention. And it is manifested in the parallels between his Star Wars project and the Disney World's fantasy called EPCOT, impelling Thompson (1987: 190) to designate him as 'an idiot savant'.

But in the context of the advancing paralysis of the Earth system, the relentless and ubiquitous games of power and the players themselves must perforce look to be exceedingly jejune. Thus, for instance, George Bush's declaration that he would do just anything to win the 1992 election could only argue his total ignorance of, or unconcern with, the mounting and defining perils of our time. In particular, because his 'anything' could well have included a diversion which Shakespeare's Henry IV recommended, while dying, to his son:

Be it thy course to busy giddy minds
With foreign quarrels.

After all, $50 billion or so of the tax-payer's money to be spent on another Gulf War would be no more than peanuts if only George Bush could manage to remain entrenched in the White House. It would be a pity to have some American servicemen killed or maimed or just lost in the process. But they would only be doing their patriotic duty to keep George Bush where he wanted to be.

Even so, the Earth system receiving many another high-tech blow from the American forces would perforce have to suffer untold damage. But that is what this system may have to suffer again and again—and again. For if Bill Clinton's missile attack on Baghdad were to be a curtain-raiser to the future, *any* American President could try to shore up sagging popularity at home simply by bullying people abroad on some pretext or other—dangerously irresponsible that such a misadventure might be. Indeed, Bill Clinton is the perfect embodiment of 'crackpot realism'. That is, realism which obliges men to get 'rigidly focused on the next step' (Mills 1959: 89) so that they become totally oblivious of the consequences of the *drift* that their cynical opportunism must perforce produce. *But what about the intelligence of the populace which can be expected to get swayed by such gimmickry?*

It is the Earth system, therefore, which can now be seen to be in a much worse state than it was even during the last days of the Third Reich. It follows that the Bushes, the Clintons, the Majors and the rest of them sticking to or scrambling for power today are also living like their Nazi predecessors in what Trevor-Roper (1975: 164) calls 'the fools' paradise'. For, as doomed marionettes, Nazi leaders were competing for nothing more than the dwindling fragments of power while Hitler was preparing to kill himself. Likewise, those trying frantically to *grab* power on a planet afflicted with creeping ecological paralysis are also living in a fools' paradise of their own. Only, it happens to be even more untenable than the one which the Nazis had created.

All this impels us to focus on the economic, political and cultural consequences of entirely unprecedented and unbridled military spending and consumerist orgies of today and all the world over. For, such reckless spending spells, if anything: an escalating destruction of resources involved in the unending fabrication of gold-plated weapons and also of gold-plated consumerist gadgetry; a concomitant ascendancy of the culture of waste generation; and a benumbing of the human spirit so thorough that it fails to see through all the propaganda unleashed in the name of 'security' and high living standards. **It follows that with the passage of time, the economic, political and cultural fallout of the Keynes–Hitler sodality has tended only to become more sinister, not less.** This is suggested directly by the nature of what Joan Robinson described in her Ely lecture as the cure for unemployment which Hitler had found: increased military spending. Evidently, if the so-called defence needs come to be inflated continuously and artificially so that military spending reaches levels which Hitler himself would not have thought possible even during his wildest ravings, the explanation must be sought in the misdoings of all the *staatliche Führungen* currently installed almost all the world over.

Evidently, militarism dovetails very neatly with consumerism *but* not without making the ecological mess even worse confounded. Indeed, on this account alone whatever military-industrialism does to enable the rich to corner the economy and lap up all they can and whatever it does to hold the rest in leash must necessarily be shortsighted and dysfunctional beyond rectification and therefore incurably irrational too. For global warming and ozone depletion apart, even such relatively localized damage as has been caused, for example, by the radioactive contamination of the Tuscaloosa Aquifer, lying at one point some 300 feet below the Savannah River nuclear weapons materials complex in South Carolina, is alarming enough. For the aquifer is a major source of drinking water from Alabama to North Carolina (Horan 1988: 28).

According to Mannoni (1968: 204), there used to be a law in Ethiopia under which a creditor could have a defaulting debtor attached to himself by means of a chain little realizing that in so doing, he too would be getting into the shackles of his own making. Likewise, little do the military-industrial orgiasts seem to realize that in creating a world of ersatz affluence for some and in condemning the rest to deprivations, they are only consolidating a state of ecological and *societal* dysfunction which would be as much of a menace to themselves as to their victims.

As *The Economist* reported in its issue of 10 July 1993 (p. 36), about half the hungry in Brazil—some 15 million people—live in the cities and the manifestations of this fact are very grim, indeed. Despair has fed crime, which in turn has bloated the security industry. Fashionable apartment buildings have been turned into fortresses, patrolled day and night by electronic eyes, and encastled by steel fences. 'Hunger imprisons us all, ' says a television commercial. But such imprisoning of the well-to-do is by no means confined to Brazil. In fact, the very model of it is to be found in the United States itself where, according to John Kenneth Galbraith (1992: 45), private security guards happen to be more numerous now than the publicly employed policemen.

In other words, in generating breathtakingly large incomes, legal and illegal, in the fabrication of gold-plated weapons—incomes which cannot but merge with those being generated in the fabrication of gold-plated consumerist gadgetry—military-industrialism does not just help create a welfare state for the rich. It also helps engender nothing less than a state of civilizational chaos which does not bode very well for the future of us all. As Werner Heisenberg once (1972: 84) put it, 'With its seemingly unlimited growth of material power, mankind finds itself in the situation of a skipper who had his boat built of such heavy concentrations of iron and steel that the boat's compass points constantly at herself and not North. With a boat of that kind no destination can be reached; she will go round in a circle, exposed to the hazards of the winds and the waves'. In sum, the military-industrial system of economic management cannot but be dysfunctional in the extreme and cannot therefore be sustained for long, much less indefinitely. But unmindful of all this, the orgiasts in power continue to generate unending avalanches of reckless waste both through military and consumerist overspending. Or, overkill.

Military-Industrial Corruption

A very large part of the explanation, at least as far as military spending is concerned, seems to lie in the kickbacks and political donations which the *Führungen* manage to reward themselves with while acquiring weapons for their respective *Staaten*. This also seems to account for a phenomenon which Joan Robinson once (1973: 101) designated as the hypertrophy of military power *after* the end of the

Second World War. Only naturally too, being by far the largest military spender ever, the American *staatliche Führung* of today must also be the recipient of the vastest military bribes in world history. But what exactly the politicians and the bureaucrats involved continue to receive from the military contractors can, of course, never be known. Even so, the tips of the proverbial icebergs which continue to become visible with a remarkably unbroken regularity do suggest that the amounts in question must indeed be breathtakingly large. How minuscule the tips are and how gigantic the icebergs is suggested by a simple and specific comparison between the fines imposed upon the contractors for fraud on the one hand and the military outlays on the other. Thus, an investigation into the Pentagon's military procurement corruption, code-named Operation Ill Wind, which became public in June 1988, had by September 1991 yielded no more than $225 million in fines, et cetera. But it had required no less than 51 actual *convictions* to produce this result and the fifty-first of these alone accounted for $190 million of the $225 million (Mann 1991: 24). As against this, the value of just *one* Pentagon contract for the supply of about 650 advanced tactical fighter (ATF) planes over the next 20 years happens now to be $93 *billion* and could turn out eventually to be much larger. Accordingly, the cost of one such plane, around $150 million now, could ultimately become much higher (Schwartz 1991: 46–47).

Besides, with the so-called Cold War having come to a close, hardly any one seems to be sure if the US Air Force at all needs the pricey ATF. In actual *need* of it rather, we are told (Schine 1991: 64), were both Lockheed and Northrop, the two military contractors competing for one of the last major contracts 'up for grabs through the end of the century'. Indeed, 'grabs' is *the* word and evidently, Lockheed and Northrop *both* would have made money flow in amounts too large and through channels too devious for ordinary mortals to comprehend. But a lot more important than the fortunes of an individual military contractor or of teamed-up contractors is the open-ended and even unboundable profligacy literally programmed into the military procurement system of the United States. For basic to this system is the unrelenting complicity between the contractors and the bureaucrats. In fact, as an internal Pentagon report, cited by the House Committee on the Budget in November 1991, noted: 'it has become difficult to determine where Government workers' functions stop and contractors' begin'. These, then are the national security soldiers of what Professor Paul Samuelson, for one, loves to see as the mixed economy of the

United States. Drawn from the private sector and the public, unelected from anywhere and also unaccountable to anyone, they continue to mug the tax-payer to be able to share the orgiastic plunder generated by the fabrication of anything from wing nuts which cost $10,000 apiece (Weiner 1992: 25–26) to 70-ton B-2 bombers, each one of which has been made to cost about three times its weight in solid gold (Sivard 1993: 56).

What exercises like Operation Ill Wind come up against, then, is a close network of collusion among contractors, military 'consultants' and Pentagon officials. Therefore, such investigations as do not question the very existence of a lavish military procurement programme must perforce let the status quo remain more or less completely unruffled. A labyrinthine procurement bureaucracy, over half-a-million strong, politicians in search of quick 'contributions' and a Pentagon budget of around $270 billion a year can only produce a hide-bound system reeking of untold corruption. In a situation like this, coffee pots which cost $7,000 apiece, ordinary hammers, $400 and paper-cup dispensers a mere $120 cannot qualify even as small beer. Nor would so qualify a variety of expenses which the NASA, for instance, incurred not long ago:

renting for $3,600,000 per year a building which the US Government *itself* had first sold away for just $300,000;

paying $159,000 for an electric cooling fan worth no more than $5,215;

buying 3-cent metal loops for $315 per piece and one-dollar worth of metal washers for $86 each.

All this, small beer or no, adds up, according to the *Editorials on File* for 16–30 April 1985, to $3.5 billion of contractual fraud over the years. But such facts, no matter how significant, must remain by and large irrelevant to the professional economists whose perceptions remain focused on such profundities as the average cost curves and the marginal cost curves and the way that they must intersect. Be that as it may, a military lobbyist did not find Operation Ill Wind to be anything other than 'bad breath'.

Once in a while, though, some leading corporation or other does *appear* to be bitten by deep remorse. But no matter how deep, and it cannot be very, such remorse cannot but be singularly misdirected and therefore entirely unavailing. For instance, as *The Wall Street Journal* reported on 22 July 1992, General Electric Co.(GE), subject of several high-profile scandals during the 1980s, has now prepared one of the most elaborate anti-fraud programmes in corporate America to avoid further embarrassments. To this end, it has decided to encourage its employees to report anything fishy to the management. But no matter how earnest the management may look to be, such programmes can only be in the nature of red herrings. For while seeking to apprehend some *individuals* guilty of fraud, they leave completely unquestioned all that *must* be questioned: the essential validity of military-industrialism itself that cannot but produce unabating orgies of waste and fraud. Therefore, even if meant to be taken extremely seriously, GE's new-found ardour for honesty is going to be very, very short-lived, indeed.

As short-lived, perhaps, as Lockheed's, for instance, has been. By far the largest grease machine in American and therefore in world history, Lockheed, during the days of its pristine glory, used to buy princes and premiers around the globe. Indeed, on its own admission, during the first half of the 1970s alone, it paid out $202 million in 'consultancy fees' and something like $38 million in what it described as 'kick-backs' and 'pay-offs,' with the hyphens still *in* there, or just as 'questionable payments'.

But then came the Church Committee investigation which, in spite of its limitations, put Lockheed in the spotlight of public attention. In consequence, the company decided, in all seriousness it seems, to mend its ways. In fact, according to David Boulton (1978: 276–77), it told its employees in the May 1977 issue of *Lockheed Life* that: 'High principles of business conduct must underline the policies of any corporation. We believe [that we have] an obligation to articulate the general principles which should guide and motivate the people of Lockheed. We are clearly stating them now as a mark of our determination to conduct the company's business on an ethical basis and as an imperative signal to every man and woman in the corporation that they must share these principles'.

Lockheed went on to declare that it would comply with the laws of the United States and of other countries with which it did business. But beyond mere legal compliance, it added, it would strive for *integrity* in every aspect of its work. Besides, taking the loyalty of its employees for granted, it said, 'Ethical conduct is the highest form of loyalty to Lockheed'. I do not know how seriously Lockheed's employees may have taken this insistence upon *ethics and integrity*. But I do know that its own definitions of these concepts have been sufficiently elastic to allow it to:

fire in 1985 three of its employees who had questioned the structural *integrity* of the C-58 aircraft it had supplied to the US Air Force and who were later awarded $45. 3 million in punitive and $376,000 in compensatory damages;

continue to buy secret government documents in order to be able to stall its rivals and thus to soak up all the lucrative military contracts it could;

make lavish political 'donations' particularly to such congressional leaders as would be in a position to 'oversee' military spending;

overprice several times over even such items as toilet seat covers it sold to the Navy; and

organize *ad hoc* espionage in collusion with the police for the apprehension of student leaders opposing its missile construction programmes.

All this would need political clout at high levels and Lockheed has never had to go short of it. But more recently, it has managed to rope in the Speaker of the House of Representatives, Newt Gingrich, who is getting to be known as the Speaker from Lockheed (Hartung 1995: 124). Even so, what we have here appears to be extremely small beer indeed in comparison with what one would expect a grease machine with the history and the size of Lockheed to be doing. But who knows? For it could well be doing all that. Only, its doings may not have surfaced so soon after the Church Committee hearings. Still, they *could* well begin to surface before long. Indeed, as Richard K. Cook, its Washington vice-president declared some years ago: 'Ill Wind has not dampened my enthusiasm for hiring the right consultants' (Griffiths 1990: 26). Nothing less than cynical contempt for ethics as also for the authority of the State would be needed for anyone to say a thing like that. But whoever takes over its Washington operations *now* could well become even more unabashed while 'hiring the right consultants'. For after its merger with Martin Marietta announced on 30 August 1994, it has become by far the largest weapons firm ever. It will now be known as Lockheed Martin and as such it had [the

combined] 1993 sales amounting to $22.5 billion, more than one-tenth
of India's GNP. Besides, out of this total, the sales to the US Department of Defence during the same year came to $11.6 billion. Evidently,
that should be good enough reason for it to begin hiring even more
and 'better' consultants and thus to continue to acquire more and more
of lobbying clout.

**What we see here, then, is not just a system *of* organized
corruption but a system orchestrated *for* organized corruption:
bateless, blatant, unboundable corruption.**

Unboundable certainly by what is known as whistleblowing. To be
sure, the Federal False Claims Act, popularly known as 'the whistle-
blower law', provides for private citizens, including company employees to file suits on behalf of the US Government and then share in
the recovered damages. But if the intention is to weed out corruption
or even to curtail it a bit, whistleblowing must perforce remain an
exercise in futility. In support of this view, let us consider a *successful*
case, which *The New York Times*, for instance, reported on 15 July
1992. CAE–Link, a contractor owned almost throughout the relevant
period of 1980-88 by the Singer Corporation, was found to have
routinely overbilled the Pentagon on contracts worth more than one
billion dollars. Under the settlement, CAE–Link and Singer were
together advised to surrender $55.9 million, with the whistleblower
and his lawyers getting $7.5 million out of this amount.

Whistleblowing would thus certainly make a military contractor
suffer more or less inconsequential penalties once in a while and at
the same time help some lucky individuals to dig gold—and lots of
it, too. But given an active and continuing collusion between corporate
America as a whole and the Pentagon for the development and
production of gold-plated but militarily superfluous weapons, open-
ended military spending and open-ended corruption must perforce
become two sides of the same coin.

*Besides, gold-plating itself could well be a grossly misleading
euphemism where weapons, such as the B-2 bomber, cost about three
times their weight in solid gold.* Those who pay all the taxes directly
and indirectly, formally and informally, and suffer all the deprivations,
are at the receiving end of this ongoing swindle. And so is an
over-ravished planet. Whistleblowing, in focusing on the relatively
minor manifestations of corruption and in leaving the root of all
corruption itself entirely unexposed, can therefore be only a red
herring so that nothing can happen to the world of business as usual.

But those in power find it eminently useful to let things remain as they are. For more and more of weapons mean more and more of slush funds. And funds, no matter how slushy, do enable the recipients to attain and retain power which in turn helps them get ever more of funds. And this cannot but produce a spiral which continues to soar upwards.

The point of it all is that, given the inexorable continuation of the Theft from those who hunger and are not fed, are cold and are not covered, whistleblowing must perforce remain no more than a cruel juridical joke, an insult to intelligence.

Indeed, if the sainted Olof Palme is any example, vast sums of money can be extracted even out of an underdeveloped country like India while inducing it to buy weapons from one's own developed country. Besides, the procedure is breathtakingly simple. Thus, shortly before his assassination, Palme, the Swedish Prime Minister at the time, happened to be visiting India to co-sign with Rajiv Gandhi and others the six-nation appeal for peace to the United States and what was still the Soviet Union. But the sanctity of the occasion did not deter the two of them from using it to finalize the Bofors–India gun deal (Subramaniam 1993: 77). This happened in January 1986. But already in the third week of December 1985, Bofors had agreed to 'donate' 50 million Swedish crowns (Sek) to Palme's Berlags Foundation (*ibid.*: 204). Evidently, it would be allowed to recover *much more* than this amount by jacking up the howitzer price that India would have to pay. This committed donation could well have been one of the reasons why the French gun system called Sofma, which had been the hot favourite in India till then, came to be dropped rather suddenly in favour of Bofors. Subramaniam (1993: 69) cites one of her Swedish sources as having said that at the final stage of decision-making, there could be no question of good guns and bad guns. For at that stage, there could only be 'good kickbacks and bad kickbacks'.

But kickbacks entail cover-ups and cover-ups entail lying. No wonder that Official India managed to surround 'itself with so many lie-mines that wherever it stepped, something blew up in its face' (*ibid.*: 132). The most incredible of all its pretences was that no Indian had taken any bribe. If so, it would be hard put to it to explain why Bofors would pay Sek 188 million 'to three women in Panama for a howitzer sale to India' (*ibid.*: 70). Evidently, and Official India would have known as much, the three musketeeresses were holding the amount—about half of the total—on someone else's behalf.

And that someone would have to be no one but one in a position to decide which gun system to acquire. This is no more than an inference, to be sure. But in such situations more direct evidence may *never* become available. For after all, no one would ever sign a *receipt* for a bribe. This being so, guilt would need to be established largely, perhaps even entirely, by circumstantial evidence. A former Law Minister of India, Shanti Bhushan, made this point while writing to the President on the Bofors issue. He also cited a number of Supreme Court judgements in support of his plea, but to no avail.

Subramaniam (1993: 158) reports that within Sweden itself Bofors was permitted to deduct kickbacks amounting to Sek 319 million from its tax liability. In other words, what began as a colossal fraud upon the people of India became before long a fraud upon the people of Sweden as well. I do not know if such tax-waivers are a general practice in that country. But even as an exception made in this case, the waiver can be seen as corruption legalized, corruption hyper-trophied—Corruption with a capital C.

But, let me repeat that it was a colossal fraud upon the people of India. For, Bofors, like any other vendor of any other ware, would have to pass on the 'burden' of slush payments to the buyer in the form of higher prices. Economists often make a distinction between the impact of an indirect tax and its incidence. The impact is on the manufacturer who has to make the payment to the revenue collector in the first instance. But the incidence falls ultimately on the consumer who has to pay a higher price. Likewise, the initial impact of slush payments might well be on the maker of weapons. But the incidence necessarily falls on the State buying them and, therefore, on the people who would have to pay more in taxes and suffer the burden of inflation and a variety of deprivations as well.

This is a situation, moreover, in which the military contractor has managed to buy all such 'protection' as people in power can provide. Therefore, there simply is no reason why he should raise his prices merely to recover the slush payments he has made, no more. That is, he can and would make the State agencies buying his wares pay much higher prices than those necessary just to recover the bribes he has given. *The metaphysic of greed suggests little else.* Nor is it a very wild speculation. Extracting a rent of $3.6 million per year from the NASA for a government building bought a little earlier for less than one-tenth of that amount or selling it 3-cent metal loops for $315 apiece can argue nothing but the power of the contractors to use slush

payments for charging whatever prices they deem fit. But the 'deci-
sion-makers', who operate at different levels and who are ever so
obsessed with the quantums of what is contained in their own coffers,
remain entirely unconcerned with and, therefore, undeterred by such
minor considerations as the burdens which ordinary people must
suffer.

Besides, if they are enterprising enough and imaginative enough,
as Olof Palme evidently was, the powers that be can easily combine
a literally Messianic crusade for world peace with fairly unabashed
gun-pushing. Little wonder, then, that Palme *could* on the one hand
seek to work out a programme for nothing less than a *downward* spiral
of expenditure on weapons (Palme et al. 1982: x) and on the other
make it so much the easier for Bofors to sell guns to India. Besides,
Palme may not have been the first nor the last of the Swedish
politicians to be making money for personal or political reasons out
of sustained gun-pushing. In fact, the Swedish politicians may well
have attained to much higher levels of finesse and sophistication in
the art of earning kickbacks than politicians in most other countries.
This could well be the reason why the neutral and peace-loving
Sweden happens to be a most important weapons exporter in the world
today. Specifically, it is the tenth biggest exporter of military equipment in the world and has firms selling arms to some forty countries
including both India and Pakistan. But on a per capita basis, Sweden
manages to move from the tenth to the first place itself among weapons
exporters (Matthews 1991: 41–42). This could well be one of the
reasons why the Swedish government has consistently refused to let
a proper inquiry be conducted into the Bofors–India scandal. For who
knows where, if once begun, would such an inquiry end? Incidentally,
Martin Ardbo, who was the Managing Director of Bofors when the
howitzer contract with India was signed, described Palme as his
company's 'best salesman' (Subramaniam 1993: xi). In the light of
all this, then, the following dedication to Olof Palme's memory must
appear to be singularly jejune: 'To Olof Palme, who with sympathy
and commitment gave so much of his talent, knowledge and energy
for a better world' (Tinbergen and Fischer 1987: v). For the same
reason, I find Bernard Lown's (1993: 1) description of Palme as 'one
of the seminal statesmen of our era', to be equally jejune. Indeed, for
this compliment to mean a thing, 'seminal' would have to be understood as something generative of just anything—even corruption.

Be that as it may, the point which needs emphasizing here is that even the democratically elected *staatliche Führungen* of our own time seem to be under no less a compulsion than the totalitarian dictatorships of the past and present to perpetuate kickbackery as an institution. For while the dictators and their coteries can use their positions to receive slush payments, rival groups of putative democrats need such payments to defend their positions: that is, they need slush funds to fight the elections to assume power and then remain installed. Military spending just happens to be a most promising source of slush payments and the *Führungen* seem to suffer no qualms in extracting and extorting what they can. For, this they see as the easiest way to ensure their own continued [full] employment. Or, full misemployment.

Indeed, even Warren Hastings would find himself to have been rather amateurish in comparison with the *Führungen* of our own time. And yet, Edmund Burke (1884: 417) insisted that Hastings had unleashed an orgy of 'fraud, guilt, corruption, and oppression' on a scale never before witnessed 'since the beginning of the world'. Would that Albert Einstein, who used to worry about the unleashed power of the atom, had also been concerned with the uncontrolled power of corruption in our time. In particular, because such corruption involves a sickening collusion between the most parasitic elements of a Third World country like India and financial sharks of the West who [or which?] manage the slush funds in, say, Swiss bank accounts. What we have here is a major but still unrecognized mode of neocolonial exploitation. Or, is it the very ultimate manifestation of constitutional liberty? For it was Edward Gibbon (1977: I-706), no less, who saw corruption as 'the most infallible symptom' of such liberty.

Surreptitious Militarization

Evidently, in a situation in which open-ended corruption and open-ended military spending are only two sides of the same coin, kickbackery cannot but spell an insidious though a most alarming kind of militarization. But militarization becomes infinitely more alarming in a situation in which nuclear weapons are also available. And this, because nuclear warheads contain large quantities of radioactive products which happen to be unbelievably dangerous and long-lived. One of these, made by man himself and named after Pluto, the god of darkness, is known as plutonium. This is the most toxic, and therefore the most lethal, product in the entire universe. Indeed, just about 150 kilograms of it, if 'equitably' distributed, could result in a high probability of every single human being on Earth dying of lung cancer. But, then, there are in existence an estimated 257 *tons* of weapons grade plutonium and probably more than 1,800 tons of highly enriched uranium, either contained in the warheads or held in storage (Renner 1994: 141). There simply is no way available to get rid of this particular legacy of the last half century though the warheads may themselves be completely 'disabled'. But the dismantling of the war-heads, even if undertaken at all seriously, would take several decades to complete and involve great expense—ironically, several times the amount spent on fabricating them! In fact, Russia would now seek massive aid from the West just to disable a large number of her nuclear warheads. The point, besides, is that the plutonium and uranium now contained in the warheads, which have been recklessly stockpiled by the leading *staatliche Führungen* of the world, would continue to menace mankind for untold millenniums.

In other words, our habitat has already been crippled perhaps beyond repair or recovery. But unmindful of all this, the security managers of the world seem hardly disobsessed with military spend-ing. And on their part, the economists, particularly those of the Keynesian persuasion, never fail to provide the moral support with the assurance that such spending is nothing but a legitimate component of 'effective demand' and has to be kept up, at least for the sake of economic buoyancy. For, what would happen to the economy, asked Lekachman (1967: 166) years ago, 'if peace broke out and military expenditure declined from $50 billion to $1 billion per year [during the late sixties]?' With him, the theoretical issue involved was that 'it is just as possible to stimulate a sluggish economy by reducing taxes as by enlarging social welfare programmes or, for that matter, military spending' (Robinson 1979: 183).

But the phrase 'or, for that matter' does *not* signify a viable option any more. Which means that the role of military spending as an economic stimulant, always dubious in nature, is in the present cir-cumstances exceedingly more dubious than ever before. No wonder. More than ever before, military spending is a major cause now of the destruction of economic opportunities for most in need of them. Nor does it fail to cripple the human habitat. This is easy to see. When politicians and military and civilian top brass, eager to swallow vast amounts of slush money, purchase gold-plated weapons, they actually divert the resources away from tasks of social construction and thus generate privations for the underlying multitudes. No wonder, they manage also to erode the political process as well. For, as Galbraith (1992: 137) has written, 'numerous legislators with no commitment either to conscience or constituency' come ardently, even automatically, to serve the military and remain indifferent to the inevitable 'military control of the legislative process'. Needless to say, what is true of the legislative process cannot but be true of the economic process as well. Which only means that the powers that be remain indifferent to the destruction of economic opportunity for ordinary people.

Besides, military spending is not just a question of spending money but of creating a variety of ever-escalating hazards as well. Thus, food chains are known to have been disrupted by the nuclear bomb tests conducted from time to time, that is, *by the money spent on conducting the bomb tests*. For instance, the nuclear tests conducted by the United States over the Marshall Islands and by the French in the area around the Moruroa Atoll are known to have produced ciguatera poisoning, the most common type of fish poisoning in the world. In fact, the intensification of ciguatera poisoning is one of the clearest pathological manifestations of military activity (Ruff 1990: 32–34).

To ignore all this and to focus instead on the narrowly economic implications of military spending is only a continuation of the economystic tradition of ignoring what ought not to be ignored. Indeed, thus alone could military spending be seen as a perfectly legitimate activity, at least from what is imagined to be the purely 'economic point of view'. For, in the Keynesian universe all that matters is the *size* of spending, not its composition. According to Lekachman (1967: 97), Keynes speaks of military expenditure in *The General Theory* itself as one of the few 'respectable' ways of increasing aggregate demand by government action. I have not been able to see where in *The General Theory* Keynes speaks of the 'respectability' of military spending. But there *is* a passage in the book (K-VII: 130) where he speaks of the political *justifiability* of it. Wars and gold mines appear to him to be 'of the greatest value and importance to civilization' apparently because they help in the 'eventual recovery'. Ecological paralysis caused by wars, or just by the fabrication of weapons which may never even get actually expended in any war, was no concern of his nor has it ever been of his followers.

But because of the job—and ecology—destroying potential of weapons-oriented activity *now*, a narrowly economystic perception of it must necessarily be misleading. For, irrespective of whether it promotes immediate economic recovery or not, an indiscriminate kind of increase in military and ordinary spending would most likely do untold damage to the ecosystem in which the economy sought to be stimulated must perforce be rooted.

Missile Mania

Let us recall in this connection one of the ostensible reasons which Ronald Reagan gave while launching the Star Wars programme in March 1983: to force the now-defunct Soviet Union into an economically ruinous arms race in space. But *that* Un-Union must already have been in a state of very advanced bankruptcy. For it came never to need a Strategic Defence Initiative (SDI) of its own to get destroyed. On the other hand, the United States itself seems now to have come to face the music of bankruptcy which *had* to be produced sooner rather than later by the SDI. According to a recent write-up in *The Bulletin of the Atomic Scientists*, within nine years, the SDI's costs had surpassed the $30 billion mark—making it by far the most expensive and also the most wasteful military project in world history (Rothstein 1992: 3–4). Indeed, as an Associated Press report of 25 May 1992 put it, a full quarter of this amount went into projects which had to be discarded as 'unneeded, unworkable or unaffordable'. Some of these projects were meant to develop the X-ray laser, charged-particle beams and electromagnetic rail guns. But they all came to naught. In fact, some SDI scientists and engineers themselves had come to realize by 1987 'that the game was over'. Kosta Tsipis of the MIT called it a fraud and Richard Garwin found the SDI goals to be technologically unachievable.

And, this in the sense that no anti-missile defence could *conceivably* stop *all* incoming warheads. This in itself would spell a kind of disaster unprecedented in the annals of war. For the target nation would be blown to smithereens even if it had been able to stop, say, 95 per cent of the incoming nuclear warheads. This is a kind of fate which, say, Britain could avoid merely by stopping one-tenth of the attacking

German planes. In fact, this interception rate *alone* was enough to ensure the collapse of the Nazi air offensive. But nine-tenths or just one-tenth of the nuclear warheads getting through would spell catastrophe for the nation under attack. [Let us ignore an eventuality like the Nuclear Winter which would not spare the aggressor itself.] But all that Ronald Reagan could say in response to this kind of criticism was, according to *The New York Times* of 12 February 1985, the following: 'I want a defence that simply says that if somebody starts pushing the button on those weapons, we've got a good chance of keeping all or at least the bulk of them from getting to the target'. It seems to have been too difficult for him to see that even a small percentage of the warheads which did get through would spell nothing but calamity. No wonder that Professor Galbraith (1992: 123) has suggested that Reagan is not someone 'given to reflection'.

Far would it be from him to see, then, that a programme like the SDI, which in principle could not succeed, would be an unmitigable ruination even if it did. This is easy to see. If a fully deployed anti-missile defence system did indeed help the Pentagon destroy *each one* of the incoming missiles in mid-flight, the plutonium contained in the crippled warheads would ultimately be scattered over the entire globe, the United States not excluded.

This is too obvious a possibility to have been missed by many. But I have heard it mentioned only once. Delivering his Nehru Memorial Lecture on 'Star Wars and Star Peace' here in Delhi, Professor Arthur C. Clarke made the following point on 13 November 1986: 'Most of [the disabled missiles] would come down on Europe. Because nobody likes to waste expensive missiles, they would probably be "salvage-fused" that is, triggered to detonate if they were attacked. And even if they fizzled only harmlessly, they would release vast quantities of plutonium—one of the deadliest substances known—into the atmosphere' (Clarke 1986: 9).

But surprisingly, even Carl Sagan (1985: 68) failed to make this self-evident point in his debate on the SDI with Edward Teller. In fact, nothing would be wrong, according to him, if *all* the incoming Soviet warheads hit the American anti-missile shield, went *boing* and slithered off harmlessly into the Gulf of Mexico. And, of course, ditto for *all* the attacking American warheads which hit a similar Soviet shield, went *boing* to slide off into the Sea of Okhotsk. In sum, he failed to see any plutonium being scattered around and claimed only that the SDI shields would not and could not destroy each one of the menacing warheads. But to my mind, a real knock-down argument against the very idea of the anti-missile defence—whether space-based or ground-based—lies in the calamity that it must perforce precipitate even in case of complete success. Perhaps, mainly in case of complete success.

But unmoved by any such consideration, the US Establishment is still far from being discharmed with the very concept of anti-missile defence. No wonder that even after the cancellation of the SDI, the fiscal 1994 allocation for anti-missile defence continued to be $3.8 billion (Smith 1993: 3). This was not a cent less than the amount which the Bush Administration had stipulated for the entire venture, Star Wars included. This should certainly enable the military contractors to continue to go to their banks still laughing all the way. And to their cash cleaners, too. In any case, the Star Wars programme was losing credibility beyond the point of redemption and the SDI officials were already being accused of falsifying data, hiding or even destroying hundreds of scientific reports critical of the programme, grossly underestimating the costs, changing plans again and again, 'consuming billions of dollars along the way' and providing an unending feast for the military contractors. Which feast was said to be 'the only reason' why the programme was not discarded altogether.

But, with even an establishment publication like the *Newsweek* coming to call it a fraud on 23 March 1992, it was obviously running out of sustainability. No wonder that, whereas a little earlier, only some of its components were discarded as being 'unneeded, unworkable or unaffordable', it has had ultimately to be discarded as a whole—and for the same reasons. However, the excuse given was the disintegration of the Soviet Union and, therefore, the disappearance of the threat in response to which it had been launched to begin with.

Evidently, it is because of its penchant for such costly and futile ventures as the SDI that the Pentagon is said to have become something of a Rumpelstiltskin in the reverse: unlike the dwarf in the well-known German fairy tale, it is spinning pure gold into plain straw.

Therefore, it cannot but threaten the United States with a most disabling kind of bankruptcy. Indeed, as Eisenhower (Renner 1991: 132) might have put it, the Pentagon would come before long to destroy from within what it is trying [or pretending] to defend from without.

The Star Wars programme certainly took long to be abandoned after the disintegration of the Union of Spuriously Socialist Republics. But, still, its conversion into a fully ground-based anti-missile defence system cannot but be as indefensible *in principle* as the SDI always was. This vindicates Carl Sagan's point (1985: 73) that a trillion dollars intended to be spent on the SDI would create a constituency with its own momentum which would have nothing to do with the originally stated purpose. No wonder that even after abandoning the SDI, the Pentagon has shifted to an equally costly ground-based anti-missile defence system. For, how exactly the programme is based hardly matters. Or, is the Pentagon persisting with anti-missile defence because it fears that, say, Rwanda might one day come to launch nuclear missiles against the United States? Who knows? But it is intriguing, nevertheless, that even an environmentally oriented politician like Senator Al Gore (1992: 321), now the Vice-President of the United States, could find the SDI research programme to be 'well-focused'. Besides, unmindful of the very ultimate environmental disruption that it must necessarily have caused, he sees in it a model of excellence for programmes of environmental protection to emulate!

Military Inexorability

As against this, what I see in the SDI or even in a ground-based anti-missile defence system is irrefutable evidence of the phenomenal momentum of military inexorability. And this in the sense that such programmes embody more than anything else whatsoever the power of the American Establishment to persist with reckless and economically bankrupting exercises even after the very excuse for them, the Soviet threat, has vanished without a trace. That is exactly what happened after it became clear that the Nazis were nowhere near making the atom bomb. But that did not persuade the powers that be to wind up the Manhattan District Project which had been launched in the first instance to beat the Nazis to the Bomb. Indeed, only one of the scientists working on the project, Joseph Rotblat, saw no point in its continuation and went back to doing normal physics.

The B-2 bomber is another manifestation of this inexorability. It was once claimed that the Soviet radar would never be able to 'see' it. But its 'stealthiness' is no longer taken very seriously. Even so, the Pentagon has long been determined to acquire more of these highly visible bombers to strike a Soviet Union which itself has become completely invisible (Hackworth 1992b: 30).

This argues the virtually unlimited power of the Pentagon to continue to override civilian authority and pre-empt resources irrespective of the existence of an enemy. Nor, for that matter, is the civilian authority overly keen on impeding the Pentagon. We are told that one evening in late June 1994, the Senate was debating the merits of producing more of B-2 bombers. Senator Dianne Feinstein of California, speaking in favour, declared that the bomber could 'deliver a large *payroll*, precision or carpet'. Later, she got 'payroll' corrected in the record as 'payload' but the Freudian slip was rather revealing (Isaacs 1994: 13).

Nevertheless, accredited scholarship remains by and large indifferent towards the fell perils of military inexorability. Epitomizing this attitude more tellingly than anyone else perhaps is Professor Paul Samuelson who, bless his skills, has come actually to personify this history-destroying phenomenon. Let me explain how. Early in the first edition of *Economics* (Samuelson 1948: 18), he makes the following point: 'If we are willing to give up some butter, we can have some guns; if we are willing to give up some guns, we can have some butter'. *In other words, we can give up either for the other*. But in later editions, beginning with the second edition itself, this option ceases to be available. For we can now give up only butter, and more and more of it, too, for more and more—and more—of guns. Call it choice, if you will, but to me it seems to be only a textbook surrogate for military inexorability. For the second edition of *Economics* carries the following affirmation: 'If we are willing to give up some butter, we can have some guns; *if we are willing to give up still more butter, we can have still more guns*' (Samuelson 1951: 18; emphasis mine). This is the form in which the guns–butter duality has remained frozen ever since.

It seems highly likely that it is this more or less instinctive preference for guns over butter which impelled Professor Samuelson to take a self-consciously hawkish position with respect to the Vietnam War. For this is what he wrote at the time: 'Those who disapprove of our war activities in Vietnam were disappointed with my analysis which showed that America could "afford" an even larger war as far as the economics of the problem is concerned. But at least they could derive comfort from my conclusion that our prosperity would not necessarily be imperilled by peace' (Samuelson 1967b: 47). However, what he calls his 'analysis' was no more than an assertion to the effect that the United States was spending 'but a small fraction' of its GNP on the Vietnam 'conflict'. *Any* hawk and not necessarily an economist could have said a thing like that. Only, he may not have dismissed, as Samuelson did, the concerns about the inflationary potential of an expanded Vietnam War as manifestations of mere 'paranoia'.

Besides, equally unacceptable was Samuelson's italicized conclusion that *'we had the power to introduce expansionary fiscal and credit programmes that would offset any decline in arms spending'* (Samuelson 1966a: 107). This was a reformulation of an earlier assertion that for 'puffing' the economy, 'There's nothing that a dollar of military spending can do that a dollar of private family spending can't also do. Or a dollar of civilian government spending' (Samuelson et al. 1966: 53). Evidently, a dollar of civilian spending cannot help organize eco-disruptive nuclear explosions and is therefore a preferable mode of spending in itself. That apart, to take 'puffing' the economy as a goal in itself bespeaks an extreme degree of unconcern with the stability and viability of the human habitat itself.

It is also worth emphasizing that what Samuelson describes merely as 'our war activities in Vietnam', and what the Robert McNamara of the mid-nineties vintage is shedding a flood of tears over, included the spraying of eleven million gallons of Agent Orange, a defoliant mixed with a cancer causing chemical called dioxin, over many thousands of Vietnamese known to be hiding in a six-million acre thick forest.

Only a mainline economist could turn a Nelson eye to the wanton genocide taking place at the time in Vietnam and continue instead to claim that the war was perfectly 'affordable' and also that its termination would not necessarily imperil 'our prosperity'. This calls for intervention by a psychiatrist like Robert Lifton. In fact, only recently (1993: 127) he has spoken of the disquieting ease with which people can develop a genocidal mentality—a willingness to participate in *or support* policies that, if carried out, would result in the annihilation of a particular human group. It is *this* aspect of the Vietnam War to which the economystic ideologues of the American ruling circles, intent on securing their supplies of tin and tungsten, continued to remain distressingly insensitive.

But, then, what Fyodor Dostoyevsky (1989: 225), for example, said a long time ago about a tyrant would be no less true of an endorser of genocide so that one could say something like the following: In an endorser of genocide, both the human being and the social being are killed for ever, and a return to human dignity, to repentance and to resurrection becomes almost impossible.

No wonder that the academic endorsers of genocide at the time being legion, the raging cult of brutality remained entirely unabated. Which provoked Bertrand Russell, according to Samuelson (1986: 262) as brilliant a mind as philosophy and mathematics could offer, to deliver the following indictment: 'I know of few wars fought more cruelly or more destructively or with a greater display of naked cynicism, than the war waged by the United States against the peasant population of South Vietnam. It is a war which epitomizes the indifference to individual freedom, national sovereignty and popular well-being—which is so characteristic of the world-policy of the military and industrial groups controlling the United States' (Russell 1967: 57).

Be that as it may, at least some of 'our war activities in Vietnam', as Samuelson saw them, did not take long to come home to roost. In particular, because several thousands of American servicemen who had ventured into or gone near the sprayed jungle to comb out the so-called Vietcong, got themselves exposed to Agent Orange. Many of these are known to have developed a variety of cancers, incurred other disabilities and fathered seriously handicapped children. One of them, Elmo Zumwalt, who happened to be the son of the Admiral who had ordered that Agent Orange be sprayed in the Mekong Delta region, died from a rare lymphoma in 1988. Ed Magnuson (1990: 27) described this incident as a tragedy, and a tragedy it was. But he made not even a passing reference to the much grimmer tragedy of many thousands of Vietnamese *over* whom Agent Orange was directly sprayed.

Some 20,000 American servicemen returning from Vietnam sued Dow Chemical and other companies and were awarded $180 million in damages (Press 1984: 56). As the *Newsweek* reported a little later on 21 January 1985, some 150, 000 servicemen and their families ultimately came to file claims with the US district court of judge Jack Weinstein.

With all this taken into account, what Professor Samuelson calls 'our prosperity' must be seen as something utterly dubious in nature. In particular, because such prosperity, whatever its intrinsic worth, could not possibly be the prosperity of the United States as a whole *but only that of the Other than the Other America.*

But how desirable would be an eco-disruptive and elite-oriented prosperity at home if it could also mean genocide abroad? Besides, a permanent war economy having already been instituted in the United

States in the form of a runaway kind of weapons production, the weapons-based prosperity at home would be of a questionable kind even without that genocide. Professor Galbraith wrote a pamphlet on the Vietnam War with, if memory serves, the following subtitle: 'A war which America cannot, will not, should not win'. And a former American military commander in Vietnam, David Hackworth (1992a: 24), found that war to be 'a criminal enterprise brought upon our nation by careless politicians [just 'careless'?] and the greed of the military industries'. He did not find America's security to be at stake at all and helped many men get out. Indeed, according to him, one would have to be brain-damaged to *want* to sink into that swamp and the only Americans who endorsed the war were the loony tunes and the John Waynes. But notwithstanding all this, Professor Samuelson continued to endorse it rather warmly and it did not occur to the self-styled radical (Samuelson 1972: 287) within him, let alone the liberal, also self-styled, to try to stir even faintly in protest. What he continued to be satisfied with instead was the 'affordability' of the Vietnam War.

Military inexorability is, of course, not peculiar to the United States. Still, it is the sheer scale of military spending and therefore the sheer *cost* of this inexorability in America which the economists in particular ought to be concerned with. Thus, over the period of the putative Cold War, the United States spent something like $10 trillion on arms and the related military activities. This amount would be enough to buy up everything in America except the land (Sagan 1992: 24). The Pentagon spending in the early 1990s used to be around $270 billion a year (Sivard 1993 : 43) and the total over the years 1993–98 is expected to be close to *one-and-a-half million million* dollars (Isaacs 1993: 12). No wonder that given a 'budgetary environment' so congenial, weapons research in America continues unabated, Cold War or no. To be sure, no new warheads are said to be rolling off the production lines. 'But that doesn't mean the warhead-development business has dried up'. For, as a Pentagon official in a written reply to a congressional enquiry recently put it: 'There will be requirements for new nuclear weapons in the future' (Grier 1992: 1). Which explains why hardly anyone at, say, the Lawrence Livermore and Sandia National weapons laboratories is unduly worried about losing his job. Rather, people there are as busy as ever trying to imagine what types of weapons the Pentagon might be abetted to have in the future. Costs to them are of no concern. For their expertise does not lie in making something cheap but in making something exotic. 'If it's gold-plated, it's gold-plated' (McKenzie 1992: 5A). Not a few of these gold-plated varieties of mini- and even micro-nuclear weapons are now being mooted for deployment and even use in the Third World. Besides, Thomas Ramos of the Pentagon argues that 'the very presence' of US nuclear weapons around the world would serve as a deterrent against proliferation (Akrin and Norris 1992: 24–25). In other words, a programme of further proliferation of nuclear weapons is being sold in order to forestall any further proliferation.

The point of it all is that military spending is not just an innocuous quantity passive in itself, which the State can manipulate to ensure economic regulation or if required, stimulation. Instead:

it has long been an elemental force with an utterly disruptive momentum of its own so that economic policy makers can do little to control, much less to manipulate it;

its size is very largely determined by the kickback giving and receiving communities;

it must perforce come to subvert in ways insidious or otherwise the basic structure of the society in question;

it cannot but deplete and destroy the terrestrial basis of human existence; and

ironically, it could well destroy many more jobs than the high-tech openings it might create even *within the military sector*.

In support of the point about job destruction, one might cite the specific case of Osprey, a pricey and highly controversial helicopter-cum-airplane being acquired by the US Navy to 'carry whatever Marines are left after the corps is cut by 25 per cent partly to pay for such fat-city frills' (Hackworth 1992b: 30). This lends credence to the point often made that a runaway kind of military spending cannot but generate burdens which even an extremely rich economy like the United States could ill-afford to carry.

In fact, in an interview with the *U.S. News & World Report*, Wassily Leontief (1981: 26) found some of these burdens to be heavy enough to threaten 'economic calamity'. The Reagan jumps in military spending, he said, would mean higher inflation, a worsening balance-of-payments gap, a massive drain on productive investment, soaring interest rates, increasing taxes, a debased currency and, in the longer term, more unemployment. Increased Pentagon spending, he added, would, particularly through stoking the fires of inflation, really cut into the life flesh of millions.

It follows, therefore, that escalating military spending should be a major source of concern, not complacency. It follows also that the Keynesian conception of military spending as a simple quantity to be manipulated for purposes of economic regulation and stimulation, not very insightful even to begin with, has continued over time to become ever more dubious. For, specifically, as a surrogate for a programme of sustained hole-digging, it has failed to produce the jobs which Keynes said it would. In fact, US military spending in our own time is by far the vastest hole-digging programme that the world has ever known. Yet, and ironically, *what it is sustaining is unemployment, not employment, at high levels.* This alone should argue the collapse of Keynesianism in general and of military Keynesianism in particular. This argues also an unending brutalization of the human condition manifested in an explosion of immiseration even within the United States itself, as also in the relentlessness of the Silent Holocaust. Which, to repeat, continues to produce worldwide at least one Hiroshima a day. That, of course, means nothing but a perpetuation and intensification of the cult of brutality which Hitler embodied and promoted.

Be that as it may, if someone were to ask me to choose one, just one, legatee of what I like to call the Keynes–Hitler sodality, I would without a moment's hesitation choose Professor Paul Anthony Samuelson of the MIT. In justification, I can do little better than to cite his complete insensitivity to the deliberately genocidal decimation of the Vietnamese as also to the process of virtually open-ended weaponization of America. Incidentally, referring to G. H. Hardy's statement that the one romance of his life as a Cambridge mathematician was his collaboration with the self-taught Indian genius Srinivasa Ramanujan, Professor Samuelson (1979: 892) makes the following observation: 'The great romance in the life of any economist of my generation must necessarily have been the Keynesian revolution.' But what would he say now that the so-called Keynesian revolution can be seen to have been little but a miserable 'irrevolution'?

2   Samuelson and Hitler*

> I dislike being wrong.
> Paul A. Samuelson (1986: 793)

Wronger and Wronger
[Lewis Carroll: O No!]

Professor Paul Samuelson speaks about his dislike for being wrong in a note dealing with his life philosophy. This is a seven-page *long* piece for the preparation of which, he tells us, he could receive no more than partial financial support from the Sloan Foundation.

Anyway, Samuelson cannot be the only one who dislikes being wrong. No one, in fact, would *like* being wrong. But still, his position in this respect is unique. For, he dislikes being wrong so much that he simply refuses to admit being wrong no matter how overwhelming and convincing the evidence which shows that he *is* in fact wrong. In contrast, A. J. Ayer has this to say: 'Why should you mind being wrong if someone can show you that you are?'

But consider, for instance, the following quotation which in the latest but one edition edition of *Economics* Samuelson ascribes to Keynes: 'For the next twenty-five years, economists will be the most important group of scientists in the world. And it is to be hoped—if they are successful—that after that they will never be important again' (Samuelson and Nordhaus 1989: 955).

But missing from this quotation is Keynes's 1932 assessment of the economists: 'at present the most incompetent [group of scientists]'.

*An earlier version of this chapter appeared in the *Economic and Political Weekly* of 29 January 1994.

Besides, in the very next sentence, Keynes referred to the economists as 'these creatures'. Evidently, phrases such as these could not possibly have been dropped through sheer oversight. Rather, they must have been subjected, in Shakespearean idiom, to a 'most foul and unnatural' excision.

I am not suggesting that what Keynes, even undoctored by Samuelson, had said was something very profound and meaningful. Quite to the contrary, in fact. For to my mind, his claim wouldn't stand a moment's scrutiny: For twenty-five years, that is, till the arbitrarily selected year 1957, he expected the economists, no matter how incompetent, to succeed [at what?] and then suddenly cease to be important. or to fail [as what?] and then continue to be important. There may not be a semanticist around who could assign any meaning to this queer collection of words. For, all that can be said for it as a collection of words is that grammatically it is not incorrect. But it still is without meaning—like Noam Chomsky's famous illustration: Colourless green ideas sleep furiously. But a misquotation remains a misquotation even if the original be something without meaning.

Be that as it may, no one contemplating 'further study' of what Samuelson calls 'our exciting science' no less than thirty-two years after 1957, the limit stipulated by Keynes himself, could be expected to take heart even from the original, much less from the expurgated words of 'this century's greatest economist'. For the words simply did never mean a thing. Even so, the 1989 edition of *Economics* expects young people to get fired with imagination and inspiration by these words, no matter how void of content they always were. But should the students not be wary of joining a profession which happens to be infested with people who, whatever the reason, are either incompetent *and* important or competent *and* unimportant?

But, given his dislike for being wrong, Samuelson responded to my letter concerning the misquotation with the verdict that in a textbook, one could do what one pleased with someone else's words. A very singular verdict, this. For in pronouncing it, one arrogates to oneself the right to go beyond even Humpty Dumpty who 'claimed the most entire freedom to give any meaning to any word' (Robinson 1970: 72). Still, Humpty claimed this kind of freedom with respect to only such words as *he* himself chose to use. In contrast, Professor Samuelson insisted on claiming the most entire freedom, even if within the confines of a textbook, to drop any of the words *which others may have used*: If, he advised me, 'you check as I have done several of the quotations that head various chapters [of *Economics*], you will find similar missing words'. But meaningwise, he added, all the quotations remain undistorted, just as what he called 'the abridged version' of the Keynes quote does.

But even the 'abridged' version of Keynes's dictum, has now been dropped from the new, 1992, edition of *Economics*, possibly in response to my letter.

But Samuelson could well have continued to stick to his guns, impelling me instead to come to agree with him that a misquotation could be a misquotation if and only if *he* chose to say that it was one. Consider, in this connection, what the Rev. Charles Lutwidge Dodgson said a long time ago, 'If I find an author saying ..."[By] the word *black* I shall always mean *white* [and vice versa]", I meekly accept his ruling, however injudicious I may think it' [Gardner 1977: 269]. Ditto with respect to Samuelson's claim *to the effect* that a misquotation would be a misquotation if and only if it occurred not in *Economics* at all but, say, in one of his scientific papers.

That is, like the one which follows: 'How majestic is the equality of the Law which permits both rich and poor alike to sleep under the bridges at night' (Samuelson 1966b: 1416). These are the words which, according to Samuelson, enable Anatole France to say all that needs to be said 'about the coercion implicit in the libertarian economics of *laissez-faire*'.

But that is just not so and Anatole France has, in fact, said a lot more than what the famous epigram by itself suggests. For all that it says by itself is no more than what a nineteenth century Lord Justice of England, Sir James Mathew, said about British justice: In England, justice is open to all, like the Ritz Hotel. Inequality in such a situation *is an immutable and static fact*; and so is the violence which goes with it. But the structured violence which the military-industrial civilization of our time generates is *a dynamic and inexorable process*; and so is the coercion implicit in the libertarian or rather libertine economics of *laissez faire*. Which from the very beginning has been a sustained apology of this civilization. This only means that the *processual* and therefore escalating violence and coercion produced by military-industrialism cannot be captured *merely* by Anatole France's epigram even in its original, let alone Samuelsonian, version.

But the situation changes considerably when the epigram is returned to its context and read along with what precedes and what succeeds it. The sentence which immediately precedes the one which Samuelson has misquoted reads as follows: 'For the poor [the pride of French citizenship] consists in supporting and maintaining the rich in their power and their idleness'. And then in the lines following the epigram which is almost always cited out of context, Anatole France speaks of the empire of wealth which in the name of equality, though, the French Revolution created for the rich who in turn have been devouring the country ever since. In other words, to the poor, the cost of supporting and maintaining the rich has continued only to mount. It is this which the epigram *alone* does not say: 'At this task [of maintaining and supporting the rich, the poor] must labour in the face of the majestic equality of the laws, which forbid rich and poor alike to sleep under the bridges, to beg in the streets, and to steal their bread' (France 1917: 75).

I did try to draw Professor Samuelson's attention to the way he had misquoted the epigram and to the crucial significance of the sentence just preceding it in the original. But, of course, there was no convincing him. Presuming that I was merely concerned with *forbid* having been misquoted as *permits*, he completely ignored the rest of the misquotation and, instead, quoted two Broadway lines with the same meaning: 'I *can* but die' and 'I *cannot* but die'. Which is to say that in using the word 'permits' in place of 'forbid' in the original and also in letting a hearsay version go in print, he had not misquoted Anatole France! Incidentally, on another occasion (Samuelson 1979: 865), he did actually admit that he was quoting Justice Holmes only from imperfect memory and could well be corrupting the text with some Freudian slips thrown in! But making a similar admission to someone relatively unknown like me appears to have been something unthinkable to him.

Involved here is a baffling refusal to admit having misquoted someone right in the face of all the evidence which shows precisely that one has. Even so, misquotation is not half so serious an academic failing as misrepresentation. Which, as we shall see, enables Professor Samuelson to see the most forbidding iniquities as unmitigable benevolences. Not just capitalist iniquities but very specific *American* iniquities. No wonder that he continues to turn out the most Panglossian pictures of a reality which in fact is menacing in the extreme.

Even so, I should like to make it clear, as best one can, that, to me, 'Paul A. Samuelson' does not *just* mean the name of an individual. For exceedingly more important, it means an ideology, a world-view, embodied in and personified by that individual. This is an ideology, moreover, which serves to put a thick and not easily penetrable gloss over the existential hazards of our time and as such is nothing less than a menace which threatens the very history of our species with termination.

It does not need a fire-eating radical to see through this ideological gloss. Just a 'bleeding-heart liberal', to use a phrase which Professor Samuelson (1986: 789) himself once used, would do. No wonder: given the mind, what matters is the heart, the more liberal the better. For such a heart *alone* can be empathic enough to comprehend the worldwide ravages of the military-industrialism of our time: Ravages which cannot but include the very extremes of poverty and immiseration even within the United States itself. It follows that Professor Samuelson's claim (*ibid.*) that his is 'a simple ideology that favours the underdog and [other thing being equal] abhors inequality' has to be taken with more than a pinch of salt. One would do well to focus instead on some of the illusions he is so fond of generating. One of the most distracting of these is the illusion of a mixed economy which, according to him, enables, say, millions of New Yorkers to continue to sleep easily at night.

The Mixed-Up Economy

Consider the city of New York, we are told (Samuelson and Nordhaus 1992: 36): 'How is it that 10 million people are able to *sleep easily at night*, without living in mortal terror of a breakdown in the elaborate economic processes upon which the city's existence depends? The surprising answer is that these economic activities are coordinated without coercion or centralized direction by anybody' [emphasis mine].

However, thanks very largely to the economists cast in the Samuelson mould, not many of the 10 million New Yorkers may have begun yet to be concerned with the imminent breakdown of the elaborate economic processes upon which the existence of their city depends much less to appreciate Issac Singer's point that this metropolis has all the symptoms of a mind gone berserk. But if as many as 10 million New Yorkers can manage to sleep easily at night, there could be no reason why any of the other Americans should have to suffer bad dreams at night or even during daytime. Only, they would have to be presumed, as the New Yorkers have been presumed, to be free from what Samuelson calls 'coercion or centralized direction by anybody'.

However, the simon-purity of the kind of market coordination that this suggests gets contaminated not a little by a variety of government interventions like 'taxes, spending, and regulation'. Such interventions produce what Samuelson and Nordhaus (1992: 741) call a 'mixed economy'. But it is only the precise content of these interventions which would determine the nature of the 'mixedness' of the economy in question. For instance, 'spending' by itself would just remain an abstract notion and tell us little about its role in the economy. But if we take care to remember that a great deal of spending can be incurred on weapons, on entitlements for the well-to-do and, Heaven forbid, also on bailouts aforethought for hordes of unscrupulous financial operators, the mixed economy ceases to be as even-handed a social formation as Samuelson and Nordhaus take it to be.

In support of this claim, one need do little more than examine the role of the US government in the actual precipitation and the so-called resolution of the savings and loan (S&L) scandal of the 1980s. For this alone should show that the mixed economy of the Samuelsonian conception is, in effect, a formal arrangement for the usurpation of gains by hordes of wheeler-dealers *but to the concomitant assumption of the corresponding costs by the State*. I do not know if Samuelson has written much on the S&L scandal. But there is a passing reference to it in the *Economics* of 1992 (p. 534) where it is described as a mere 'fiasco'. That is, something understood as a ludicrous and humiliating failure of policy all right but still a failure which is purely incidental to that policy. However, something which Galbraith (1992: 61), for one, has described as 'the largest and costliest venture in public misfeasance, malfeasance and larceny of all time' could not just be taken to be an incidental fiasco. Rather, it would need to be taken to be something actually built into the cynical mixture of the elements of the American mixed economy.

No wonder that the bailout of the S&L depositors has already produced what is called the Son of the S&L scandal. But first, let us have a look at the way that the parent itself came into the world. Well, putting it a bit picturesquely, it was born of an apparently very odd congress. That is, the one between capitalism's bitch-goddess called *laissez-faire* and its *bête noire*, the State. Of course, it was the US Congress itself which abetted the consummation by causing *both* the goddess and the beast to come to a state of heightened excitation: the goddess, by a complete deregulation of the S&L's; and the beast, by raising the deposit insurance protection, *provided at public expense*, from $40,000 to $100,000 *per account* held by a depositor. A more brazen arrangement than this for the generation of booty by swarms of scoundrels with the State assuming all the losses, and a more cynical scholarship than the one which could designate this kind of existential reality as a 'mixed economy' would be hard to imagine. No wonder that interested no more in the little guy nor even in the middle-class borrowers wanting money for mere homes, the S&L's began lending it to reckless developers with big, speculative, wild and weird dreams. Or even to people who would use the money to buy high-yield, high-risk junk bonds. Besides, 'men without the slightest bankerly inclination' (Glassman 1993: 24) began to buy small S&L's and pump them with thousands of government-insured deposits in $100, 000 increments. Evidently, all this was done for purposes of pure plunder. For, the best way to rob an S&L would be to buy it. Thus, according to Glassman (*ibid.:* 23), one Don Dixon and his cronies defrauded their S&L of over half a billion dollars. They made loans up to $90 million *each* to friends without 'any reasonable basis for concluding [that] they were collectible'. In addition, Vernon Savings and Loan, which Dixon owned, bought a $2 million beach house for his use. He had another house built in California, flew with his wife to London to consult an interior decorator and buy $489, 000 in furnishings. For the walls, he acquired $5. 5 million worth of Western art. And, not finally, he took his wife and friends on a two-week tour of France. Needless to say, all these extravagances were duly paid for by Vernon Savings and Loan.

But by no means was Vernon an exception. Instead, it was the rule —a rule which enabled an operator like Charles Keating, for instance, to rake in $34 million for himself and his family in return for generating losses amounting to $2. 5 billion (Glynn 1993: 18). Keating also made Lincoln, the S&L he had acquired, contribute generously to the campaign coffers and political committees of as many as twenty-four members of the US Congress. Among them were five senators, the Keating Five, who took $1.3 million from him (Day 1993: 263). In return, he got political protection from them, though at a hefty cost of $2 billion to the tax-payer. One of the Five was the former astronaut Senator John Glenn—a sort of a peacenik to boot. It is easy to see that only the gung-ho operators of an S&L could lend millions of dollars to a car dealer who didn't even exist. And only one such operator could indulge in the sickening luxury of a bullet-proof bathroom.

Besides, thanks only to the weird generosity of an S&L could Neil Bush, a classic babe in the woods, dream of making millions in business. For in spite of his abnormal difficulty with reading and spelling, a disease formally diagnosed as dyslexia, he was found to be perfectly fit to be a director of a Denver S&L called Silverado but locally known as Desperado. Nor did this third and the only non-intelligent son of George Bush, the US Vice-President at the time, fail to see the reason why he was being so elevated. Moreover, his lack of brains did not stop him from realizing that it was 'a little fishy' for him to be able to borrow $100, 000 from one Kenneth Good for a high-risk venture and be required to repay it if and only if the venture succeeded. It didn't; and he didn't repay. But whether it was fishy or not, Bush did help Good in due course to borrow several millions from Silverado—millions which never were repaid (*ibid.*: 364). In the meantime, Silverado swelled from under a $100 million in more or less genuine loan assets in 1980 to billions in entirely spurious loan assets by 1988 (Glynn: 1993 17).

The mixed economy is thus coming to look more and more like an arrangement conditioned and defined by plain crime and financial manipulations of a most remorseless kind. In sum, wheeler-dealing seems to have emerged as a prepotent culture-category of contemporary capitalism. Samuelson and Nordhaus seek to explain the massive S&L larceny of not easily exceedable proportions partly in terms of 'high salaries for the directors' of the loan associations and partly in terms of the principle governing their operations: 'Heads I win, tails the government loses'. But, then, that exactly is the principle which the mixed economy of their conception must be governed by. Indeed, the 'heads tails' syndrome congeals nothing less than a redefinition of the Samuelsonian mixed economy. *Which means, to repeat, a remorseless juxtaposition of the private appropriation of benefits and the public assumption of the costs involved.* Besides, by no means could such juxtaposition be explained in terms of 'some frantic perversion of business arithmetic', as Keynes (K-XXVIII: 342) perhaps would have put it. For it is not any latter-day perversion but the congenital dynamic of the 'Arithmetic of Acquisition', with capital A's, which impels people to turn into larceners big and small. This is what, say, the Michael Milkens in America and the Harshad Mehtas in India have in common. Entirely to blame is what, in a 1920 letter

to H. G. Wells, William James described as 'the squalid cash inter-
pretation put on the word success'. Only naturally, then, and in a hurry
to make millions, the S&L operators continued to indulge in reckless
speculation in real estate and created an excess of commercial office
space in the cities, expensive condominiums in the suburbs, the
'architecturally questionable skyscrapers in New York City and [the]
admittedly hideous gambling casinos in Atlantic City'. All this 'set
the stage for what was by far the most feckless and felonious dispo-
sition of what, essentially, were public funds in the nation's history,
perhaps in any modern nation's history' (Galbraith 1992: 59, 63). A
misadventure of such proportions was bound to collapse in a rash of
insolvencies and leave the S&L depositors high and dry.

But the State decided once again to play its traditionally selective
role, provide the insurance cover to the well-to-do depositors, force
the underclasses to continue to suffer the deprivations and make
tax-payers in general take on the money cost. Which in this case turned
out to be rather mind-boggling. Thus, according to Kathleen Day
(1993: 375): 'With interest added, realistic estimates of the tab easily
exceed $500 billion in ten years, or more than $1 trillion in several
decades, enough by some calculations to add $13 billion a year in
interest—for ever—to the national debt'..Besides, in 1990 and 1991,
'with estimates of the bailouts' ultimate cost reaching into the trillions,
the Bush administration abandoned [all] pretence of limiting tax-payer
liability. [For it] was generally accepted that the public would foot
most, if not all, of the cost'. Indeed, busted S&L's in Texas *alone*
could cost the US tax-payers some $560 billion over the next forty
years (Corn 1993: 488). Incidentally, the public rescue of just *one*
S&L, known as American Diversified, cost the Federal government
as much as the bailouts of New York City, Chrysler and Lockheed
combined. Evidently, but not incidentally, the 'morals and working
morale' of the rich rentiers are not thought to be in any way damaged
by deposit insurance provided at public expense. For, the compara-
tively 'affluent can withstand the adverse moral effect of being sub-
sidized and supported by the government; not so the poor' (Galbraith
1992: 15).

Such, then, are the bare bones of what to Samuelson and Nord-
haus(1992: 535) was no more than a 'sad episode'. That is: something
which was but a break in an otherwise unbroken chronicle of economic
bliss; something during which people with state-insured deposits did
not lose their sleep but during which the economists brooding over

the wayward behaviour of the S&L operators probably lost theirs; something which still was no more than a relatively marginal aberration; something, moreover, whose occurrence in future could be prevented if only the banks and the public could continue to behave as 'cooperating partners' in the process of money creation: the banks by creating it through a 'multiple expansion of reserves', and the public by continuing to hold it 'in depository institutions'.

It is out of a collocation of innocences of this kind, then, that neoclassical wisdom is formed: innocences which can make sense only in the halcyon pages of textbooks like the *Economics* of 1992. But they stand not a chance in the murky world of reality, which is to be found beyond the pages of such books. Consider, then, a situation in which a hyperactive wheeler-dealer of Washington, who is made the Commerce Secretary of the United States, turns out to be 'the best spin artist in Clinton's cabinet', and is accused of influence-peddling and in fact of accepting $700, 000 in one deal alone. Or, a situation in which a former S&L owner, who is made the Treasury Secretary— yes, the *Treasury Secretary*—in the Clinton Cabinet, allows his son to make off with a $4. 25 million loan on which payments need not be made, and himself manages to stand by while, as David Corn (1993) insists, 'a scandal of tremendous and costly proportions is occurring'.

This is the Son of the S&L scandal which is centred round the Resolution Trust Corporation [RTC] overseeing the S&L bailouts. The RTC is reported (Corn 1993: 488) to be infested with corruption and incompetence. It continues to waste hundreds of millions of dollars by deliberately finalizing bad deals and has repeatedly punished and impeded lawyers and investigators trying to win back some of the money stolen by the S&L operators in the 1980s. Indeed, its own Inspector General's office has spent 'more time covering up, or committing fraud than it ever spent investigating it'. Specifically, this office has kept itself busy rewriting reports to avoid embarrassment and to mislead the Congress, covering up high-level misconduct, shredding incriminating documents and helping rig a report on Neil Bush. Added to the foregoing are the furtive purchases of RTC properties by its own chairman. Michael Koszola, a special agent for the RTC's Inspector General, testified to all this before a· hearing of a Senate subcommittee on banking. But the members of the committee merely heard him in silence.

In the meantime, mainline economics insensitive to iniquity, no matter how glaring, continues to sing paeans to the sheer benignity of market coordination. Benignity, moreover, remains unmitigated by State intervention and allows ordinary people to remain undisturbed and unbothered by all kinds of deprivations and highly organized crime including rampant larcenies of high finance. Which larcenies, as noted, Professor Galbraith, in particular, has taken so much care to focus on.

Concerning New York

But irrespective of all these inexorable iniquities, Professor Samuelson, as we have seen already, thinks that millions of New Yorkers in any case continue to sleep easily at night. And this, in spite of the following: New York which accounts for no more than 3 per cent of the population of America has lost as many as one-third of *all* manufacturing jobs lost in the country as a whole since 1969; the city is living with a heavy budget deficit of $2.7 billion in 1995 while the rich continue to get a bulk of $1.1 billion tax cut; and public hospitals have been closed down throughout the city (Fitch 1995 : 628–32). Therefore, for anyone who cares to see, the imminence of a major breakdown of the economic processes is writ very large on the face of New York. Only, in letters of muck, filth and garbage. Over the years 1993–96, a sum of at least $520 million would have to be spent on the construction and renovation of several incineration plants. But there is no way to compute the public health costs of congenital deformities, widespread brain damage and an excess of cancers which those having to live in the vicinity of the incineration plants would perforce have to suffer. Note may also be taken of mercury contamination which could taint fish and mothers' milk as well (Amron 1992: A14). Given the onslaught of 26,000 tons of trash every day (Coletti 1992: A14), the city is clearly running out of options. In particular, because it may no longer be able to *export* its garbage to the hinterland and may have to find waste disposal locations within its own increasingly choked confines. In fact, as *Time* reported on 27 July 1992, New York did try to pass off 2,200 tons of garbage in June to *some* landfill facility in the country which would be prepared to receive it. But as many as three states rejected the detritus occupying 30 railway wagons. In consequence, having made a 3,000-mile trip, the bug-infested cargo 'wound up back home' to the Staten Island landfill called Fresh Kills.

Besides, thanks to a Congress ban on ocean dumping, New York would now have to handle vast quantities of thick greasy sludge on land itself. But while it would be nearly impossible to export, bury or burn this material, it would be hard to find a New Yorker willing to live near a plant designed to process it. Also, sludge disposal would now cost over $250 million a year as against less than $20 million earlier. But using the ocean as a municipal chamberpot has its own ecological costs, unbearable in themselves (Specter 1992: A16).

But what has all this to do with Professor Samuelson? A great deal. For all the solid waste and sludge which New York like other metropolises has to contend with is by no means a necessary product of city life as such. It is a product instead of a culture informed and conditioned by orgiastic waste. For what Samuelson sees as New York's elaborate economic processes are in fact a set of cynically orchestrated procedures which cannot but produce overconsumption and therefore uncontrollable waste. The recklessly throwaway culture of which New York is a major exemplar can be seen to be not just wallowing in waste but to be choking on its own vomit, too. Here, then, is a most important reason why not one of the ten million Americans now cooped up in New York would before long be able to sleep easily at night. Notwithstanding the illusion mongering which happens to be the passion 'par unexcellence' of the economics profession.

But there is an important reason—homelessness—why *even now* not a few of the New Yorkers may not be sleeping easily at night. For instance, according to an Associated Press release of 4 June 1991, police in riot gear raided the Tompkins Square Park the previous night and evicted some 150 squatters from there. But the Park Supervisor, Michael Napa, told the reporters, 'Personally, I don't think it's over. You might be back here tomorrow for the riot'. The squatters could well have been sleeping pretty easily at night to be rioting against their eviction from the park. Even so, those in the social sciences who manage to elide and ignore the phenomenon of homeless squatting in a city like New York must indeed be quite insensitive to brutality and brutalization as such; in particular, because the Tompkins Square Park squatters could not possibly have been an exception. Nevertheless, in spite of his unconcern for the raging iniquities of our time manifested in his claim about the New Yorkers sleeping easily at night and in spite of his claim about America being able to 'afford' a much bigger war in Vietnam, Professor Samuelson (1979: 895) has this to say about himself as an economist: certainly 'the blend in economics of analytical hardness and humane relevance was tailor-made for me and I for it'.

To be sure, what is called 'the homeless caseload' is said to have decreased during the year 1991 in some places such as Westchester County, a New York City suburb otherwise awash in people without homes (Mathews 1992: 2). But the reasons given do not all suggest an irreversible and sustainable subdual of the scourge. A three-day medical, psychological and occupational check-up which this county now insists upon may in itself be screening out not a few of the shelter-seekers. Many of them stay away 'when told that they must undergo drug treatment and other forms of rehabilitation'. The basic causes of homelessness such as poverty and lack of education and jobs are as unabating as ever so that job-training programmes of this county may at best have a cosmetic value.

But the homeless in New York, as elsewhere, are not mere numbers. Rather, with their crimes induced by a kind of poverty which only the reckless orgies of the consumerist crust of a military-industrial society can generate, their addictions and their ailments, they are a catastrophe which flows torrentially and remorselessly through, say, the ten 'pre-arraignment holding pens' in the basement of the New York City Criminal Courts Building in Brooklyn. On a typical day, in each of the pens, more than 200 suspects contend for standing room only as they wait to be charged or discharged (Cowley 1992b: 53). Every month, the homeless in their thousands pass through these windowless, 10-by-15-foot cages and in the process carry and convey a variety of contagions like tuberculosis. These inhuman conditions are now inciting great alarm, except in the ranks of the economists, of course.

Now, all this cannot but spell a systemic generation of brutality which only someone unshakeably determined to gloss over the grim and the macabre could ignore. Regrettably, Professor Samuelson happens to be so determined; and this may well be the reason why, normally, he does not *just* turn a Nelson eye towards evil but manages somehow to see it as actual benefaction instead.

Man's Humanity to Man?

Consider, for instance, his claim (Samuelson 1986: 966) that inflation is actually *rooted* in nothing else but what he calls 'man's humanity to man'.

But, even in a narrowly technical sense, this is a flawed position to take. Besides, given the myriad manifestations of cruelty, of insensitivity to suffering, which inform and define the leading industrial society of the world today, what Samuelson simply takes to be a humane state is anything but.

The technical weakness of Samuelson's position is self-evident. For all that he is saying is that unemployment insurance and public welfare payments enable the unemployed worker to afford a minimum living standard, to ward off starvation and thus to refuse to accept a painfully low wage that may be offered. In consequence, he no longer puts a downward pressure on wages and prices. This can only mean inflation. Which to Samuelson becomes something born out of man's humanity to man.

Few, saith he soon after, would wish to turn the clock back to the inhumane society; nor would it be politically feasible to do so. But, then, there is no need for anyone to turn the clock back to the inhumane society. *For, precisely such a society is already there.* Verily, the sheer inhumaneness of the contemporary American society does not inhere just in the weapons-mania of its ruling circles but also— and mainly—in an extremely marked predilection for the well-to-do, which has been very carefully programmed into the very structure of the American social security system. Thus, in 1992, and according to Samuelson himself, payments made under unemployment insurance came to no more than 4. 4 per cent of the total welfare or 'entitlement' spending in the United States (Samuelson and Nordhaus 1992: 369). I do not know what the corresponding percentage was for 1979 when Samuelson wrote his 'roots-of-inflation' article. But I think it fairly reasonable to presume that it could not possibly have been *so* high as to have become a great inflationary force to the complete exclusion of the rest of the entitlement spending and military spending as well: the two major sources of the Budget deficit to which, at least in this article, Samuelson does not make even a passing reference. How serious this omission could be is suggested by the following specific instance given by the November 1991 report of the US House Committee on the Budget. According to the report, early in 1987, McDonnell Douglas, teamed up with General Dynamics and won a $4. 2 billion contract for the supply of Advanced Tactical Aircraft (ATA) to the Navy, and this contract is expected eventually to become worth $40 billion. As against this, the 1992 outlay on unemployment insurance, according to Samuelson, came to $27.2 billion, that is, an

amount much smaller than the expected *increase* in the value of just
one of the smaller military contracts. Accountancy is not my cup of
tea, so I do not know if this comparison is technically very correct.
But at least from a broader point of view, it does help us put figures
in perspective and see that 'man's humanity to man' could only be a
most distracting metaphor.

Strange that it may seem, Samuelson does not say anything in this
article about entitlement spending other than the outlays on unemployment insurance. What he does say instead is the following: 'If
people spend their money more rapidly or if the central bank prints
billions of new dollar bills for release from helicopters, enhanced
demand will bid up the prices of goods once all labour and capital
resources have become fully employed and further increases in output
are severely limited' (Samuelson 1986: 964–65). He does not consider
the very marked possibility that on account of the raging military-
industrial profligacy and the concomitant misdirection of resources,
labour will *never* get fully employed. That is why the minimum
irreducible rate of unemployment has continued only to rise since the
end of the Second World War. So, inflation has to be explained some
other way. But that is not what I wish to do here. Instead, what I do
wish to do here is to critique the very idea of 'man's humanity to
man' in the sense in which Samuelson has for long been purveying
it unquestioned.

Anyway, helicopter dollars are no different from the dollars which
are printed to cover the deficit caused by military and entitlement
spending. Besides, to say that unemployment insurance not only
embodies 'man's humanity to man' but is also nothing less than *the*
'root cause' of inflation is to say in effect that only such helicopter
dollars as happen to be picked up by the unemployed workers can
become inflationary while those picked up by the rest must necessarily
remain to be non-inflationary. This is to claim that while the jobless
workers must perforce spend their welfare dollars, the rest must
necessarily save theirs.

But it would be wrong to make a claim to this effect in the 'Age
of Rampant Overconsumption.' Or, rather in the 'Age of Pathological
Overconsumption' as Professor Samuelson (1967c: 53) himself came
remarkably close to designating it at least once: 'Look around you in
the subway or at the club', he said, 'and you will see that we generally
eat too much. Some lima beans substituted in our diets for creamy
milk and filet mignon would lower our cholesterol levels and add to

life expectancy'. One would only have to carry this remark to its logical conclusion to see all the dysfunctions which the overspending and overconsuming sector of the American economy happens to be conditioned by these days.

For, there *also* is a sector of the American economy which does anything but overspend and overconsume. And which, as we have seen earlier, Noam Chomsky describes as America's domestic Third World: 'A corollary to the globalization of the economy is the entrenchment of Third World features at home: the steady drift towards a two-tiered society in which large sectors are superfluous for wealth-enhancement for the privileged'. Besides, we find that in Samuelson's easily sleeping New York the proportion of children raised in poverty more than doubled to 40 per cent between the 1960s and 1982, and nationwide the number of hungry American children grew by 26 per cent. In a more focused instance, the number of malnourished, low-weight children at the Boston City Hospital jumped dramatically when parents had to face the agonizing choice between heat and food. Even more shocking, the wait for care at the Hospital reached two months, compelling the staff to resort to 'triage' (Chomsky 1993: 275, 281). Which meant abandoning those who in any case could not be saved, sorting out those who were well enough to do without medical attention and focusing such attention only on those who couldn't do without it but could still be expected to respond to it positively.

Ironically, William and Paul Paddock once (1968: 206) advised the United States, 'the sole hope of the hungry nations', to distribute food among them in accordance with the principle of triage. Little might they have anticipated at the time that one day a hospital in Boston itself would actually be forced to follow their advice with respect to medical attention. Life does after all imitate art once in a while, to adapt a point which Oscar Wilde once made. But the imitation in the present case happens to be exceedingly grim.

But Samuelson, able to see only the overeating and prosperous 'we' would not find it easy to cognize the very existence of the undereating and poverty-stricken 'they'. It seems he has yet not tried fully to appreciate the meaning and significance of what Benjamin Disraeli said way back in 1845 about England's 'Two nations ... THE RICH AND THE POOR'. Nor may he have bothered about what in our own time Michael Harrington has designated as the Other America, nor about the profounder political and economic implications of what Noam Chomsky says about America's Third World at Home.

Be that as it may, let us come back to the American leisure class which cannot possibly be much bothered today about saving its entitlement dollars nor about their inflationary reverberations. It may seem incredible, but this class can manage to spend a good part of its entitlements even before actually receiving them.

This is how: A sum of approximately $200 billion gets distributed every year in the form of tax subsidies to individuals *to cover the expenses already incurred*. These tax subsidies are also known as 'tax expenditures' and their beneficiaries are the individuals who claim the home-mortgage deduction as also deductions for such endeavours as financing a built-in sauna, hiring an au pair and so on. To meet these tax expenditures, other people's taxes have to be raised or deficits increased.

Verily, the United States is a welfare state for the affluent. More specifically, the cost of gold-plated pensions of the rich came to $9.2 billion in 1991—twice the cost of abolishing poverty for the American elderly. Besides, enough to dispel the illusion of 'man's humanity to man' would be the over one million dollars in lifetime benefits which would accrue to a typical Congressman retiring in 1991. By 1993, the figure is likely to have crossed the $1.5 million mark. All told, and including the tax expenditures, the entitlements have become a trillion-dollar river (Howe and Longman 1992: 89–92). *That is, a river more than three times as large as the Pentagon drain*. With the well-to-do coming to generate veritable torrents of state-subsidized consumption, it doesn't seem to make much sense to trace the 'roots of inflation' to the unemployed workers consuming their doles.

Be that as it may, the cost of the booty embodied in entitlements could not but continue to mount inexorably. It is only natural that a system of lavish and even orgiastic entitlements, meant very largely for the relatively well-to-do, should not only be the main source of the gargantuan budget deficit and, therefore, of inflation, but should also be heading towards its own bankruptcy. Just in 24 years from now, as Bruce Schobel (1992: 41) has written, the social security programme will begin running a cash deficit. In the year 2030, the shortfall would grow to $700 billion and in 2035, to almost $1, 000 billion. By the early 2020s, if not earlier, benefits will almost certainly have to be cut back. That is, the social security system would have to be drastically trimmed if not wound up altogether.

I do not know how Professor Samuelson would see all this. But in a *Newsweek* column some years ago (1967a: 88), he did find social

security to be the 'most successful' programme of the modern welfare
state. Besides, he insisted that it would always remain 'untouched by
inflation'. In view of the impending bankruptcy of the system, that
does not seem to be very reasonable. Also, if the social security
benefits were to remain untouched by inflation, what is the one
hundred per cent cost-of-living adjustment—COLA—in aid of? **But
what Professor Samuelson did not see was the much greater
significance of social security *causing* inflation than of social security remaining 'untouched' by it.**

It is surprising how Samuelson could ignore the much greater
inflationary impact of rich people's entitlements and instead get fixated
on a mere molehill—the poor man's dole. Besides, in getting fixated
on the molehill and in blowing it up into a mountain, he managed
also to push the mountain of the rich man's entitlements into complete
oblivion.

But surely, whatever enlarges the budget deficit and therefore directly pushes the prices up ought to have merited much greater
attention than something which merely abetted the unemployed workers not to push them down. Besides, in Samuelson's assertion that
inflation is caused by the failure of such workers to put a downward
pressure on prices is an implicit admission *that they are in any case
being pushed up by forces over which the unemployed workers have
no control*. Therefore, what he mis-sees as 'man's humanity to man'
is only a fib to cover a major dysfunction built into the American
economy in the form of the overbloated entitlements of the rich.
Indeed, even Peter Peterson, a conservative Republican of the Nixon
vintage (Peterson 1984: xi), considers the entitlements-produced
budget deficit to be a progressive, if silent, *disease* which threatens
to metastasize throughout the American *and even the world economy*.
More recently, he has found entitlements to be an entirely 'unforgivable way of allocating resources'. For there simply is no justification,
he says, that the rich should be getting three to five times what they
have put into Social Security, plus interest, plus the company contribution, and that also plus interest. Nor is there any reason, he adds,
that they should be receiving a lot of it tax-free (Peterson 1988: 66).

This unforgivable way of allocating resources as we have already
seen adds up now to about $1, 000 billion of entitlements per year.
Entitlements which in 1996 would in terms of Bill Clinton's election
platform get cut by no more than two billion dollars. Entitlements
which have continued to grow more rapidly than the GNP itself, thus

destroying any chance of deficit reduction. Entitlements which no Presidential candidate could ever dare to point a finger at, much less try, if elected, to trim. Entitlements which embody the immense power of the American elite actually to *grab* whatever unearned wealth they want. But entitlements which Samuelson manages somehow not to see at all so as to be able to designate the poor man's dole as a manifestation of 'man's humanity to man.'

Evidently, nothing but sheer contempt for the intelligence of his readers could impel Samuelson (1986: 966) to make claims of this kind and designate as 'the humane state':

a state which could wantonly bring a situation to pass in which the very existence of the human race cannot be taken for granted any more;

a state which could dump at least 250, 000 of its own troops who had been deliberately and directly exposed to atomic radiation during seventeen years of nuclear testing with a Pentagon official claiming 'We're not in the health effects business—we're in the defence business' (Wasserman and Solomon 1982: 33, 35);

a state which could deliberately use some 300, 000 people living around the Hanford nuclear weapons production complex as human guinea pigs with Tom Bailie, one of the victims of the 'experiment', asking recently in a *New York Times* op-ed article: 'Is this what it feels like to be raped?' (Ackland 1990: 2);

a state which would *not* warn its own citizens living downwind from the Nevada test site of the biological consequences of the nuclear fallout (Begley 1984: 37);

a state which could spray millions of gallons of the cancer causing Agent Orange over many thousands of human beings known to be hiding in a thick forest in Vietnam and then refuse to look into the fate of many thousands of its own soldiers who, while going into the sprayed forest, became exposed to the same cancer causing Agent Orange (Magnuson 1990: 27–28);

a state which could create an eight hundred billion dollars per year medical booty for such special interests as the pharmaceutical companies, members of the Medical Association of America as also of the Health Insurance Association of America (Marmor and

Godfrey 1992: A15) and at the same time leave thirty-seven million Americans without any health insurance at all and many more millions with too little of it (Terris 1990: 14);

a state which may well come to impose much stiffer taxes upon the rich but which also takes care to allow them 'a way to find their taxes much less taxing' though 'ultimately at the expense of everyone else' (Stiehm 1993: 422–23);

a state which could let the average real Aid to Families with Dependent Children decline by 37 per cent from 1975 to 1994 and fail to help the welfare receiving families come up to the poverty line (Sidel 1994: 712); and

a state which just in order to find ways of spreading disease once decided to release several million mosquitoes over an exclusively Black American community living in Carver Village with disastrous consequences for the victims (Cockburn 1994: 116).

But nothing of this could possibly wean Samuelson away from the verbal anodyne he calls 'man's humanity to man'. For, such jargon, no matter how pseudo, is required for the spiritual palliation of the ruling classes. Which explains why he continues to Panglossify reality in spite of all the existential perils of our time and remains committed to an ideology *so* refractive as to make him see as 'man's humanity to man' something which in fact is a massive and intensifying fraud upon the American underclass.

Guns and Butter

Professor Samuelson's misperception of the United States as a humane state could well be a major reason why he can manage to endorse the weapons-mania of its rulers as a legitimate preoccupation and to tell them, in effect, that their mania no matter how maniacal is not maniacal enough.

One may refer in this connection to a report on the 'Prospects and Policies for the 1961 American Economy' which he prepared as Head of a Special Task Force set up by President-Elect John F. Kennedy, and which appears as the one-hundred-and-eleventh of his collected papers under the title 'Economic Frontiers'. He noted, to begin with, that the American economy was in a state of recession and went on to insist that America needed a great deal of worthwhile governmental programmes without having to push the panic button and resort to 'inefficient spending devices'. But, then, the one efficient spending device which he could think of was the Pentagon itself. Military spending, he certainly did say, ought never to be used as 'the football of economic stabilization'. But, he added, it should also not be kept below the optimal level needed for security 'because of the mistaken notion' that the economy would not be able to bear any extra burdens.

But in a situation infested with and brutalized by voracious military contractors, Pentagon 'consultants' and swarms of lobbyists, military spending would perforce remain open-ended, excessive and reckless, but never be suboptimal. Besides, with veritable hordes of these moochers continuing inexorably to batten on its very vitals, the economy would perforce and before long come to suffer and not just bear the 'extra burdens' of stepped-up military spending. Evidently, Samuelson was seeking just to tell the powers that be that increasing military spending, if 'deemed desirable for its own sake', could 'only help rather than hinder the health of [the US] economy in the period immediately ahead' (Samuelson 1966b: 1484–85).

But why just 'immediately ahead'? Why not always? With unbounded military spending deemed to be desirable by military contractors and the recipients of slush payments; with the scholar refusing to do his paramount intellectual duty to critique and question something which always was and continues to be nothing but open-ended waste: the Pentagon, that is, Samuelson's 'spending device', no matter how efficient he took it to be, would for ever remain not just profligate but completely out of control, too. No wonder that even after the collapse of the Soviet Union and hence of even the putative threat to Europe, a sum of $120 billion has been earmarked for the so-called defence of that continent. 'That is more money', we are told, 'than the federal government will spend on educating our children; *and* cleaning up our environment; *and* rebuilding roads, bridges and sewers; *and* providing the nutrition and Head Start programmes that help kids come to school ready to learn; *and* aiding research and development in health, energy, the environment and all other civilian areas combined' (Borosage 1992b: 616). That explains why, according to Borosage, America was mugged once again and that too in the halls of the US Congress on 31 March 1992.

But from Professor Samuelson's point of view, I think, merely because it was deemed to be desirable for its own sake by the Pentagon itself, the expenditure of $120 billion on dispelling even an imaginary threat to Europe could only help but not hinder the health of the US economy. The appearance of Eisenhower's guns-as-a-theft-from-those-who-hunger statement as one of the epigraphs in *Economics* (Samuelson and Nordhaus 1992: 19) is therefore a bit intriguing. Incidentally, just after the dislike-being-wrong passage, Samuelson describes himself as an eclectic economist. Could it be, then, that he is trying to force the legitimacy of the deemed-to-be-desirable-by-the-Pentagon military expenditure and the Guns-as-Theft metaphor into the same conceptual holdall? But, to my mind, no such holdall of ideas, no matter how elastic, could be elastic enough to contain both these opposing paradigms: Weapons-as-Theft paradigm and Weapons-as-Boon paradigm. The former sustains a social critic, the latter, an apologist; the critic takes weapons to be a source of *insecurity*, the apologist, of *security*. The one takes it to be his inalienable *right* to critique the reigning metaphysic of destruction; the other just cowers behind what the powers that be have deemed to be desirable levels of military spending.

In any case, Samuelson ought to have known that the 'desirability' of stepped-up military spending is determined, on the one hand, by the clout which the contractors, using their money power, can wield; and, on the other, by the cynical and misanthropic men of science who, having developed exotic and expensive weapons systems, are only too eager to prescribe uses for them, too.

Which only means that the one thing the desirability of increased military spending is *not* determined by is *authentic* security. What it *is* determined by instead can only be the considerations which can have little to do with security. Besides, the kind of military spending now taking place, particularly in the United States, produces not security but actual insecurity. A relentless destruction of opportunities at least for those confined to the Other America and the creeping paralysis of ecology could mean little else. Nor could the menacing possibility of total annihilation spell security even for the merchants of death themselves.

Surprisingly, the *Economics* (1992) chapter, at the head of which the Eisenhower quotation appears, deals with the Guns–Butter duality which was first posited by the redoubtable Hermann Göring and to which Samuelson himself has added his own bit. Or, is it just a bit?

Göring's version appeared in a 1936 radio broadcast: 'Guns will make us powerful; butter will only make us fat'. But twelve years later, Samuelson (1948: 18) lifted the duality out of the realm of the Nazi metaphysic and inducted it into the realm of the liberal metaphysic. But merely because he could do it so easily and without any fear of the 'transplant' being in any way 'rejected' by the recipient clearly shows that the two sets of illusions, each equating national strength and security with guns, were not mutually incompatible. In Samuelson's hands, moreover, the duality became 'the famous pair, butter and guns'. He has continued to use it over the years to elucidate what he calls the basic problems of economic organization. Only, he no longer describes it as 'famous'. Besides, having borrowed it from the ghost of a Nazi tantric called Göring early in the Nuclear Age, Samuelson has continued ever since to use this duality in order to sell little but mystification pure and simple.

Evidently, the exceeding ease with which Samuelson could borrow something from Göring seems to argue at least a minimal commonality of perceptions between the neoclassicists on the one hand and the Nazis on the other. For there is no ideological barrier which can conceivably block a to-and-fro of ideas between the two sides. No wonder that Keynes himself expected 'less resistance' to his theory in Nazi Germany than in liberal Britain. No wonder, too, to cite an instance of a reverse flow of ideas, that the 1933 programme of the Nazis for the extermination of those whom they could brand as genetically unfit even among the non-Jewish Germans (Bullock 1992: 144) was but a logical and natural culmination of 'a modest proposal' for a selective breeding of humans which Alfred Marshall (1974: 207) had once made: 'Thus progress may be hastened ... by the application of the principles of Eugenics to the replenishment of the race from its higher rather than its lower strains...'

Let us remember, too, that Göring, who harangued the Germans against butter which would only make them fat, himself had a very large girth, indeed, both physical and metaphorical. The latter in particular appears to have been truly gigantic in size. He acquired a vast country palace called Karinhall where 'in scenes of Roman luxury, he feasted and hunted and entertained, and showed his distinguished guests round the architectural and artistic wonders of his house—a study like a medium-sized church, a domed library like the Vatican library, a desk twenty-six feet long, of mahogany inlaid with bronze swastikas, furnished with two big golden baroque candelabra, and an inkstand all of onyx, and a long ruler of green ivory studded with jewels'. Meanwhile, it was to this palace that 'his art-gangsters came continually in from Paris and Rome, from Athens and Kiev, and some also from the museums of Germany, with their tribute of jewels and statuary, of old masters and *objets d'art*, of Gobelin tapestries and altar-pieces, of goldsmiths' work and Augsburg work, and old Roman bishops' staves, from the looted museums and gutted palaces of more ancient, famous states'. It was at Karinhall, too, that Göring, presuming that the war was won, dressed 'now like some oriental maharajah, now in a light-blue uniform with a bejewelled baton of pure gold and ivory, now in white silk, like a Doge of Venice, only studded with jewels'. And, as would be necessary and natural for someone wallowing in luxury so morbid and pathological, Göring took cocaine. Besides, dressed up in a toga, he '[would paint] his finger-nails red' (Trevor-Roper 1975: 77–78, 150n).

By the sheer vastness of his loot, Göring alone would be enough to show that those who order more of guns manage more or less inevitably to get more of butter as well and leave the rest to suffer and to starve—*without any guns and without any butter*—that is, without any power and without any luxuries or even such necessities as could be included in butter. As per his own boast, moreover, Göring was able to swallow a lot of butter in the form of an accumulation of the art treasures of Europe. In money terms, this amounted to a far from modest sum of fifty million reichsmarks (Shirer 1990: 945). Needless to say, this systematic plunder could only be effected with the help of the mounting piles of Nazi guns.

Such, then, were the moral and intellectual credentials of Göring, the sage who inspired Samuelson to fashion his explanatory pedagogy. However, it is the Führer himself and not just the Reich Marshal who Samuelson thinks invented the guns–butter duality. For this is what he wrote to me once: 'Guns and Butter was the famous choice of Adolf Hitler in 1933.' But whether Hitler invented the duality in 1933, or Göring in 1936, is not something worth bothering about: in particular, because Göring himself would not mind Hitler claiming the priority. In fact, he once went so far as to declare: '*I have no conscience*. My conscience is Adolf Hitler' (Rauschning 1939: 84). As if Hitler had any. In fact, even before coming to power, he, according to Rauschning, made the following disarming declaration: 'I have no scruples, and I will use whatever weapon I require.'

Be that as it may, does the guns–butter duality help us comprehend the basic problems of economic organization? Samuelson thinks it does. For to him it is an excellent pedagogical example which—and I am quoting from another letter of his—has great dramatic force. But to my mind, this duality has a confounding power of a kind which can only make one mis-see reality. What Samuelson has written, then, is not drama but farce. The reason why lies in the way the duality is actually worded. [Cited earlier in connection with the phenomenon of military inexorability, it has to be reproduced here as well]: 'If we are willing to give up some butter, we can have some guns. If we are willing to give up still more butter, we can have still more guns' (Samuelson and Nordhaus 1992: 22). But who does the 'we' in this statement stand for? For someone sleeping easily at night under a New York bridge as also for the consultant-hiring Washington vice-president of Lockheed Martin? Indeed, little could be more misleading than Samuelson's seemingly innocuous 'we' standing for a seamless mass of humans with no class distinctions and with no pre-emptions of privileges by the overlying minorities. Also, there is nothing to distinguish it from Göring's 'us'. Therefore, just as in Göring's formulation, guns made *us* strong and butter made *us* fat, so in Samuelson's formulation, it is *we* who are willing to give up some butter and then still more butter to get more guns and then still more guns. Besides, under the totalitarian dispensation, as we have seen, Göring could pile up all the butter he wanted in the vast expanses of his palace and at the same time continue to sell the illusion of strength through guns to his fellow Germans. Likewise, under the liberal dispensation, arms dealers like Adnan Khashoggi can come to wallow in 'a dazzling and ostentatious realm of luxury beyond the dreams of Croesus'. Khashoggi, for one, has a luxury jet bought and reconfigured in 1982 for a mere $40 million. The plane has three bedrooms one of which has a ten-foot-wide bed with a $200,000 Russian sable covering it (Stengel 1987: 8). Besides, even in such luxurious and unearthly surroundings he takes all the care to remember his Maker.

In the meantime, scholars like Samuelson continue to generate illusions about the *we* who have all the power to give up ever more of butter for ever more of guns, *ad absurdum* or *ad nauseam*. Or, perhaps both. It seems that George Bernard Shaw's Andrew Undershaft would scarce be prepared to have himself impounded in the neoclassical economist's 'we'. For describing himself as 'a profiteer in mutilation and murder', he said: 'No, my friend: you will do what pays u s. You will make war when it suits us, and keep peace when it doesnt. You will find out that trade requires certain measures when we have decided on those measures. *When I want anything to keep my dividends up, you will discover that my want is [no less than] a national need.* When other people want something to keep my dividends down, you will call out the police and military. And in return you shall have the support and applause of my newspapers, and the delight of imagining that you are a great statesman [or a great economist?]' (Shaw 1962a: 360, 416; emphasis mine).

It follows that one can do little better than to reject the fiction of an undifferentiated and homogeneous mass of people embodied in Samuelson's 'we' and in Göring's 'us', and with that to reject the guns–butter duality as well. For it is the ruling minorities which manage more or less effectively to corner *both* the guns and the butter with the result that *for the rest there would be no choice at all but to suffer deprivation and inflation.* Indeed, the duality becomes all the more dubious in a situation in which the butter being produced happens to be as poisonous as that which Hitler produced.

All the more curious or rather shocking, then, is Professor Samuelson's insistence, in one of his letters to me, that at first Hitler could have both guns and butter by reducing unemployment from its 25 per cent depression rate, but 'later he was prepared to sacrifice welfare for glory'.

But far more important than a mere statistical achievement, no matter how impressive, was the *kind* of butter which Hitler began producing the very moment he rose to power and which Samuelson mistakenly says he would before long be prepared to sacrifice for 'glory'. In this connection, one may cite a passage from a 1934 Hitler monologue which Hermann Rauschning (1939: 139–41) has recorded in all its sickening and gory details: '*We are obliged to depopulate*', Hitler said emphatically, 'as part of our mission of preserving the German population'. And then: 'We shall have to develop a technique of depopulation. If you ask me what I mean by depopulation, I mean the removal of entire racial units. And that is what I intend to carry out—that roughly is my task. Nature is cruel, therefore, we too, may be cruel. If I can send the flower of the German nation into the hell of war without the smallest pity for the spilling of precious German blood, then surely I have the right to remove millions of an inferior race that breeds like vermin!' Except suggesting that Hitler could well have spoken of 'the smallest remorse' in place of 'the smallest pity', one could do little to improve upon the quality of the butter which Samuelson says Hitler managed to acquire and which he would later give up for greater glory.

Only naturally, Hitler's actions for the production of butter very closely matched his intentions. For a beginning, he organized the Blood Purge of 30 June 1934 for the elimination of Ernst Röhm, once a very close friend of his, and some 150 others. But someone who could spill so much of the precious German blood without experiencing the smallest remorse, would also have to show how ruthless he could be towards the inferior 'racial units'. This Hitler would do through a long chain of concentration camps organized for purposes of extortion and sheer sadism and brutality. Indeed, during the very first year of Hitler's rise to power, these camps sprang up like mushrooms and by the end of 1933, there were some fifty of them already in existence (Shirer 1990: 271). *But that precisely would be the year during which Samuelson would imagine Hitler to be promoting welfare!*

However, Hitler did not have to 'sacrifice' even an iota of the 'butter' thus accumulated to achieve what Samuelson claims was 'glory'. *On the contrary, he would need and continue to get ever more of it.* No wonder that in an escalating fury of barbarism, he ordered that the eight condemned men who had taken part in the 20 July 1944 plot against him be hanged like cattle. A noose of piano wire was placed around each prisoner's neck and then attached to a meat hook. A movie of the proceedings was also prepared for Hitler to watch the same evening (Shirer 1990: 1071).

That was a congelation of glory within Germany. Without—one need mention only one of the uncountable many: Auschwitz. We are told that at the height of its operations, the average 'output' of this complex of four gas chambers and ovens rose to 20,000 bodies a day. Besides, of the total of 18 million Nazi victims in the whole of Europe including Russia, as many as 11 million perished in Poland alone. Of them, over 5 million were Jews, the majority of them Poles (Bullock 1992: 808–09).

Some of those who perished there as part of the Final Solution could well have been fairly closely related to Professor Samuelson himself. In any case, the possibility of such a thing having happened cannot be excluded altogether. For after all, it was only his parents and no earlier forbears who had left Poland for America. It is strange that even his dictionary, instead of making a sharp distinction between brutality and butter, should actually impel him to see all that was brutal as pure butter. Which may well be the reason why he is so unconcerned with the *brutality* which the sheer fabrication of modern weapons cannot but entail for ordinary people, though not for the military contractors and their ideologues.

The basic issue, besides, does not concern just the accrual of power to the State Establishments which are busy acquiring the guns. Rather, it concerns the way this power is actually used. It is dismaying in the extreme that in taking on this exceedingly notorious duality and in designating it as famous, Professor Samuelson forgot all about the misanthropic crimes which Hitler and his cronies had used their power to perpetrate. William Shirer (1990: 964) reproduces the following order which Göring once gave to Reinhard Heydrich: 'I herewith commission you to carry out all preparation with regard ... to a *total* solution [to] the Jewish question in those territories of Europe which are under German influence ... I furthermore charge you to submit to me as soon as possible a draft showing the ... measures already taken for the execution of the intended *final* solution [to] the Jewish question'.

It follows that in branding his book with this disgusting Nazi duality and in making quite literally millions of young students internalize it, Professor Samuelson has been much less than respectful to the memory of his own relatives as also of millions and millions of other human beings, Jew and Gentile, who perished at Auschwitz and elsewhere. More specifically, as Simon Weisenthal, who played an active role in the apprehension of Adolf Eichmann, would say, Samuelson forgot his people.

Even so, he mistook my protest against the use of the guns–butter duality as a plea for silence about the Nazi crimes and wrote to me as follows: 'Victorians thought, ostrich like, if they spoke not of evil that would weaken it. Students should understand that resources can be used for what good people want *or for what they do not want*' [emphasis mine]. I cannot figure out how resources can be used for what good people *do not want*. Perhaps Professor Samuelson could. Also, in keeping quiet, ostrich like, over such considerations as kickbacks and cost overruns which impel 'good people' to indulge in successive sprees of fabricating and acquiring extremely costly weapons systems, one does not in any way help the students to *understand* the prevailing reality. One manages only to elide its horrid nature and in fact to *so* invert it that the students do in effect get confounded. In sum, they too begin to see crass iniquities as unmitigable benefactions.

Production Impossibilities

But no matter how strange, this optic inversion is suggested by the word 'we' which Samuelson uses as many as four times in the articulation of the guns–butter duality: 'If *we* are willing to give up some butter...' In terms of intellectual finesse, this 'we' is not at a level much higher than Göring's 'us' in 'Guns will make *us* powerful...' Evidently, since 'decisions are shaped by insular weapons establishments with special interests' (Perkovich 1992: 16), such terms as 'us' and 'we' can come *only* to mislead. Samuelson makes the *we* stand for a single, well-integrated decision-making unit *so that the costs are borne and benefits enjoyed more or less equitably.* But that hardly is the case in fact. Rather, what is the case in fact is the pre-emption of all the butter by the Görings and the Khashoggis and the rest—that is, the very people who are in a position to acquire and peddle the guns. This means that it would be impossible for anyone to abstract from all the raging iniquities of the times, put guns along one axis and butter along the other and then claim that he had fabricated a pedagogic device of untold power.

Besides, not a few of these iniquities are produced by the continuing conjuration of demons which, in General Colin Powell's view, noted earlier, the American military cannot do without.

But even if we ignore all this and let Samuelson's 'we' be a truly meaningful term, there is yet another reason why his pedagogic device must perforce fail to take off. And *this* reason lies in the durationlessness of the instant of time at which the so-called alternative production possibilities along Samuelson's Production–Possibility or P–P Frontier are supposed to be available as so many choices. Only one of these is meant to be taken up even on paper. But such a choice does not, *indeed cannot*, allow any movement—any transition—whatsoever. Therefore, what Samuelson and Nordhaus simply presume to be the transformation of butter into guns, 'not physically, but by the alchemy of diverting resources from one use to the other', is no more than a sturdy illusion. For, the diversion must take time and *time* has been frozen in the very conception of the P–P Frontier.

But no matter how obvious, the sheer impossibility of the P–P Frontier as a conceptual construct has, to my mind, never been taken any note of by any economist. But already in a 1938 publication, that is, ten years before Samuelson came to articulate this idea, Alfred North Whitehead (1968: 152) had dismissed its very possibility in no uncertain terms: 'It is nonsense to conceive of nature as a static fact, even for an instant devoid of duration. There is no nature apart from transition and there is no transition apart from temporal duration. This is the reason why the notion of an instant of time, conceived as a primary simple fact, is nonsense.'

Economists have not always failed to cognize the time-orientation of the economic process. Indeed, Keynes himself (K-XXI: 245) speaks of this process *as by nature being rooted in time*. But perhaps it is only natural that in order better to serve as an ideological gloss, economics should still refuse to reject the very notion of an infinity of options imagined to be available at one durationless and frozen instant of time, absurd and inconceivable that it does happen to be. To my mind, this alone should be more than enough to argue the conceptual unviability of the P–P Frontier or of any of the if-then kind of curves contained in the mainline economist's 'tool box'. Along any one of these concoctions one can continue merrily and freely to jump backwards and forwards and forget all about temporal transition which can never occur backwards. As Erwin Schrödinger (1984: 452) has written: 'Nothing could ever happen in exactly the opposite way it does happen, because that would involve a decrease of entropy'. In other words, that would involve an increase of order rather than disorder.

Elsewhere, but I cannot recall where, Schrödinger also makes the point that the concept of approach to the limit is not always very useful. Which is but a way of saying that at least in some situations, one would do well to avoid using a mechanistic tool like the differential calculus. For in these situations, it could only generate not understanding but misunderstanding. That is, instead of insights, it could produce only mystifications.

Specifically, situations in which the differential calculus comes to play a negative role, that is, situations in which its use becomes a veritable insult to intelligence, are those which *exclude reversibility*. It follows, therefore, that any attempt to treat inherently and abidingly irreversible phenomena as reversible could at best result in mock-precision and pseudo-mathematization; but it could not possibly help us understand reality. To be sure, the 'Earth', for instance, 'could have very well moved in the opposite direction on its orbit without contradicting any mechanical laws' (Georgescu-Roegen 1974: 135).

But the P–P Frontier is a different kettle of fish altogether and even if we allow it to be constructed in total disregard of Whitehead's warning about the conceptual absurdity of a durationless instant of time, it cannot be treated as a two-way street, which precisely has Samuelson been doing for long if only to generate illusions about the prevailing order. That should be something which even an economist, no matter how uncritical of the status quo, should not find impossible to understand.

Would that Erwin Schrödinger had abetted his famous cat to eat up all the economystic rats which never tire of making wayward and even conceptually preposterous movements! For it is only after these enthralling distractions had been put out of the way that the economists could come to focus on the quintessence of the existential reality of our time. That is, only then could they begin looking into the utterly reckless misdoings of the reigning pyramids of economic and political power. In other words, only after giving up their conventional concerns could they begin raising non-trivial questions which alone can yield non-trivial answers.

Gunnar Myrdal, for one, took great care to emphasize the necessary and absolute priority of questions over answers. Which only means that every care should be taken to ask the right questions. For wrong questions cannot but generate wrong answers. Indeed, only critical questions can produce non-trivial answers as to the nature of the prevailing order. But intent on promoting conformity to this order, its ideologists cannot but continue to ask wayward questions and remain reassured of the harmlessness and triviality of the answers which their victims might give. As Thomas Pynchon once put it: 'If they can get you asking the wrong questions, they don't have to worry about the answers' (Jensen and Anderson 1990: front cover).

Joan Robinson once (1966: 7–8) referred to a common confusion between logical definitions and natural history categories, *the point* being the exemplar *par excellence* of the former, *the elephant* of the latter. But the P–P Frontier happens to be a catastrophic mix-up of shaky logic and contorted natural history. Its construction starts with a vast multitude of alternative possibilities—a set of choices— presumed to be available at a single durationless instant of time. And then an unbounded natural history transformation in either direction, which in itself violates the entropy law, is melded into it. In other words, one impossibility is fused into the other. That *alone* could be the meaning of combining the stipulation of a durationless choice-set with what Samuelson and Nordhaus call the alchemy of diverting resources from any one of the two uses to the other.

By now it should be evident that Whitehead and Schrödinger together confront Samuelson and Nordhaus with an utterly unsolvable dilemma: if they consider, as they do, different positions along the P–P Frontier as so many possibilities supposed to be available at a durationless instant, they invite the Whiteheadian charge of generating nothing but nonsense; and, if in a natural history manner, they try to make a temporal transition from one point to the other in either direction, Schrödinger would not let them move back. As a result, they must perforce come to abort their mission to produce even a conceptually coherent and definable P–P Frontier.

But even if it had been a definable concept, the P–P Frontier would only make us forget all about an existential limitation which we as a race have to contend with. Samuelson has for long been claiming that through an ongoing technological development, as also through successive discoveries of natural resources, we can always keep pushing the P–P Frontier itself to the right. But he manages somehow to keep quiet over the relentless attrition and destruction of the terrestrial ecosystem the integrity of which happens to be so essential to the process of production or rather of fabrication. Far would it be from him to see the absolute incompatibility between the need for ecosystemic integrity on the one hand and the idea of a continual rightward shift of the P–P Frontier on the other.

The essential problem, in other words, does not inhere in continuing indefinitely to push a conceptual anomaly like the P–P Frontier to the right but in actually curbing the rampancy of the contemporary civilization. In the evocative formulation of Paul Ehrlich's (1991: 35): 'The indispensable strategy for saving our fellow living creatures and ourselves in the long run ... is to *diminish* the scale of human activities. Both the size of the human population and the environmental impact of the average individual must, I believe, eventually be reduced to well below what it is today. The task of accomplishing this with wisdom, fairness, and without racism, sexism, and gross economic inequity will involve a global effort unprecedented in human history. But unless humanity can start moving determinedly in that direction, all of the efforts now going into *in situ* conservation will eventually be for naught, and our grandchildren's futures will remain in jeopardy'.

Lest this should appear to be a plea for some sort of a Malthusian agenda, one should take care to emphasize that a reduction in the scale of human activities which Paul Ehrlich is asking for requires much more than mere NPG—or Negative Population Growth. Indeed, above all, it requires a drastic reduction in military spending and fat-city consumption. For thus alone can the impact of human activity on the Earth system as a whole be attenuated. Which only means that an NPG programme confined to Asia would mean not a thing if the United States continued to be as impervious as ever to the hazards posed by, say, space shuttles, Concordes and energy-devouring motor cars, or what Georgescu-Roegen (1986: 276) calls 'two-garage cars', that is, cars requiring two garages each.

It is this kind of reckless and wasteful consumption which obliges us to insist with the Ehrlichs (1989) that there are not just too many people around but that there are too many *rich people* around. In fact, they single out the United States itself as the world's *most heavily overpopulated nation* in terms of the impact on the Earth's fragile environment and limited resources. Which it has to be. With more than 250 million people, an entirely 'unprecedented affluence [of its upper classes] and reckless use of environmentally malign technologies' (Ehrlich and Ehrlich 1991: 224), the United States cannot but continue to be far guiltier than most other nations combined of an inexorable attrition of the human habitat and therefore of a remorseless attenuation of the very possibility of Man's future itself. New World Order, indeed!

A recognition of this kind entails a self-conscious abnegation of value-free scientism which can spell nothing but psychic desiccation. And *that* in turn is something which, as we have seen, Professor Paul Samuelson, for one, seems actually to enjoy. The only way out would be to combine science with conscience or as Victor Weisskopf (1972: 364) would have it, curiosity with compassion. **In his own words: 'Human existence depends upon compassion and curiosity. Curiosity without compassion is inhuman; compassion without curiosity is ineffectual'.**

Part Two: Keynes — A Limping Pangloss

Frank presentation of ominous facts was never more necessary than it is today because we seem to have developed escapism into a system of thought.

Joseph Alois Schumpeter (1961: xi)

The free enterprise system fully embraces the right to inflict limitless damage on itself.

John Kenneth Galbraith (1992: 59)

3   The Third Crisis

> The second crisis is quite different. The first crisis arose from
> the breakdown of a theory which could not account for the *level*
> of employment. The second crisis arises from a theory that cannot
> account for the *content* of employment.
>
>   Joan Robinson (1973: 99–100)

Reckless Profligacy

And a few sentences later, she said: 'Now that we all agree that
government expenditure can maintain employment, we should argue
about what the expenditure should be for.' She said this just about
twenty-five years ago. But even over such a relatively short period,
government spending, particularly in the United States, has got more
or less completely out of control and ironically has become even a
source of actual job-destruction. Besides, since such spending has
soared to levels of profligacy which have never been known before,
Joan Robinson's question about what [government] expenditure *should*
be for admits of no coherent answer as long as we continue to accept
the basic legitimacy of the status quo. The unique and utterly chaotic
and critical situation, which lies beyond the power of the received
theory to explain, certainly merits a name. Let us call it 'the third
crisis'.

It is as different from the second as the second was from the first.
The first crisis, as Joan Robinson saw it, arose out of the abysmal
failure of the then reigning orthodoxy to account for a drastic fall in
the *level* of employment; and the second, out of a similar failure of
the Keynesian orthodoxy to account for, much less warn against, the
exceedingly dangerous *modes* of employment informed as they are by

what she called the continuing hypertrophy of military power *after* the end of the Second World War. But, then, she ought also to have said that such hypertrophy was but an inevitable outcome of military Keynesianism itself. Anyway, as I see it, *the third crisis arises out of the complete unconcern of the received theory with state profligacy so reckless that it cannot but culminate in a virtually terminal bankruptcy of the status quo.* Unfortunately, Joan Robinson focused only on the smaller of the two components of such profligacy, weaponization, and ignored the much larger one: entitlements of the well-to-do. Together, financed through relentless budget deficits, they generate a sky-rocketing spiral of state profligacy—and thus the third crisis.

In brief, the short-term remedies which Keynes happened to prescribe could not but produce the tenacious and long-term problems of our own time. Exceedingly important should it be, therefore, to find a place for *The General Theory* itself within this series of daunting crises. Evidently, the book was, if within the sturdy confines of neoclassicism, a direct intellectual response to the first crisis. But it is rarely, if ever, appreciated that it was not just a response to the first crisis. Far more important, it was the genesis of the second and the third crises. For Keynes, like economists in general, came to count without the ecological host and thus to ignore the way that the Earth system could and inevitably *would* retaliate against the inexorably mounting orgies of consumerism and militarism combined. At least in retrospect, then, his plea for hole-digging can be seen to have been anything but innocuous.

It is in this context that one would do well to focus on the economically disruptive role of entitlements. They have been described as 'uncontrollable budgetary monsters' which by 1992 came to 'swallow up almost half of all federal spending' in the United States and which threaten now to consume one out of every seven GNP dollars by the year 2000 (McNamee 1992: 74). Besides, in 1991, the Medicare component of social security in the United States accounted for nearly $19 billion subsidizing the health care of households earning $50,000 a year and above. The mounting cost of Medicare for the rich could well cause the system to collapse within fifteen years and, if the present trends continue, 'total health-care spending would rise to an economy-shattering 44 per cent of the gross national product by 2030' (Howe and Longman 1992: 89). Already in 1981, as *The New York Times* noted editorially on 10 May that year, the cost of social security was rising by $45,000 *a minute* and it would probably be rising a great deal more rapidly by now. Concluding its editorial entitled 'Time for Surgery on Social Security', the paper said: 'These days, time for reflection does not come cheap.' But Joan Robinson, concerned as she was with the continuing hypertrophy of military power after the Second World War was over, failed to make even a passing reference, at least in her Ely lecture, to the much greater and concomitant hypertrophy of state subsidized consumption of the well-to-do, particularly in the United States.

I am not trying to dismiss social security *per se*. What I am trying to do instead is to dismiss the economically, socially and ethically unviable kind of social *insecurity* which the Other than the Other America, having hijacked the US economy, has managed to create for the rest and ultimately for itself also. This is something which even the non-Americans cannot afford to remain unconcerned with. For, as per Peter Peterson's warning noted earlier, this is a pathology which cannot but metastasize before long throughout the world economy. In view of this, we in the Third World cannot but insist as follows: *De nostra res agitur*: It all is our own concern. The point of it all is that with a 'budget bursting with entitlement programmes running on autopilot' (Howe and Longman 1992: 89), public spending can no longer serve as a tool of fiscal policy. For what are entitlements to the recipients but commitments to the State. Which, with its resources being *largely and increasingly committed to the well-being of the well-to-do*, can come only to lose whatever room for manoeuvre it ever had. In fact, even the powers that be while pleading for social security reforms take every care to keep entitlements out of the picture. No wonder that Bill Clinton, for one, while talking of ending 'welfare as we know it' (Besharov 1993: 95) seeks only to do away with the benefits accruing to members of the American underclass who after receiving two years of job training and education, according to him, can very well give up 'welfare as a way of life'. But he is not in the least bothered about curtailing the escalating entitlements of the well-to-do. For he seems to believe that the affluent need not give up 'welfare as a way of life'.

It is the American State, then, which bifurcates the economy into two sectors with a Chinese Wall in between. Entitlements, which are but a major exercise in subsidizing fat-city consumption, and the very lucrative military contracts together ensure buoyancy and high profits in one of the sectors while the other can only continue to languish. This explains what has been called the paradox of 'weak economy, strong profits'. The United States is not doing very well, we were told in mid-1992, 'but its corporations are doing just fine' (Norris 1992: C1). Evidently, as Norris says, these two trends cannot co-exist indefinitely. But there is still no reason why their co-existence should be taken to be a paradox of 1992 only. On the contrary, it is a paradox, as Noam Chomsky (1993: 280) suggests which can only become ever more absurd as the architects of policy invoke their wonted remedies. For the corporate sector, thriving on a market dynamized by entitlements as also on the Pentagon largesse, must still continue to cause devitalization—i.e., depletion and contamination taken together—of the human habitat and in the process come to condemn itself to paralysis, too.

Incidentally, and putting it a bit schematically, state-subsidized fat-city consumers in the United States happen to be more than three times as profligate of resources as even the Pentagon itself. Therefore, and contrary to what Ruth Sivard (1991: 7), for instance, thinks, it is *not* militarism but consumerism which is 'King in America'. Still, from the point of view of resource-destruction, it does not seem to be very reasonable to make any distinction between the civilian and military sectors of the American economy. For, it is *together* that the two are at war with the Earth as also with what Frantz Fanon would call the wretched of the Earth—the wretched of the United States itself not excluded.

Lethal Misemployment

No wonder that military-industrialism remains, and by definition too, as enamoured as ever of weapons-making, with its scholarly ideologues continuing to concoct the glibbest and the most specious conceivable apologies. One such is that weapons industries help maintain high levels of employment and trade surpluses, too. For instance, one Philippe Moreau-Desfarges, said to be a leading French expert on military matters, while venting his worries about his country's growing trade deficits and the severity of the unemployment problem during the 1980s, insists that 'Any reduction in arms production means that people will lose their jobs and export earnings will fall. France simply cannot afford to stop selling weapons' (Evans 1989: 14).

But if that be taken seriously, what about Britain, Germany, the United States or, for that matter, even the late haven of socialism in the world? For, by the same spurious token of employment generation, how could any one of them be expected or persuaded to stop selling weapons? Nor is it clear as to how Britain, for one, could use employment as a pretext for selling some of the Soviet weapons, it had acquired earlier, to Azerbaijan which in turn would use them to kill some thousands of Armenians (Sampson 1992: 10).

Let us remember too, that socialist humanism as an ideology never came to stand in the way of the erstwhile Soviet Union making massive exports of death in the form of weapons. Evidently, to the *nomenklatura*, valuta mattered much, much more than employment at home or lives in the Third World whither most of their deadly equipment was sent. Nor would they bother about some of their erstwhile client states refusing to pay for the weapons acquired earlier: $5 billion in the case of Egypt and $3 billion in the case of Indonesia (Kaldor 1984: 37). Besides, with the former Soviet republics vying frantically with one another to sell weapons abroad, the total for the region of the old Union could well become larger than ever. Already, there are reports to the effect that Iran has been conducting secret negotiations to buy nuclear warheads from the cash-starved Kazakhstan and that Russia itself may be tempted to sell at least nuclear weapons technology and to send its out-of-job nuclear scientists and engineers abroad (Rossolimo 1993: 6).

Weapons exports, in brief, have become an international obsession. Bill Clinton, for instance, didn't take long to forget all about his campaign promise to 'press for strong international limits on the dangerous and wasteful flow of weapons to troubled regions'. Instead, during the very first year of his Presidency, such exports reached an astounding $33.2 billion—more than double the $15.2 billion George Bush had approved in 1992. Further, about three-quarters of these sales went to governments deemed repressive or undemocratic in the State Department's own human rights reports. And not surprisingly, as Lawrence Korb, an Assistant Secretary of Defence under Ronald Reagan, put it, Clinton has made the United States 'the world's leading merchant of death'. Suddenly, according to a senior executive of a weapons firm, 'we have a government that will actually help you in a transaction'. And according to another, 'The President and Cabinet officials have become personally involved in major potential aerospace sales' (Press 1994: 340).

No wonder that in the pursuit of military Keynesianism as a *policy*, not a few mixed-economy governments themselves come often to connive with arms dealers and exporters to contravene their own officially declared embargoes and restrictions. But once in a while such contraventions do break out into embarrassing scandals for those in power. One such having emanated from Britain is known as the Matrix Churchill affair which has put John Major in an awkward situation. As *The Guardian Weekly* put it on 15 November 1992, in claiming in the House of Commons a few days earlier that it was not clear if the Matrix Churchill Company had violated any official guidelines, John Major was 'being less than honest and shamelessly economical with the truth'.

But John Major's troubles in this connection at least are probably not of his own making but of Margaret [now Lady] Thatcher's. For not long ago, she personally abetted and encouraged some British arms manufacturers to finalize many illegal deals with Iraq. It is one of these which was later to become the not-so celebrated Matrix Churchill affair. The more generous of the commentators suggested that she was not in this scandal up to her eyeballs. But even if she was only waist-deep in it, she could not possibly have been motivated by a burning desire to reduce the rate of unemployment in Britain. In fact, there were demands that Mark Thatcher, her prodigal son, be compelled to give evidence before Lord Justice Scott who was looking into this affair (Lewis 1992: 3). Which suggests that much of what the lady did towards gun-pushing as Britain's Prime Minister was inspired—or triggered—by her Motherly Affections. How else could the Son earn nearly $19 million as commission in a *single* British arms deal (Singer 1995: 20) with Saudi Arabia?

To my mind, this specific instance alone should help us see that those who make and sell weapons are really not concerned with assigning top priority to levels of employment at home. Too much money is involved for these people to take this economystic hobby-horse very seriously. Highly exaggerated, indeed, are the benefits which arms exports may bring to the economy in question. For such exports involve enormous government largesse and numerous hidden costs, benefitting a few dominant corporations all right, but draining nearly everyone else. Among the least known but most significant hidden costs are industrial offsets which weapons manufacturers routinely make available to foreign governments as enticement for buying their wares (Press 1994: 340). A specific [American] instance is the following: In 1992, McDonnel Douglas and Northrop contracted to sell $3 billion worth of F-18 aircraft to Finland. To fulfil *part* of its offset obligation, Northrop offered a 3 per cent cut on $50 million worth of paper-making machinery if it was purchased from a Finnish rather than a US manufacturer (*ibid.*). The implication is obvious: Even if this particular deal helped sustain the level of employment in the aerospace industry, it would have destroyed not a few jobs in the paper-making machinery industry. Besides, because of the higher capital intensity of the aerospace industry, this specific deal could well have caused *a net destruction of jobs in the economy as a whole*. In any case, when these offsets or the so-called giveaways can be as high as 100 to 150 per cent of the face value of the contract itself (Lumpe 1994: 30, 32), there must, at least prima facie, be something fishy. It seems reasonable to presume that the cost of the giveaways has already been included in the jacked-up prices of the weapons to be supplied. So the giveaways are anything but things being given away. If anything, being given away could be the jobs in the exporting countries. For while every billion dollars spent on fabricating weapons [for exports] could well create 25,000 jobs, the same billion spent on a socially productive pursuit like mass transit could create 30,000 jobs; on housing, 36,000; on education, 41,000; and on health care, 47,000 (Press 1994: 342).

Besides, one of the giveaways happens to be production of weapons under licence in the importing country. Which has resulted in a proliferation of military-industrial complexes around the world. In the 1950s, only five Third World countries made small arms and ammunition, and a couple of these made even major military equipment. But by the early 1980s, the number had increased to 54 with 36 of these making major military equipment (Lumpe 1994: 34). Such proliferation cannot but destroy jobs everywhere, just as in the United States.

It follows that the supposed nexus between weapons fabrication and exports on the one hand and employment generation on the other is little more than a tendentiously maintained fiction. Thus, in 1987, Lady Thatcher, among others, did help Britain sign weapons export contracts worth $8.6 billion so as to close in on the United States with its $9.2 billion. Britain in the process almost became Number Two in terms of weapons export orders. But during 1990–92, that is, when those orders could well have at least begun to be executed, John Major couldn't do a thing to stop the rate of unemployment in his country rising from 6 per cent to 10 per cent (Skidelsky 1992: 4). This means that as far as job generation for the British economy as a whole is concerned, the government preaching 'virtue in public while conniving with exporters to outwit its own embargo' would be of little avail. The phrase in quotes is from a [London] *Times* editorial of 11 November 1992. Which, however, was not being very perceptive in saying that for a weapons exporting nation jobs at home tend to weigh heavier in the scales than deaths abroad. For it is not jobs but absolutely rampant greed—uncontrollably wild greed—of the captains of military-industry which does not just tend but invariably does happen to be much heavier in the scales than deaths abroad. On this account alone must these captains be presumed to have generated not employment but misemployment: misemployment, moreover, which cripples the global ecology as well. More specifically, the destruction of jobs in the economy as a whole, caused by relentless misdirection of resources towards fat-city consumption and open-ended military spending, is manifested in a continual and inexorable rise of what is generally accepted as *the very minimum or irreducible rate of unemployment*. To the proponents of full employment legislation in the United States, it was 2 per cent in 1945. It became 4 per cent in the 1960s and exceeded 9 per cent during the early 1980s (Leontief 1982: 190).

Keynes himself would have been scandalized by the very idea of the acceptability of an irreducible rate of unemployment. For as he saw it, the 'complaint against the present system' is not that those who are in fact employed 'ought to be employed on different tasks', but that it fails to make tasks available for all those who are not employed, allowance being made for 'errors of foresight'. He would also have been scandalized by the suggestion of large-scale misemployment of resources. For he saw 'no reason to suppose that the existing system seriously misemploys the factors of production which are in use'. To cite an example which he himself gave: 'When 9,000,000 men are employed out of 10,000,000 willing and able to work, there is no evidence that the labour of these 9,000,000 is misdirected'. In sum: 'It is in determining the volume, not the direction, of actual employment that the existing system has broken down' (K-VII: 379).

Only someone unsheakably fixated on some quantities and utterly unconcerned with others could have argued like that. For there *are* quantities which are not known to draw the mainline economists into a state of intellectual animation: quantities such as billions of tons of carbon dioxide in the atmosphere and millions of tons of CFCs in the stratosphere as also the disappearing stocks of minerals in the crust of the Earth. Remember Robert Solow's assertion cited in the Preface that: 'The world can, in effect, get along without natural resources, so exhaustion is just an event, not a catastrophe'? This leaves only some quantities for the economist to bother about, such as the GNP no matter how amorphous and imprecise, the growth rate but not the concomitant rate of consumption of the terrestrial capital, employment but not the content of it, and so on. Which argues nothing but absolute unconcern with the relentless deterioration of the human habitat and the concomitant existential hazards.

Keynes may not have heard of the CFCs which Du Pont introduced some sixty years ago (Elmer-Dewitt: 1992) that is, not long before *The General Theory* came to be published, and which by now are playing havoc with the Earth's ozone shield and promise nothing less than a civilizational collapse. But at least as an enlightened citizen, if not as an economist, he ought to have known about the fell perils of a more or less indiscriminate production and use of a large number of chemicals—perils such as a rash of cancers of different kinds, brain damage, digestive disorders, reproductive problems and so on. Some 70, 000 of such chemicals are now in regular use in the United States, little being known about the health effects of as many as 80 per cent of them, though a great number are already suspect (Sivard 1991: 38).

An indiscriminate and unabating unleashing of chemicals is, of course, not the only instance of the way that 'the existing system seriously misemploys the factors of production which are in use'. For the list of such instances could be extended almost *ad infinitum*. But the one I have given alone must suffice to help us see how wrong Keynes was in refusing to bother about the serious and systemic misemployment of the factors of production which are in actual use. In particular, because such misemployment comes in fact to define the existing system. In an obituary which has been reprinted in a popular collection, Paul Sweezy (1983: 76–77) said that a socialist could only blink his eyes in astonishment over Keynes's dismissal of the very possibility of misemployment, and further, that several 'other examples of the insularity and comparative narrowness of the Keynesian approach could be cited'. **Besides, had the existing system been as innocent of misemployment as Keynes claimed it was, we would never have been experiencing the very ultimate existential crisis we now are.**

It follows that we have no option but to recognize the extremely menacing nature of the problem of misemployment in comparison with which the problem of unemployment as such pales into insignificance. Would that Robert Oppenheimer, and certainly Edward Teller, had remained unemployed than misemployed the way they were. To my mind therefore misemployment merits much greater attention now than unemployment. In fact, the resources to be released, once the menace of misemployment is brought under control, should go a long way in helping to convert the now-intractable problem of unemployment into one which is relatively manageable. Also, this could well be the only way to reverse the relentless increase in the irreducible rate of unemployment. *Which means that Joan Robinson's demand that we should argue about what government expenditure is for should make us argue about what employment ought to be for.* That in any case is the implication of her concern with the *content* of employment. As far as I know, mainline economics has never raised this unexceedably important question. In fact, it seems to have taken all the care to avoid raising it. But it no longer can, even if in the very process of raising this question it has to cease to be itself—an apology—and become instead an abiding exercise in dissent. For a focus on the content of employment must perforce make it see the continuing increase in the irreducible rate of unemployment, say in the United States, as an inevitable consequence of the ever-mounting military-consumerist waste. Which, in turn, must make it question nothing less than the legitimacy of the status quo. And that is exactly what an exercise in dissent has to do.

However, even when a mainline economist comes to be concerned with the sheer tenacity of the problem of unemployment manifesting itself in the continual increase in the irreducible rate of unemployment, he would think in terms of any but the most obvious explanation: open-ended military and consumerist spending. A typical but still a most important example is Wassily Leontief. In a 1981 interview with the *U. S. News & World Report*, cited in Chapter 1, he did make the point that the Reagan jumps in military spending would necessarily starve the rest of the economy of the investible resources which it desperately required.

But strangely enough he did not take any notice of the ravages of the entitlement-based consumerism which starve the economy of resources a lot more thoroughly than mere militarism could.

Still, there is no gainsaying Leontief's suggestion to the effect that while creating large-scale misemployment for the development and fabrication of exotic, expensive and militarily dubious Star Wars weapons, Reagan came actually to create general and widespread unemployment as well. Even so, just a year and a half later, and in a *Scientific American* article referred to a little earlier, Leontief came to ascribe the phenomenon of a rising rate of irreducible unemployment exclusively to automation.

The Myth of the Multiplier

I am not trying to deny the very possibility of the technologically generated increase in unemployment which may already have become a chronic malady. What I am asking for instead is the recognition of increasing overall unemployment caused jointly by militarism and contemporary consumerism. Evidently in a situation like this, the very idea of the multiplier effect of stepped-up spending which the Keynesians have never ceased to celebrate fails to cut much ice. It may well appear to the unwary as a tidy and slick paper-and-pencil exercise that is, an exercise very much within the realm of symbols and definitions. But as ideated by Keynes, it cannot conceivably become an 'open sesame' to comprehending and manipulating a world conditioned and defined by military-industrial profligacy. *Dynamizing the profligacy is greed; and there can only be a metaphysic of greed, no mathematics of it.* It follows that as a formal mathematical concept, the multiplier can only obscure but not illumine the prevailing reality. For there simply is no reason why the most highly paid high-tech jobs created to produce weapons for the Star Wars programme, for instance, should have imparted any expansionary impulse, via the multiplier, to the economy as a whole. On the contrary, as already indicated, job-generation of this kind could only starve the economy of resources to the point of what Leontief described as 'economic calamity'. Besides, with the powers that be given to a psychically disoriented military profligacy, Keynes's 'normal psychological law' (K-VII: 114) itself cannot but come to naught.

What is needed, then, is a sustained and self-consciously empathic critique of the dysfunctional political hierarchies of our time and a concomitant disemphasis on bogus and misleading quantitative precision. As Keynes himself once wrote, a comparison between the

personalities of Queen Victoria and Queen Elizabeth I, no matter how
interesting [and even tempting], would be 'unsuitable as material for
the differential calculus' (K-VII: 40). All the more puzzling, therefore,
that like the rest of his profession, he remained fixated on sheer
quantity manifested in such terms as 'employment', 'consumption',
'saving', 'investment', and so forth and never came to be concerned
with the *composition of output*, the *content of employment* and so on.
Indeed, it was only because of his total unconcern with existential
quality thus understood that he came to popularize the idea of the
multiplier, though in a philosophically dubious manner. For whatever
I have said in Chapter 2 about Samuelson's Production–Possibility
Frontier, in the light of A. N. Whitehead's dismissal of the very idea
of a durationless instant of time as also in the light of Erwin Schrödinger's dismissal of the idea of reversibility, would apply, *mutatis
mutandis*, to Keynes's multiplier and, indeed, to much of mainline
economics, too. Which only means that as long as one chooses not
to break out of orthodox economics *altogether*, one cannot possibly
hope to be able to generate a genuinely new mode of thinking.
Specifically, what Keynes saw as a powerful and mighty citadel is in
fact only a sand-castle; and, as such, it could stand only superficial
and not fundamental architectural alterations. This simply means that
there was hardly a point in his being so self-conscious of what he and
many others took to be the extreme novelty of his theorizing. For as
long as he himself remained absolutely unconcerned with gross and
widespread *misemployment*, he would merely be superimposing a new
grotesquerie upon the old. Therefore, his 'assault' upon his readers,
far from liberating them from the exceedingly dense illusions of the
past, would and merely did burden them with many more.

It follows that what Keynes wrote to George Bernard Shaw about
The General Theory still in preparation at the time must be dismissed
as a flamboyant flourish, no more. He was writing a book on economic
theory, he said, which would largely *revolutionize* [his word, this]
within about ten years the way the world thinks about economic
problems. Further: 'When my new theory has been duly assimilated
and mixed with politics and feelings and passions, I can't predict what
the final upshot will be in its effect on action and affairs. But there
will be great change ... I can't expect you, nor anyone else, to believe
this at the present stage. But for myself I don't merely hope what I
say, in my own mind I'm quite sure' (K-XIII: 492–93).

Nevertheless, Keynes's theoretical innovations, no matter how sweeping they might have seemed to himself and the rest, could only be, indeed had to be, pathetically irrevolutionary. To be sure, they were intended primarily to help one take a macro—in place of a micro—economic view of the status quo. But that view could not be macro *enough* to let one see that the status quo itself was but an inherently unsustainable exercise in the remorseless consumption of the terrestrial capital. Indeed, entirely unconcerned with the basic problem of resource exhaustion, Keynesianism, given its recipe of *just any kind of increased public spending*, could well cause and did in fact cause a further intensification of depletion and pollution and therefore a still further deepening of the existential crisis of our time. In other words, in trying to cope with short-term problems, it could only make those of the long term even more menacing. The reason is simple: Keynes was concerned with a mere *symptom* which he called involuntary unemployment and was not even trying to diagnose the malady itself, which even then could have been seen to be little but a gross misemployment of men and materials.

Maybe, in the 1930s, primacy seemed to lie with putting idle but already available resources to work: Which could be done without much ado by stepped-up government spending even on hole-digging and hole- filling. But the crisis generated by reckless profligacy of the State and of the upper classes, that is, the crisis of our own time, is a lot more complex and incomparably more menacing. For it inheres not just in an explosion of idleness and the concomitant increase in the irreducible rate of unemployment, but in a relentless attrition of the human habitat as well. It is easy to see that stepped-up spending, unless it is intended specifically and self-consciously to rectify the ecological damage already done, cannot but add to the gravity of the prevailing situation. What we have at work here is a sort of a perverse multiplier which not only continues inexorably to destroy jobs but to cripple the human habitat too. Whether stepped-up and ecologically disoriented spending takes place in the public sector for the construction of, say, a nuclear power plant at Chernobyl or in the private sector for the construction of an MIC plant at Bhopal hardly matters. For each one of them was violative of the cardinal imperative of ecology: 'Enough is Beautiful'. But uncontrolled spending makes a mockery of economic theory and policy and also impedes the culture of enoughness.

No wonder. For during the ascendancy of the military-industrial civilization, the very idea of enoughness has come to lose all meaning so that now there is not a trace of it left as a culture category. Only naturally, therefore, as *The New York Times* reported on 4 July 1992, some leading bankers did not feel enthused by the interest-rate cut announced by the Federal Reserve System on the 2nd. For they did not expect it to trigger a 'big [spending] spree'. What the spree, as a link in an unending series of sprees, could and would do to the ecosystem was not their concern. Nor, indeed, of the hard-nosed economists like Francis Bator and Robert Solow (1992: C4) who insist in a joint little note that under the prevailing conditions of economic stagnancy, 'almost any kind of prompt action to increase total demand [would be] desirable' not only in the short run but also in the long. For, they claim, it would necessarily add to the future production capacity as well. But in order to be able to recommend just *'any kind of prompt action'* for immediate demand stimulation and also to insist that it would be useful in the long run too, one would have to be completely innocent of the imperatives of ecology and those of physics and at the same time to be innocent of the unavoidable penalties which their violation must necessarily invite.

For it is not just ecology but physics also which entails an unwavering commitment to a culture of enoughness. Specifically, what I am referring to here is the second law of thermodynamics or the entropy law which is generally recognized to be the premier law of all science. Indeed, it is only total insensitivity to the entropic constraints on human activity which could make one recommend just any kind of prompt action for demand stimulation. For such stimulation cannot but accentuate the deterioration of ecology, both national and global. Which already can be seen to be taking place inexorably very much in accordance with the law that order must spontaneously and irreversibly dissipate into disorder.

I am not saying that it is the mainline economists alone who are insensitive to the entropic nature of our existential reality. Rather, it is the military-industrial civilization of our time which as a whole is so insensitive. It is only natural, then, that as professional apologists of this civilization, economists too should choose to be insensitive to the stark implications of the entropy law. In this context, one may refer to the warning which Arthur Eddington (1929: 74) once gave: If your theory is found to be against the second law of thermodynamics, I can give you no hope; for there is nothing for it to do but to collapse in the deepest humiliation. Much more than a theory, it is a profligate civilization which is now found to be disregarding the demands of the second law. Which means that it is this civilization which is bound to collapse in the deepest humiliation. As an apology of a civilization hell-bent on precipitating entropic collapse, economic theory too must perforce be condemned to collapse in the deepest humiliation. Which is why it would not do just to rethink this theory but to 'unthink' it altogether. For it is only then that its practitioners will begin raising questions they have never raised and begin seeking answers they have never sought.

It seems to me that during the last phase of her professional career, Joan Robinson, for one, kept busy doing just that. 'I am talking about the evident bankruptcy of economic theory', she said at the end of her Ely Lecture, 'which for the second time has nothing to say on the questions that to everyone except economists appear to be most in need of an answer' (Robinson 1973: 105). But as of now, the economists cannot but fail even to see something which would make them extroject all that they have been trained to introject and absorb. For they take for granted the legitimacy of the status quo which is in fact caught in the throes of an unprecedented legitimation crisis: a crisis which has become worse confounded on account of the ascendancy of public spending gone completely out of control—taking both entitlements and military spending together. Perhaps, Joan Robinson herself would have spoken of the evident bankruptcy of economic theory which for the *third* time has nothing to say on a vital question in urgent need of an answer.

Sustained Dysfunction

But the economists, and the Keynesians very much among them, appear to be light years away from even a foggy perception of the fell perils which the prevailing situation happens to be heavy with. For no one could be at all aware of these perils and still continue to be indifferent towards their horrendously grim implications.

But some people, economists in particular, try, if pressed, to explain such indifference in terms of a paucity of evidence. Paul Samuelson, for instance. I did try to make him shed his sustained apathy towards the fate of the Earth and therefore also towards the fate of the human race which is very much bound to it. But in response, all that he has said is that 'ecological diseconomies' notwithstanding, one must draw a line between plain hysteria and 'documentable concern'.

Certainly one must. But very evident here, to begin with, is a misperception of sheer ecological *dysfunction* as no more than a set of more or less innocuous and more or less manageable *diseconomies*. For instance, it has long been known that people exposed to asbestos dust may come to suffer from pleural, lung and other forms of deadly cancers. The late Irving Selikoff, a great authority on asbestos disease, once estimated that of the twenty-one million living Americans occupationally exposed to asbestos, between eight and ten thousand would continue to die of cancer every year for twenty years after 1980. Besides, asbestos having been widely used in the construction of school buildings, several millions of children have been and are still being placed at potential risk of dying of cancers like mesothelioma [pleural cancer]. No wonder that most asbestos companies have been sued for damages and even the Manville Corporation, the world's largest such, having assets of more than $2 billion at the time, decided to file a debtor's petition under the federal Bankruptcy Code in 1982. But 'few people were aware that the bankruptcy filing was simply the latest episode in a fifty-year history of corporate malfeasance and inhumanity to man that is unparalleled in the annals of the private enterprise system' (Brodeur 1985: 3, 6, 339).

Not unnaturally, those at the receiving end of such inhumanity, entirely unmindful and perhaps even unaware of everything that Professor Samuelson has written about man's humanity to man and about the humane state, have continued to file claims for damages caused by asbestos. Indeed, according to the *Time* of 27 July 1992, quite literally tens of thousands of asbestos cases are pending in US courts. Evidently, all this is built into the very logic of making profits from wherever and whatever possible. **I am sure therefore that even the economists would find it hard to transmogrify this menacing internality into a manageable externality, irrespective of the size and sophistication of the mathematical armada deployed**.

Or, consider the catastrophic destruction of the Earth's ozone shield caused by the apparently harmless chemicals known as chlorofluorocarbons or CFCs. A single atom of chlorine could destroy as many as 100,000 molecules of ozone and thus continue to produce an artificial rate of ozone-destruction far in excess of the natural rate of ozone-formation. But since 20 million tons of CFCs are already there in the stratosphere, ozone-depletion must continue unabated for several years to come and ozone-holes continue to menace mankind in different parts of the world even if CFC production is stopped forthwith.

More specifically, the level of chlorine concentration in the stratosphere at present is reported to be around 3.4 ppb. But even if the CFCs are completely eliminated by the year 2000 in terms of the Montreal Protocol, chlorine concentration will rise to about 4.1 ppb. (Kerr 1992: 798). But then the ultraviolet radiation of the Sun, which the ozone shield alone can block, must threaten people with cataracts, skin cancers *and* damaged immune systems more commonly known as AIDS, and so on. All this means a rain of destruction from the skies far deadlier than the one which Truman caused to fall on the Japanese. Indeed, the situation is so alarming that early in February 1992, even the US Senate by a 96–0 vote called for a faster phase-out of the CFCs (Lemonick 1992: 60–63).

I can only hope that Professor Samuelson would take the concerns which all this suggests to be fairly well documented rather than dismiss them as evidence of plain hysteria. In particular, because in a situation like this, it does make a lot of sense to err on the side of caution. As Claude Bernard put it around 130 years ago, 'True science teaches us to doubt and in ignorance to refrain' (Ritchie-Calder 1970: 18). But that is not likely to amuse the US Establishment very much. In fact, at the Rio Earth Summit of June 1992, it took the position that 'scientists don't know enough about global warming to justify expensive CO_2 controls'. Besides, George Bush was reported personally to have desired that as much uncertainty be created at Rio as possible with respect to global warming. And yet, he used to describe himself as the environmental president and just before the Rio Summit, as the Associated Press reported on 31 May 1992, he claimed that he was a 'sound and hopefully sensible environmental president'.

That apart, the insufficient knowledge plea could *also* be used to justify stringent CO_2 controls, no matter how expensive. For even if we agree that overwhelming scientific evidence is not there to suggest an intensification of global warming, enough of it is also not there to exclude the precipitation of this scenario altogether. What if it does take place after all? Too much is at stake for anyone to insist that since it may not necessarily take place, greenhouse gases may continue to be released into the atmosphere as before.

In other words, one need not argue that global warming will definitely come to pass but only that, given the prevailing situation, it *could* come to pass. According to Jeremy Leggett, climate models suggesting this possibility may not be perfect but ignoring them altogether 'means taking an appalling gamble with the environmental security of the generations to come'. Besides, in a poll of 400 climatologists conducted by Greenpeace, 45 per cent said that 'a runaway greenhouse effect is possible if action is not taken to cut greenhouse gas emissions' (Leggett 1992: 30). We have been reminded, in fact, that about half the US population lives within fifty miles of the coastline (Satchell 1992: 75). Global warming actually coming to pass and ocean levels rising as feared would evidently spell a major disaster for vast sections of the American population. **Is the US Establishment even remotely as keen on warding off such a disaster as it is on shooting down all the incoming missiles with the help of its anti-missile defence system?**

It follows that a demand for ever more of documentation and what Samuelson would call 'documentability' cannot but distract attention from the essential issues involved and must on this account alone turn out to be plainly counter-productive. Enough, for instance, is already known about the causes and potential consequences of ozone depletion. What this knowledge argues is the need for a withering critique of the status quo. But what the NASA does instead is to send up, as the *Newsweek* reported on 13 April 1992, *ozone-depleting space shuttles to study the phenomenon of ozone depletion*! What I wish to suggest is that beyond a point, reached fairly early, ever more of evidence spells merely an ever-expanding *file*. Which can only be the dream of the clerk, not of the scholar whose dream is profundity of understanding. And for purposes of understanding we need a model into the construction of which only the essentials have gone. But, in contrast, the file must suck in everything, essential *and* non-essential alike.

I do believe, therefore, that I am not hearing voices in the air and also that what I am saying is based on solid and well-documented evidence. Incidentally, Samuelson's position is strongly reminiscent of a 1952 letter which Albert Einstein wrote to Max Born (1971: 192). Einstein found it rather puzzling that, always inclined to overestimate mere measuring accuracies, people should normally remain absolutely deaf to the strongest arguments. He could well have found it puzzling too that people should normally remain completely blind to the unbounded brutality of a recklessly weaponized reality which is at the same time choked with a plethora of gold-plated gadgetry.

Einstein could also have added that stark deafness to reason and total blindness to brutality have not a little to do with professional advancement in the world of mainline scholarship. But sensitivity to brutality needs a heart which, as Oscar Wilde once (1970: 65) put it, doesn't go with the modern dress. Rather: 'It makes one look old. And it spoils one's career at critical moments'. In this world of apathy and indifference the world of economics scholarship is, of course, very much included. In fact, the apathy of the economists may even be a lot more pronounced than the apathy of the rest of the literati. This should explain, I think, why Samuelson (1986: 798), for instance, finds the period 1932–75 to have been a favourable one for economists like himself 'in that it was an epoch of tremendous university expansion and job opportunity'.

But what he is not concerned with at all is the sharp precipitation *during this very period* of the existential crisis of our time. Such complacency could be the reason why something like a union of concerned economists has never been constituted and perhaps never even been thought of. In contrast, a union of concerned scientists, for instance, has long been in existence. No wonder that the economists who have 'made it' are legion and their dubious hallmark insensitivity. To my mind, in this insensitivity lies the superfluity of what Joan Robinson once saw as the superfluous economists. In refusing to question and critique a dysfunctional order and in becoming its apologists instead, they themselves become dysfunctional. Which is of course much worse than being just superfluous. Be that as it may, it is only insensitivity to an exceedingly critical situation which makes them continue to do all that she once dismissed as 'totally beside the point' (Robinson 1983: 15). As a result, many, many more of them would have to suffer a total loss of credibility *now* than those who had to suffer it in the 1930s (Robinson 1973: 92).

No wonder. For in failing or perhaps refusing to critique the doings of Mammon, economists come inevitably to celebrate brutality. *In a formal sense*, the way they celebrate it may not have much in common with the way Hitler did. But in a substantive sense, and thanks to all the cynicism and callousness involved, there is little to distinguish between their way and Hitler's.

The Anoosphere

The environment of utter dysfunction engulfing mankind today merits a name. The one which I propose is 'anoosphere', the exact opposite of 'noosphere'. Which in turn the French Jesuit scholar, Pierre Teilhard de Chardin derived way back in 1925 from two Greek roots, *nous* for 'mind' and *sphaira* for 'ball' or 'sphere'. The term 'noosphere' thus came to signify the sphere of the mind.

Besides, in Greek, the antonym of a given word is obtained simply by prefixing an 'a'—denoting 'not'—to it. Some of the examples are 'a-trophy', 'a-tom', 'a-gnostic', and 'a-theist'. So, if in Teilhard de Chardin's coinage, 'noosphere' signifies 'the sphere of the mind', in my own coinage, 'anoosphere' signifies the sphere of the anti-mind.

It seems to me that the term 'anoosphere' helps us to manifest, as nothing else can, the essential nature of the supposedly macrocosmic world-view of John Maynard Keynes as also of the kind of theorizing it has spawned: his own and that of his followers. For they manage always to unsee the real wood for the purely imaginary trees: the real wood being a set of mounting perils which threaten our very existence as a race and the imaginary trees, such conceptual red herrings as the economystic tool box happens to be packed with.

No wonder that Keynes, for one, having very consciously ruled out even the possibility of misemployment, came to create a theory which would have something to say about the first crisis all right but not a thing about the second nor the third. *Indeed, his basic prescription for the attenuation of the first would in due course come actually to trigger both the second and the third.* 'An expert is someone', Werner Heisenberg has written, 'who knows some of the worst mistakes that can be made in his subject and who manages to avoid them'. But Keynes, no matter how great an economist he has been taken to be, could not even see the kind of problems his short-term and short-sighted remedies would come inevitably to generate. For while enhanced public spending would certainly cause the already available but idle resources to get activated, it could not possibly avoid escalating resource-exhaustion. Besides, such spending would come inevitably to assume explosive proportions and spell utter dysfunction as it now does.

In other words, quite literally built into Keynes's remedies for the first crisis were the causes of the second and the third. It is this inexorability of the eco-ecological process over time which Keynes could not perceive and which renders his programme for the perception of the economy as a whole to be rather dubious in nature. For in dealing in its own unholistic way with such macroeconomic categories as the level of employment, national income, national saving and so on, *Keynesianism continues to count without the ecological host*. That is to say, it actually ignores what cannot be and ought not to be ignored and manages still to congratulate itself on its macrocosmic sweep. That is why Keynes and the Keynesians would perforce fail to see that mainline economics has *little* to say and military-industrialism *little* to do about the inexorable severity of the second crisis. That, to my mind, is the essential message of Joan Robinson's lecture on the 'Second Crisis of Economic Theory' which she gave on 27 December 1971.

But about nine months earlier, on 5 March 1971 to be exact, Paul Samuelson had given a lecture on 'Liberalism at Bay' insisting that after Keynes there was little to be said on a question like the power of the modern state to cure unemployment. Evidently in order to remove all doubt about what he was saying, he put it with prolonged emphasis, too: *'More importantly, after Keynes no one could fail to realize that it is within the capability of a modern mixed economy to contrive fiscal and monetary policies designed to iron out the cruel business cycle and achieve a more tolerable approximation to full employment and vigorous growth'* (Samuelson 1979: 866).

This passage may not have holes as numerous as a garden sprinkler or a kitchen sieve, but it still has quite a few. Thus, while Professor Samuelson is trying to convince us that after Keynes, quite self-evident ought to be the power of a modern economy to achieve a more tolerable approximation to full employment, *the prevailing reality is informed by a persistent rise in the rate of the minimum irreducible unemployment*. What this means is that such monetary and fiscal policies as fail to control the pre-emption of resources by the over-consuming rich and by the military must perforce remain more or less ineffectual. The importance of the destructive role of fat-city consumption and military spending, therefore, can never be over-emphasized.

Nor can be over-emphasized the dangerously toxic nature of many of the components of the industrial output of the military-industrial state. Let us recall, for instance, the sustained corporate cruelties in the form of cancers and cover-ups which the asbestos industry has long rewarded its workers and the rest of the community with. Or, look at the intense contamination of the global environment caused by the polychlorinated biphenyls better known as the PCBs. Like the DDT, they are extremely toxic and extremely long-lived. This explains why years after the discontinuation of their production in the leading industrial nations, a mere one per cent of the total ever produced which has reached the oceans so far is playing havoc with many of the life-forms there. In fact, the oceans may be suffering from a kind of AIDS on account of the PCB blight alone. Besides, women who happened to consume very moderate amounts of the Lake Michigan fish and had very low PCB levels in their blood are reported to have given birth to babies with reduced psychomotor function and subnormal powers of visual recognition (Stone 1992: 798–99).

It follows that Samuelson's 'vigorous growth', unless it excluded industries of this kind, would by itself produce cruelties in comparison with which the cruelties of the business cycle would come to be seen as minor irritants. **In fact, to consider the very ultimate theoretical possibility, even if the military-industrial state of our time were to wipe out the business cycle for all time to come but were not to renege the military and industrial activities on which it is so completely hooked, a variety of cruelties would continue only to mount.** In such a situation, it would entirely be beyond the power of 'a modern mixed economy to contrive fiscal and monetary policies' to rectify the relentless generation of cruelties. In fact, it would continue only to lose that power even if it ever had any.

The essential gravity of the problem lies in the longevity of many of the toxic products which have been released into the environment of late so that fiscal measures cannot be introduced early enough nor effectively enough. The PCBs, for instance, were found to be so dangerous that their manufacture in the USA was actually banned by the Congress way back in 1976. But no legislature in the world could stop the PCBs already produced from reaching the oceans in due course of time.

One may refer in this connection to Professor Samuelson's claim (1979: 701) that '*at least after 1940*' [his italics], capitalism ceased to be in need of 'imperialistic foreign investments and war expenditures for its creation of adequate purchasing power'. His point was that public spending within the domestic civilian economy would be enough to dispel the old spectre of underconsumption.

In fact, he went so far as to suggest elsewhere that only if the Weimar Republic had pursued forceful counter-cyclical stabilization policies to bring down the then prevailing unemployment rate of 25 per cent, Germany might not have turned to Adolf Hitler's Fascism. That is: 'Had John Maynard Keynes's *General Theory* appeared in 1930 and not in 1936, World War II might well have been avoided' (Samuelson 1983: 49). But if this hypothesis were as reasonable as Professor Samuelson thinks it is, how could one explain America's war with Vietnam more than thirty years *after* the publication of *The General Theory*? Even more important, how could one explain the mindless pursuits of the Cold Warriors, who, in utter disregard of the central message of *The General Theory* brought about a breathtaking destruction of resources which the economists tell us are inherently scarce? Nevertheless, Professor Samuelson would have us believe that 'imperialistic foreign investments and war expenditures' have been rendered totally obsolete by Keynesianism which finds them unnecessary for the purpose of creating additional purchasing power.

But, then, the defining problem of our own time is not underconsumption but overconsumption. For a combination of orgiastic militarism and orgiastic consumerism could not but produce overconsumption. Overconsumption, that is, of the terrestrial capital itself. Overconsumption thus understood signifies not only the reckless running down of the stocks of minerals but also the unending disruption of the cyclical flows of what not long ago used to be renewable resources. This only means that in order to see the relentless running down of the terrestrial capital as escalating Gross *National* Products, the economists manage also to *unsee* the actual fall in what might be called the Gross *Natural* Product.

But only a Rip Van Winkle, to use Professor Samuelson's favourite metaphor, or a Pangloss, to use my own, could ignore all this and instead continue to celebrate the everlasting glory of Keynesianism. Which, according to Professor Samuelson, has cured capitalism of a variety of ailments—ailments peculiar to a system of unbridled *laissez-faire* all right, but not to a system of free enterprise judiciously mixed with public economic activity. In fact, rejecting his teacher Joseph Schumpeter's view of the so-called mixed economy as 'capitalism in an oxygen tent', he once insisted as follows: 'Had Schumpeter lived for a quarter of a century after the first publication in 1942 of his *Capitalism, Socialism and Democracy*, I think he might have been truly astonished by the invalid's vitality'. And further: 'For the world as a whole, the third quarter of the twentieth century outshone any epoch in the annals of economic history. As far as [the] growth of total world output is concerned, we did not see its like before.

Perhaps we shall not see its like again. But let us not fail to notice what its record did show' (Samuelson 1983: 45–46).

But Samuelson *did* fail to notice an unexceedably important part of the record of the third quarter of the twentieth century. For this precisely was the quarter during which a rapidly precipitating crisis of global ecology *began* to be recognized. Rachel Carson published her great book entitled *The Silent Spring* in 1962 and less than a decade later, Barry Commoner came out with *The Closing Circle*. Within economics itself, Joan Robinson spoke of the second and completely bankrupting crisis of the received theory. Capitalism itself might not have been confined to what Schumpeter had called 'the oxygen tent'. But it still had created a sphere of toxic matter around the globe which could not but create problems for us as a race. Included in this toxic sphere are the CFCs which are known to have created large enough holes in the ozone shield—holes which cannot but let in massive doses of ultraviolet radiation from the Sun.

'All this', as Schumpeter himself (1961: 91) perhaps would have said, 'is of course nothing but the tritest common sense. But it is being overlooked [particularly in mainline economics circles] with a persistence so stubborn as sometimes to raise the question of sincerity'.

In the paragraph immediately preceding these lines, he speaks of the process of creative destruction in which many firms may have to perish and create avoidable unemployment. There would be a case therefore, he says, for turning a rout of these firms, which may become a centre of cumulative depression effects, into an orderly retreat. Likewise, he argues for an orderly advance 'in the case of industries that have sown their wild oats but are still gaining and not losing ground'. However, the wildest of the wild oats appear to have been sown while Schumpeter was still alive by most of the offshoots of the petrochemical industry, for instance, and these were oats so wild and poisonous that they would begin before long to blight the planetary system itself. In cases like these, therefore, there would be no question of an orderly advance but only of retreat. More specifically, the production of the PCBs, as we have noted a little earlier, had to be banned rather suddenly in 1976. But they still continue to play havoc with marine life and food chains, terminating in a variety of congenital malfunctions from which not a few human infants are known to be suffering. This, then, is the 'atmosphere' in which capitalism would work *not* with what Schumpeter (1961: 70) merely described as 'decreasing efficiency', but rather with increasing virulence.

This explains why we have no option but to focus on misemployment as the paramount problem of our time, not the business cycle. And since capitalism as such cannot do and is not doing a thing about this problem, it must continue inexorably towards a paralysis of the human habitat and therefore towards its own destruction, too. It follows that Professor Samuelson's (1979: 867) insistence to the contrary notwithstanding, capitalism or rather military-industrialism *is* getting inexorably closer to the day when the Extreme Unction would have to be administered to it. But by whom? For in its own termination, it could well spell the termination of the evolutionary history of the human race as a whole, leaving no one to give it a decent burial. No wonder. For all the misemployment which military-industrialism has generated in our time could not but have created a virulent anoosphere—a vicious sphere of the anti-mind. Which, unlike the noosphere which Teilhard de Chardin thought to be outside and above the biosphere, is very much *within* the biosphere which it is also destroying from there.

Paul Baran once (1969: 436) made the point that 'American capitalism, cornered, threatened and frightened may be incapable of leaving the rest of the world alone without so slamming the door that the entire building collapses'. It is this act of ultimate despair, he added, which had to be prevented by all available means. But no longer cornered today, American capitalism is the reigning and rampant segment of military-industrialism now running riot through the world. Currently, it is wallowing in a glut of what Noam Chomsky calls 'triumphalism'. And it may not have to slam any door to bring the entire building down. For it has both the propensity and the power to so run down the system's structure, to so deplete it, to so erode it, that it collapses on its own. But perhaps, to borrow a phrase which Keynes (K-X: 4) used in a different context, if we all 'shout loud enough', our race *might* become sufficiently aware of the existential hazards of our time to prevent the collapse. This requires what Paulo Freire calls 'conscientization' and that in turn entails, if it is to see us through the present crisis, an educational exercise on a scale entirely unprecedented in all our evolutionary history. In particular, because what we have to overcome is a kind of insidious brutality also unprecedented in all our evolutionary history.

And this is a brutality which, even if relatively subtle, is further compounded by mass entertainment corporations which use, say, camcorder-TV combinations to project the violent and the macabre right into people's living rooms. Not violent and macabre in a physical sense, to be sure, but still no less insidious and destructive of human sensibilities and sensitivities is sheer cacophony which passes for music as are the TV–projected gyrations which pass for dancing: gyrations which are *so* wild and uninhibited that they make much apter than ever before George Bernard Shaw's definition of dancing as 'a perpendicular expression of a horizontal desire'. Evidently, this kind of bizarre entertainment cannot but make it increasingly difficult for millions of ordinary people to perceive the essential nature of the evolving or rather dangerously involuting reality. Commercial generation of insensibility and insensitivity, then, is very much a part of the third crisis: a crisis caused in the main, as we have seen, by State and upper class profligacy. Indeed, contemporary showbiz produces a vulgarization of leisure and in the process *that* state of mass insensitivity in which alone could the prodigal and the profligate continue to flourish unimpeded.

4   The Pangloss Complex

'Optimism!' said Cacambo, 'what is that?'

'Alas!' replied Candide, 'it is the obstinacy of maintaining that everything is best when it is worst: ' and so saying, he turned his eyes towards the poor negro, and shed a flood of tears...

Voltaire (1969: 57)

The Cassandra Who Never Was

Early in *The General Theory* (K-VII: 33), John Maynard Keynes speaks of the 'celebrated' [*sic*] optimism of the traditional economic theory 'which has led to economists being looked upon as Candides, who, having left this world for the cultivation of their gardens, teach that all is for the best in the best of all possible worlds...'

This passage contains two schoolboy bloomers which, to my mind, no one seems to have bothered about so far—not even the editors of Macmillan nor of the Royal Economic Society. The first of these involves a mix-up between the two main *Candide* characters, Candide and Pangloss. In *Candide* itself, the protagonist of optimism is Pangloss not Candide who in fact is the antagonist of it. Keynes's mix-up here is rather intriguing. For as the passage cited above shows, it is to Candide that Voltaire assigns the task of dismissing the Panglossian optimism as an 'obstinacy'. In fact, the phrase 'All is for the best in the best of all possible worlds', which Keynes himself reproduces, is a typical, though a little doctored, Panglossian assertion, not a Candidean one. But when at the very end of the book, Pangloss says that there is 'a concatenation of all events in the best of possible worlds' so that Candide may have lived through all that he actually has just to be able to eat 'preserved citrons and pistachio-nuts', the latter is brought to the very end of his tether. 'Excellently observed', he responds sarcastically, 'but let us take care of our garden'. Which means: Let us forget about the abstract concatenations and get concerned instead with our concrete, this-worldly affairs.

And this brings me to the second of Keynes's two bloomers I have referred to: his utter misuse of the phrase 'let us take care of our garden'. To Voltaire himself, it means, as just noted, focusing one's attention on one's own *worldly* affairs. But, as against this, to Keynes, the phrase signifies an actual escape from the world of reality and its problems. Which means that according to him, the economists have abandoned the real world which has problems for the imaginary world which has none. Having done that, they find it easy and natural to continue to believe, in the manner of Pangloss, that all must always be for the best in the best of all possible worlds. And this, in turn, enables them to continue inexorably to indulge in free-wheeling fantasies which, according to Keynes, are their gardens—gardens in which, he could also have said, such unwelcome conceptual plants as Say's Law are cultivated. Or at least used to be till not very long ago.

To be sure, with respect to the *one* question of unemployment, Keynes did take a much grimmer view of the world of reality than most of the professional economists of his time were wont to. Thus, in a BBC discussion with Josiah Stamp, he found the mere existence of general unemployment to be 'an absurdity, a confession of failure, and a hopeless and inexcusable breakdown of the economic machine'. But Stamp found these terms to be 'rather violent' and advised Keynes not to 'expect to put an earthquake tidy in a few minutes' (K-XX: 321). But it would occur to neither Keynes nor Stamp that what merited attention much, much more than the symptomatic earthquake of unemployment was the underlying seismic fault of widespread and growing misemployment. Indeed, in our own time, as we have seen in the previous chapter, the malady of misemployment has become so virulent that even a complete eradication of unemployment as such would not bring about an end to the profounder problems of existential importance our race is now facing. These are the problems, moreover, which the standard Keynesian prescription of stepped-up public spending, including stepped-up military spending, could only make worse through a further intensification of depletion and pollution.

In other words, Keynes could well have taken a more serious view of the prevailing situation than the Panglossian advocates of Say's Law. But fixated as he was on the short run to the point of being actually contemptuous of long-run concerns (K-IV: 65), he hardly was in a position to perceive the essential gravity of the evolving situation. It seems it was not just in his early days but throughout his life that he continued to be a mere water-spider, casually skimming, as light and unpenetrating as air 'the surface of the stream without any contact at all with the eddies and currents underneath' (K-X: 450). That is, without any concern at all with the deeper problems of existence—problems which, to repeat, his own remedies would continue to make grimmer and grimmer. Paradoxically, it is *his short-run remedies* which have imparted a macabre kind of *immediacy* to the long run itself so that even he perhaps would have been impelled to revise his most frequently quoted remark as follows: 'Even in the *short* run we *can* all be dead'. The collapse of the Earth-system, irrespective of whether it is brought about by the nuclear Bang or the ecological Whimper, can promise but little else. Besides, in the present situation, the expression 'we are all dead' cannot mean what it used to. For, in the earlier situation, our children and our children's children would still be around after we were all dead, though in the long run. But all being dead *now* means the extinction of the species itself, leaving no children and no children's children as survivors.

It is this kind of existential gravity which Keynes as a self-designated water-spider would not be in a position even to perceive, let alone get concerned with. Consider in this light his own description of some of his essays as 'the croakings of a Cassandra who could never influence the course of events in time' (K-IX: xvii). At the time he wrote these essays, he might have imagined himself to be a Cassandra whose pessimistic predictions were not being taken seriously enough. But since, in his own words, he did not have 'any contact at all with the eddies and currents' beneath the surface of the prevailing reality, he could never make dire enough predictions. In fact, soon after declaring himself to be a Cassandra, he came to pronounce his 'profound conviction' to the effect that the economic problem understood as 'the problem of want and poverty and the economic struggle between classes and nations' was nothing but 'a frightful muddle, a transitory and an *unnecessary* muddle' (K-IX: xviii). This was a muddle, moreover, in order to clear which, he declared, mankind would need to use no more than the power of compound interest. This led to the apparently evocative declaration that the economic problem is not the permanent problem of the human race. But his perception of himself as a Cassandra notwithstanding, he never could see that compound interest or exponential kind of increase in the size of the cake, even if equitably shared by members of the human race, would not and could not come to solve the economic problem. Indeed, given his failure to perceive the prevailing reality as a whole, he could not but *fail* to see the equally exponential exhaustion of the mineral reserves of the Earth as also the concomitant erosion of its life-support systems. His pessimism, then, was no more than skin-deep. In sum, Keynes was not a Cassandra at all but, perhaps, some sort of a limping Pangloss!

Keynes the Immoralist

In the 1938 essay on his early beliefs, which I have already cited from, Keynes described himself as an immoralist. He and his Bloomsbury friends, he said, entirely repudiated customary morals, recognized no moral obligation, obeyed no inner sanction, and were not much bothered about the consequences of being found out. As far as he was concerned, he added, it was too late to change: 'I remain, and always will remain, an immoralist' (K-X: 446-47). Evidently, what we have in Keynes is an embodiment of the very ultimate kind of ethical relativism with each individual creating his own ethical norms and thus destroying the very possibility of societal existence.

I am not going to dwell upon a very specific and a bit too notorious manifestation of Keynes's self-proclaimed immorality. What I am going to do instead is to try to manifest a fairly precise nexus between his 'immoralism' on the one hand and his economics on the other. For, irrespective of the supposedly macrocosmic orientation of his theorizing, his economics remains woefully reductionist in nature; and to my mind, given his immoralism, this could not but be so. I am not trying to suggest that every reductionist thinker has to be an immoralist as Keynes was. What I *am* saying instead is that anyone and everyone as incorrigibly immoral as Keynes said he was, has no option but to be a reductionist thinker, if even that.

This is suggested directly by Roger Sperry's insights into the working of the human brain. A major psychobiologist of our time, he won the 1980 Nobel Prize for Medicine for manifesting the distinct functions of each of the hemispheres of the brain, the left and the right. For according to him, each hemisphere is the locus of a specialized kind of intellection. In his own words: 'The left and right hemispheres of the brain are each found to have their own specialized forms of intellect. The left is highly verbal and mathematical, and performs with analytic, symbolic, computer-like, sequential logic ... The right, by contrast, is spatial, mute, and performs with a synthetic, spatioperceptual, and mechanical kind of information processing not yet simulatable in computers' (Sperry 1983: 55). At the head of the chapter in which this occurs is a quotation about 'where really our values come from'. The burden of Sperry's argument is that the right hemisphere is the only 'ethicizer' we have.

I am in no position to go into the technical details of this argument. Even so, it does seem to yield a very reasonable and important epistemological inference. Which is that the articulation of values can now be recognized to be a very legitimate and indeed a perfectly respectable kind of intellection; *and also that a synthetic and therefore holistic mode of thinking alone can yield values which would be particularly appropriate to our tormented times*. In other words, the 'left hemisphere' may be taken to signify not just the left segment of the cerebrum as such but also an abiding and more or less exclusive preoccupation with overly reduced technicism and therefore with technofixes. Likewise, the 'right hemisphere' may be taken to signify not just the right segment of the brain but above all a paramount concern with well-articulated values which the sheer gravity of the prevailing situation obliges us to cultivate. It follows that it is only when value-articulation is recognized as a legitimate concern of intellection that one comes to see the essential gravity of the existential predicament of today. This is something which must remain beyond the perceptions of those who are given to unholistic and supposedly value-free thinking.

Sperry (1982: 1225) has also warned that 'The left-right dichotomy in cognitive mode is an idea with which it is very easy to run wild'. Besides, he says that *in the normal state*, 'the two hemispheres appear to work closely together as a unit, rather than one being turned on while the other idles'. But Keynes's was *not a normal state*. For involved in his case was a very self-conscious cultivation of immorality and that meant, in his own words, a refusal to recognize any 'moral obligation' or to obey any 'inner sanction'. Which is why it seems to be reasonable enough to presume that Keynes had in fact turned off the right hemisphere of his brain. Which, as far as I am concerned, would signify no more than a studied suppression of one's ethical and value generating faculties. That alone should explain his well-known fixation on the short run to the concomitant disdain, as noted a little earlier, for the long. For according to Sperry (*ibid.*), it is the right hemisphere alone which is the locus of concern for the future and therefore is also the locus of the worries about the hazards which might lie in store for us in the future.

All that this means to me is that a self-consciously ethical and value-oriented intellection alone can be comprehensive enough to enable one to spare thought for the future and for all that it might portend. No wonder that his marked antipathy towards ethics impelled Keynes to eschew all concern with the long run. Indeed, it may not have even occurred to him to try to anticipate the long-run consequences of the short-run remedies in the form of stepped-up spending on anything whatsoever which he was prescribing so enthusiastically.

There are, then, two broad and distinct kinds of intellection—one which is ethically oriented and the other which is technicistically oriented. It seems to me that the very point of suggesting that they are located in different parts of the brain is to recognize the paramount and indeed the unmitigable importance of value-articulation as a perfectly legitimate category of thought.

In particular, because it is such articulation alone which could help us see the essential elements of the prevailing reality as a whole and thus comprehend the true gravity of our predicament today. Indeed, such comprehension could well be our only hope for survival as a race. In other words, a self-consciously value-oriented and holistic intellection alone could help us affirm our humanity and contain and perhaps even undo the devastation caused by the utterly reductionist preoccupations of the military-industrial civilization of our time. Which also means that holistic intellection alone could help us dismiss the pseudo-scientific pretensions of the ideologues of this civilization.

But to make a plea for an inquiry which is holistic is not to ask for knowledge which is total for the simple reason that there can be no knowledge of this kind. As Bertrand Russell once (1979: 714) put it, 'If all knowledge were knowledge of the universe as a whole, there would be no knowledge.' It ought to be evident therefore that if someone with a complete and encyclopedic knowledge of reality were ever to come into being, he would be more of a freak than an exceptionally knowledgeable individual. This means that the claim that 'she knows everything' which has been made on behalf of *Encyclopaedia Britannica*, for instance, can never be made on behalf of any individual.

Perhaps, this impossibility of total knowledge is what Goethe is seeking to emphasize in his *Faust*, when he lets 'Professor and Doctor' Wagner produce a 'chemical man', a nimble and well-formed little dwarf who embodies a universal world calendar and can tell all that has occurred among men since the creation of Adam. Evidently, no normal historian would accept the dwarf as desirable company. Nor is his stature or rather the lack of it without considerable symbolic significance. For, in spite of all that he 'knows', he remains, from the intellectual point of view, only a lilliputian.

In sum, what holism asks for is no more than a model of reality into the construction of which everything that can be shown to be significant has been incorporated. Holism thus conceived has an extremely important role to play in the prevailing situation. For it alone can help us cultivate criticality sharp enough to enable us to distinguish between right and wrong; and an ability to make this distinction is our paramount need as a sapient species.

In fact, our present predicament may be due in no small measure to our calamitous failure to make this distinction. In *Major Barbara*, George Bernard Shaw (1962a: 415) makes Andrew Undershaft insist that what has 'puzzled all the philosophers, baffled all the lawyers, muddled all the men of business, and ruined most of the artists' is 'the secret of right and wrong'.

Consciousness: Naive and Critical

But a self-consciously and abidingly holistic world-view alone can be critical enough to help us see and tell right from wrong; and as George Bernard Shaw himself would have been only too keen to agree, an ability to do this was never needed more urgently than now. For such is the power of modern technology for good or evil that the consequences of doing what is not right can now be unthinkably grim and calamitous.

Involved here are not just two levels but two *kinds* of consciousness: naive and critical. These terms are Paulo Freire's (1976: 44). But I have taken some liberty and defined them my own way. Naive or uncritical consciousness, in my usage, signifies in effect a state of somnolence so heavy that one suffering from it cannot perceive, let alone question, the misdoings of the status quo. Rather, one who is only naively conscious cannot but get co-opted into the prevailing order to the point of taking its legitimacy for granted. In other words, naive consciousness is co-opted or complacent consciousness. Or, as Paulo Freire would put it, it is massified and domesticated consciousness. Or, like that of Keynes as a water-spider, who keeps 'casually skimming' but never piercing the surface, it is floating consciousness—that is, consciousness which is largely at peace with the prevailing reality whose total loss of legitimation it is simply not concerned with.

University degrees and even positions of academic importance provide no protection against the naivety of such consciousness and may actually help accentuate it. For, they increase one's stake in the continuation of things as they are. Indeed, if the universities everywhere had taken care to dispel naive consciousness and to make the cultivation of criticality their primary profession, we would not be facing the threat either of ecodoom or of global holocaust. It follows, therefore, that naive consciousness can only increase our vulnerability to and defencelessness against the hazards of contemporary military-industrialism.

In particular, because for the production of such consciousness, the ruling circles everywhere have available, in Georgescu-Roegen's coinage, a truly vast and expanding 'armamentarium' of newspapers, glossy magazines, TV, radio and so on. As Keynes (K-XXI: 245) himself would have put it, this 'is the modern method—to depend on propaganda and to seize the organs of opinion'. For, 'it is thought to be clever and useful to fossilize thought and to use all the forces of authority to paralyse the play of mind on mind'. Little wonder that naive and captivated consciousness must become 'falser and falser' and what passes for education degenerate into a mere exercise in the assiduous cultivation and promotion of conformity. But given the sheer ultimacy of the existential crisis we are now facing, such conformity is not just a case of the underlying populations coming to introject or subconsciously to incorporate or imbibe the ideas and values of the ruling minorities as, for example, they do in the Freirean situation.

Rather, it is a case of the ruling minorities themselves, no less than the rest, getting immersed in a situation which promises nothing but the extinction of our race. Masses of people so immersed can only fall to the level of what is sometimes called 'the vegetative soul' or 'life not aware of itself'. This *alone* could explain why the reign of Death has become a menace of global dimensions.

In contrast, critical consciousness signifies a state of awareness so acute that one never can fail to perceive the true meaning of the counter-existential pursuits and propensities of the managers of the status quo. For this to become possible, Doubt has to be installed as a fundamental methodological principle.

But Doubt as I take it, has nothing to do with the Cartesian Doubt. Doubt of my conception is intended to be focused on the credentials of the prevailing system which are taken to be in constant need of verification.

Thus conceived, Doubt cannot but necessarily impel one towards non-conformity. Besides, this seems to be the only way that one can hope to acquire and develop the faculty of critical consciousness. Which means making a quantum jump and not just undergoing a gradual transition from a state of naive consciousness.

Having made such a jump, one gets transformed into an 'intellective soul' and becomes a bearer of 'thinking life'. Evidently, Doubt can produce criticality if and only if one takes into account everything that can be shown to be significant *in the given context*, that is, if and only if one takes a holistic view.

Prima facie, a statement like this might appear to be totally pointless. For who would actually say that one ought to leave out of account anything and everything that could be shown to be significant in the given context? Even so, since mainline scholarship manages always to elide all that is significant and at the same time never fails to focus on whatever is trivial, the epistemological importance of the holistic viewpoint of my conception becomes self-evident.

Our concern at the moment is the elimination of the threat to our existence, and the primacy of this concern has to be taken for granted. For, it is a fundamental value premise which, to borrow a telling expression from Albert Einstein (1973: 272), 'reason cannot touch'. Rather, all reason must flow from it and thus help us comprehend the Shavian distinction between right and wrong. Perhaps, one ought to emphasize here a distinction between reason and intellect. For as Max Born has said: 'Intellect distinguishes between the possible and the impossible; reason distinguishes between the sensible and the senseless. Even the possible can be senseless' (Weisskopf 1972: 334). At least, there is no reason why the possible should necessarily be sensible, too.

But an ability to make the distinction between right and wrong lies far beyond the realm of pure thought in which technique alone can be cultivated and from which all concern for doctrine has been banished. Indeed, as Keynes (K-XII: 856) himself once put it: 'The theory of economics does not furnish a body of settled conclusions immediately applicable to policy. It is a method rather than a doctrine, an apparatus of the mind, a technique of thinking, which helps its possessor to draw correct conclusions.' But being a mere technique, it cannot but be innocent of morality; and it therefore must lack such power as alone could have helped its possessor to tell right from wrong, the sensible from the senseless, and draw correct conclusions. That is, conclusions properly and not spuriously understood to be correct. *Anyway, the precipitation before long of the second crisis and then of the third as a direct consequence of the remedies which Keynes had proposed is enough to show that the theory of economics understood as a mere technique did not help him, for one, to draw conclusions which would be safe enough to be designated as correct.* In other words, the theory of economics understood as an apparatus of the mind and as a technique did *not* help Keynes to tell right from wrong.

All this apart, Keynes was woefully mistaken in presuming that economics is not a doctrine. For, it very much is one and that, too, in the very specific sense that it takes for granted both the status quo and its everlasting validity.

Indeed, on this account alone, it ceases to be a mere doctrine and becomes a dogma instead: a dogma which is stark blind to all the pathologies comprising the prevailing order. This means that only those who are victims of naïve consciousness, and therefore do not find it possible or even necessary to examine the credentials of the status quo, may get enthralled by the charms of the theory of economics as a method, an apparatus of the mind, a technique of thinking.

Lord Bacon and Lord Keynes

And this suggests a very close parallel between Lord Keynes on the one hand and Lord Bacon on the other. For, both took method *per se* to be the very quintessence of scientific intellection; both were prevented by this mania for method from perceiving the precise nature of reality; and, finally, both happened to be morally unsound and therefore destitute of any power to tell right from wrong.*

It could be no more than an interesting coincidence that the philosopher and the prophet who gave modern science 'its method and its inspiration' (Cranston 1972: 235) was as much of a moral bankrupt as the one who is generally referred to as the greatest economist of the twentieth century. But still it is by no means a *surprising* coincidence. For each of them could well have turned off the right hemisphere of his brain in Roger Sperry's terms or strangled his faculty of telling right from wrong in Shavian terms and then cultivated immoralism as a metaphysical principle of prepotent power. We have already had a look at Keynes's immoralism. Bacon's was no less blatant. For 'Bacon seeking the truth and Bacon seeking for the Seals' was but a 'union of high intelligence with low desires' so that 'he had only to look within' to find both 'the soaring angel' and 'the creeping snake', the one the philosopher, the other the Attorney General (333), the two together producing a 'checkered spectacle of so much glory and so much shame' (410). Bacon betrayed friendships, embraced sheer unscrupulousness as a way of life, was fearful of offending the powerful (304), chose very consciously to flatter possible patrons and used his brilliant wit to 'cultivate the art of thriving in the world far more effectively than any plodding dunce could have done (341).

Or, did he? For, as part of the art of thriving in the world, he took bribes and through bribery would he come to meet his nemesis before long. Soon enough, with the House of Lords examining the charges of corruption against him, he descended into his own conscience, only to come out with an ingenuous confession of guilt and, renouncing all defence, beseeched his peers 'to be merciful to a broken reed' (350).

No wonder that it was a man like Bacon who came virtually to identify science with method just as Keynes would be identifying economics with method three hundred years later. But method alone would not force either of them to cultivate an in-depth analysis of the prevailing reality nor make him tell right from wrong. Nor was either of them in a position to do so.

* My comments on Bacon are based largely on T.B. Macaulay's famous essay of July 1837 (reprinted 1937 : 289–410), citations from which are followed by page numbers given in parentheses.

Be that as it may, not everyone believes that Francis Bacon actually launched induction as the new method of science. For, as T.B. Macaulay put it rather irreverently, '[every] infant, we imagine, is led by induction to expect milk from his mother or nurse, and none from his father'. Further, induction is something 'which we are all doing from morning to night, and which we continue to do even in our dreams. A plain man finds his stomach out of order. He never heard of Lord Bacon's name. But he proceeds in the strictest conformity with the rules laid down in the second book of the *Novum Organum*, and satisfies himself that minced pies have done the mischief'. Macaulay then carries this argument to the point where a hypothesis or what Bacon calls the *Vindemiatio* or the First Vintage can be proposed: 'Our invalid ... pronounces that minced pies do not agree with him' (391–92).

This would suggest that Bacon's induction was little more than common sense made *formal* which he nevertheless wanted to use to generate 'dry light', that is, 'the light of the intellect, not obscured by the mists of passion, interest, or prejudice' (387–88n). But having been produced without any regard whatsoever for wisdom or values since at least the time of Bacon, that very dry light has in our own time degenerated into what Robert Redfield (1959: 572) once called 'darkened light'. That is, knowledge which has been produced by naive and uncritical imagination and which has in our own time come to imperil our very existence as a race. What we now need more than anything else to dispel this threat is empathy. Which, according to the new, 1989, edition of *The Oxford English Dictionary*, signifies 'the power of projecting one's personality [and so fully comprehending] the object of contemplation'.

This only means that at least from our point of view, the Baconian project, utterly shorn of empathy, can be seen to have been a rather dangerous undertaking. Which may also have been informed in no small measure by some of Bacon's most outrageous prejudices and misconceptions. Thus, his fixation on scientific method notwithstanding, he continued unwaveringly to deny the possibility of the circulation of blood although William Harvey himself was his personal physician; *nor did he ever come to renounce his cussed commitment to the geocentric dogma.* He managed also to reject Gilbert on magnetism, Kepler on the planets and Galileo on everything (Gillispie 1973: 74).

Besides, Bacon's pronouncements on the nature of heat were no less scandalous or rather bizarre. The motion of heat, he claimed in the *Novum Organum*, is not from a higher temperature to a lower temperature, but is always 'tending upwards' from a lower level in space. For the verification of this hypothesis, he even suggested a specific experiment which would have sent shivers down the spine of any normal schoolboy of his own time.

But as if his hypothesis concerning the movement of heat were not enough, Bacon insisted a little later that it is only the 'greater degree of heat' which causes 'the genitals to protrude in the male, whilst the heat of the female being too weak to effect this, they are retained internally' (Bacon 1952: 152, 158). He did not see though that the 'greater degree of heat' had not effected any protrusions in the *trunk* of the body masculine.

Besides, his enchantment with induction never persuaded him to examine, in the light of his peculiar thermodynamics, the reproductive systems of hens and roosters to be found aplenty at Twickenham, the estate which the Earl of Essex had presented him with.

In sum, method *alone* provides no protection against obscurantism and even against sheer grotesquerie.

Bacon might well 'have taken all knowledge to be [his] province', to cite an oft-quoted phrase which he included in a letter he wrote to not a very beloved uncle of his. But not a small part of his knowledge, as we have just seen, happened to be nothing but crass ignorance. Which only means that his mind could not possibly have been as 'nimble and versatile' as he once said it was 'to catch the resemblances of things'. Besides whatever else his mind might have been gifted with, it was *not gifted*, Farrington's (1973: 32–35) eulogies notwithstanding, with any 'readiness to reconsider'.

All the more reason why one must take care to dismiss Bacon's oft-mentioned claim to the effect that in launching his particular method, he had rendered genius almost entirely unnecessary for the doing of science. In his own words: 'Our method of discovering the sciences is such as to leave little to the acuteness and strength of wit, and indeed rather to level wit and intellect. For as in the drawing of a straight line, or accurate circle by the hand, much depends on its steadiness and practice, but if a ruler or compass be employed there is little occasion for either; so it is with our method' (Bacon 1952: 113). Which means that all that one has to do to be able to write like Dryden is to master the rules of grammar and to be able to speak like Burke, the rules of rhetoric (396).

Such, then, was the new method as Francis Bacon using high intelligence and low empathy claimed to have produced. No wonder that instead of bringing about 'the relief of man's estate', as he expected it to do, it has brought about nothing but the threat of extinction itself. *Likewise*, Keynes, also using high intelligence and low empathy, came emphatically to dismiss the very possibility of any, much less large-scale, misemployment and failed as a result to foresee that his short-term remedies would before long come home to roost in the form of utterly unexpected and intractable crises: the second and the third. Inevitably, in our own time, this combination of high intelligence and low empathy has been the bane of no less than Paul Samuelson himself who is not just one of the cardinals but the very Pope of the 'Methodist Church' within economics. Remember with what exceeding gusto was he able to combine in 1967 his concern for weapons-based American prosperity with a most unabashed endorsement of the genocide which had then been unleashed in Vietnam?

The point of it all is that it is nothing but naive consciousness, that is, a status-quo-endorsing consciousness, which produces an addiction to method irrespective of whether it is induction as in the case of Bacon or an excessively mechanistic reduction as in the case of the economists. The reason is not far to seek: a relentless focus on method is but a device, even a subterfuge, to avoid critiquing the prevailing order. For there is nothing whatsoever in method *per se* which could produce enough of empathy and comprehension and therefore criticality. In consequence and entirely contrary to Bacon's design (1952: 113), an overriding concern with method has produced only an unrelenting conformity to the mores of the status quo and therefore a 'long and general ... unanimity in error'. For conformity argues but a determination to unsee any of the defining pathologies of the prevailing order and therefore cannot but engender error in one form or other. In sum, conformity to the status quo and an overriding commitment to method cannot but mutually reinforce each other.

The Inversion of Mechanics

In particular among the economists. For, they have not been fixated on just any method randomly chosen but on a *wrong method very deliberately chosen*. No wonder that impeded by a general unanimity in methodological error, they continue to be rather insensitive to the essential gravity of the existential crisis of our time, no matter how sophisticated the techniques at their disposal.

In fact, the greater the sophistication, the greater the insensitivity. For, the very 'skill and swiftness of [those who run] not in the right direction must [continue to increase their] aberration'. Incidentally, it was Bacon (1952: 113) himself who warned against the danger of this methodologically produced aberration.

Still, the economics profession remains more or less completely stupefied by the charms of mechanics which can sometimes be beguiling in the extreme. Indeed, profoundly disturbing questions have sometimes been raised about the most forbidding abstractions of mechanics. 'What becomes of velocity at an instant?' A.N. Whitehead (1968: 146) once asked in a trenchant tone: 'Again, we ask—What becomes of momentum at an instant?' Incidentally, some twenty years ago when I had not yet seen Whitehead's *Modes of Thought*, I put a similar question to Paul Samuelson: 'What is the meaning of marginal cost at zero output?' He responded with a verdict to the effect that the destruction of marginal cost at zero output would spell its destruction as a concept at all other levels, too. To my objection that since it was only a concept, not a sacred cow, it could well be allowed to be destroyed as a whole, he made no reply.* But, then, what I have said in Chapter 2 about the P–P Frontier in the light of Whitehead's dismissal of the very idea of a durationless instant of time and Schrödinger's rejection of the very possibility of reversibility would apply to, and therefore destroy, marginal cost as a concept—and the rest of the contents of the economystic 'tool box' as well. Besides, no amount of mathematical sophistication could work out the marginal cost of, say, the ozone destroying CFCs at *any* level of output, zero or any other. Which also goes, naturally, for the PCBs and all the pursuits and processes from which the greenhouse gases emanate in amounts too vast to be ignored. Nothing could justify an abstraction from these most obvious limitations.

In any case, I am not primarily concerned with the inherent untenability of the economystic tools but with the basic unviability of the prevailing military-industrial civilization which those tools can only divert our attention from. Even so, I do wish that Bertrand Russell who found mathematics to be an embodiment of truth and supreme

---

* A brief account of this exchange appears in Singh. 1989: 167–68n.

beauty (Johnson 1990: 199) had also spoken of its inherent vulnerability to extreme misuse by the economics profession. In particular, because the beauty of mathematics being 'cold and austere' would destroy all empathy which is needed so sorely for an intuitive grasp of all the iniquities defining the human situation today.

Be that as it may, mechanics needs the durationless instant of time only as *a limiting case* and has used the differential calculus or the idea of *approach to the limit*, that is, the idea of getting to the neighbourhood of the limit, to achieve astoundingly powerful results.

For, only in a tightly determined Newtonian universe, for instance, could an astronomer predict the existence as also the position and orbit of a previously unknown planet but without actually observing it. That is exactly what a young English astronomer, John Adams, did in September 1845. But the Astronomer Royal didn't take his mathematical calculations very seriously; so his work remained unrecognized. Later, in the summer of 1846, the French astronomer, Urbain Le Verrier was luckier with *his* calculations which came to be taken seriously. For, guided by these, the German astronomer Johann Gottfried Galle was able to discover this planet through actual observation on 23 September 1846. Thus, it was not John Adams but Le Verrier who could become known as the astronomer who had managed to discover Neptune quite literally at the tip of his pen.

The achievements of mechanics such as this raised sanguine hopes of precision and predictive powers even among the economists. Stanley Jevons (1957: 21) was not deterred by *The Coal Question* and spoke of his intention to reconstruct economics as the mechanics of utility and self-interest. Frank Knight (1951: 85) went further and designated *mechanics* as the sister-science of economics. And, then, Lionel Robbins (1949: 83) also made the following claim: 'In pure Mechanics we explore the implication of the existence of certain given properties of bodies. In pure Economics we examine the implication of the existence of scarce means with alternative uses'.

But 'sanguine hopes are sanguine hopes' (Georgescu-Roegen 1974: 39), so that the plans of the economists, no matter how sophisticated, were bound to go awry. The reason is not far to seek. Mechanics, concerned with locomotion, could afford to ignore friction altogether. But in order to work out 'the implication of the existence of scarce means with alternative uses', economics came to ignore all that is incorrigibly wrong with the prevailing order. Not just the societal wrongs but the environmental wrongs as well: disappearing resources and the vanishing power of the biosphere to absorb and rectify the escalating effluence produced by the military-industrial affluence. In sum, while mechanics ignores only the ignorable, economics manages to ignore all that is unignorable and in the process cannot but become meta-mechanical in nature.

It is this kind of a meta-mechanistic world-view which makes the economists lose all 'readiness to reconsider'. But the consequences of Bacon refusing to reconsider his commitment to the validity of, say, the geocentric dogma could not be remotely as dangerous as the consequences in our own time of the economists refusing to reconsider the validity of, say, the growth dogma. Even so, it is precisely this which they refuse to reconsider.

Here, too, our obvious and natural exemplar is Paul Samuelson (1967a: 88). For, according to him, national product can be expected to continue to grow at compound interest 'for as far ahead as the eye cannot see'. To be able to make a claim like that, one would have to assume that mineral reserves do not get exhausted over time and certainly not at compound interest. Besides, with such mounting threats as global warming, biological extinction, ozone depletion, soil erosion and PCB contamination, et cetera, notwithstanding, one would also have to assume that the capacity of the environment to absorb effluence *per se* remains completely undiminished. But given the obvious absurdity of both these assumptions, even Pangloss himself would be hard put to it to perceive compound interest growth continuing to take place 'for as far ahead as the eye cannot see'. Perhaps, Macaulay (293) too would have said that for a claim so grotesque 'there is not a tittle of evidence' available.

In the light of all this, it seems a bit of a joke to speak of the moral and technical powers of *The General Theory*. Which is exactly what Robert Heilbroner (1994: 9), no less, has recently done. Even so, about the morality of anything having emanated from Keynes the less said the better. For it is simply not conceivable that anyone as morbidly *and* as remorselessly corrupt at the personal level as Keynes would be able to imbue anything he did at the public level with other than the most spurious kind of morality. The reason: psychically depleted by personal pathologies, he would just not have the kind of imagination which alone would help him empathize with the existential reality so as to comprehend it in all its hideous and escalating grimness. No wonder that Michael Holroyd (1971: 242), having cited Bertrand Russell's well-known paean to Keynes's intellect and having himself spoken of the lightning rapidity of his brain, speaks also of some deficiency of imagination which he nevertheless suffered from. To my mind, it was this deficiency of imagination which prevented Keynes from making the absolutely crucial distinction between employment and misemployment and thus from turning out a relentlessly ethical examination of the status quo. To be sure, his reference to unemployment, cited a little earlier, as 'an absurdity, a confession of failure, and a hopeless and inexcusable breakdown of the economic machine' could well be taken to be a moral condemnation of the prevailing order. But the extinction of the normative fire of this indictment took no more than the following sentence already cited in Chapter 3: 'It is in determining the volume, not the direction, of actual employment that the existing system has broken down'.

In our own time, this unconcern with *the direction* of employment would perforce mean an unconcern with the Imperative of Ecology and therefore with the existential ethics so essential to our survival as a species. It is this kind of ethics which the morally desiccated Keynesianism cannot possibly help us evolve. *Indeed, it cannot even help us see that the paramount problem of our time is misemployment, not unemployment per se.*

But written into the refusal to cognize the very possibility of misemployment was and is a catastrophic misdirection of intellectual effort. In Keynes's case, for instance, it led to the curious speculation (K-VII: 375–76) that the stock of capital could be increased up to a point where 'it would mean the euthanasia of the rentier, and, consequently, the euthanasia of the cumulative oppressive power of the capitalist to exploit the scarcity-value of capital'. But he failed altogether to see that such abundance of capital stock would necessarily entail the *completest* possible consumption of the terrestrial capital—the italicized coinage being Daniel Defoe's, not mine. Besides, part of the capital thus consumed has been and would continue to be in the form of fossil fuels now known to have seriously disrupted a variety of biospheric processes. What all this can be seen to promise is the euthanasia of the biosphere, not *just* of the rentier: euthanasia of the biosphere not in the literal sense of the term but still in a sense critical enough to spell the destruction of the human habitat. But the lightning rapidity of his brain notwithstanding, Keynes remained entirely oblivious of this possibility. However, today, no one, much less an economist, and still less an economic philosopher of the stature

of Robert Heilbroner, can afford to continue to be so oblivious of the
menacing dimensions of the human situation.

So much, then, for the moral overtones of *The General Theory*. Its
technical powers are even easier to dispose of. For the existential crisis
of our time is defined not by a deficiency of aggregate demand but
by an excess of overconsumption of the terrestrial capital and a
concomitant attrition of the biospheric processes as well. Which
only means that an enforcement of the prescriptions of *The General
Theory* in the present situation could only make the crisis, *at
least ultimately*, exceedingly more critical. This further means that
Keynesianism cannot possibly solve the *long-term and inherently
non-cyclical problems generated very largely by its short-term
solutions to the inherently cyclical problems*. For, as suggested a little
earlier, the logic of stepped-up spending on just about anything and
everything cannot but be exceedingly inimical to the logic of conservation. In sum: the life-menacing drives of the Upper Circles delight-
ing in what Nicholas Georgescu-Roegen has designated as the Square
Dance of Effective Demand cannot but be entirely incompatible with
the life-sustaining ethics of those who swear by the laws of Ecology
with a capital E.

Reductionism as Bestism

But those steeped comically in the lore of the mainline or meta-
mechanical economics remain blissfully unconcerned with such issues,
no matter how serious they may happen to be. That is only natural.
An unholistic—and therefore uncritical—world-view does not even
permit them to see anything that is wrong with the prevailing order.
Therefore, all they can possibly do now is to put on the mantle of
Pangloss and take everything to be for the best in the best of all
possible worlds. No wonder that Samuelson, for one, had no option
but to take the everlasting continuity of compound interest growth for
granted.

This, then, is the fell bane of the reductionist imagination: it cannot
see the seamy side of the status quo. Or rather, it perceives as perfectly
unseamy whatever is in fact irredeemably seamy. It is in this very
specific sense that reductionism and 'bestism' cannot but appear as
two sides of the same, singularly ill-conceived, ideological coin.

'Bestism' is, of course, no different from 'escapism', which, as we have seen, Schumpeter once described as a veritable system of thought. But at least in the present context I find bestism to be a more useful term than escapism. For it helps one focus directly on the Panglossian fixation of mainline economics or the lore of the nicely calculated less or more as—if memory serves—Wordsworth once described it.

Remember two of the 'bestist' claims cited earlier in the Preface? Robert Solow's claim to the effect that the substitutability of some unspecified and even unspecifiable 'other factors' for natural resources renders the latter completely dispensable? The sheer profundity of this Nobel Memorial Prize winning discovery lies in the breathtaking simplicity of the realization that the substitutability of some mythical 'other factors' is but the dispensability of natural resources: in fact, even of such literally vital resources as ozone in the skies, top-soil on the Earth and water in the aquifers deep below. Which is the reason why from now on, natural resources must necessarily cease to be indispensable.

The other of the bestist claims is, of course, Wilfred Beckerman's that, one day, it might become possible to mine the Earth to a depth of one mile *at every point in its crust*. The actual mineral reserves, he suggests, might then turn out to be one million times larger than those which are currently known to be available. Sorry to repeat, but, unbothered by the seismic consequences of that kind of mining, he says that when we come to AD one *hundred* million, 'we will think up something'. That is, till then we should enjoy unharried sleep.

Even so, Paul Samuelson (1967c: 53), eager not to let us suffer a wait so long, has already 'thought up something' which he expects will quite effectively substitute for the disappearing reserves of fossil oil. Before cheap oil shales get exhausted, he says, 'our school-children will be synthesizing hydrocarbons from the atmosphere and from the oceans'.

But in order to do this, Samuelson's school children will need to charge the atmospheric carbon dioxide with the oceanic hydrogen. I do not know how, if ever, any direct reduction, that is, hydrogenation, of carbon dioxide will come to be effected. But an indirect method, involving the reduction of biomass which is already available, does not seem to make the prospect of direct reduction very promising.

'Biomass' is the name commonly given to the mass of dry plant materials and organic wastes of all kinds. Of the two categories, dry plant materials are the stores of carbon which was once directly captured by living plants from the atmospheric carbon dioxide; and organic wastes are the stores of carbon collected indirectly by the plant-eating animals. Together, they can be chemically reduced with carbon monoxide and steam under pressure equal to 100 atmospheres so as to produce what is called heavy oil. This is an extremely heavy and viscous hydrocarbon also known as synthetic crude or 'syncrude'. But evidently, it is not a very viable energy option (Schumacher 1985: 170), particularly in the context of an energy-guzzling civilization.

Much worse, it is a red herring which can only divert attention from the basic issue involved. Which is that the solution to the energy question is to be sought not on the side of supply but on the side of demand. For a world whose pistons, according to Samuelson himself, are exploding petroleum products recklessly away would be *structurally incapable* of keeping its energy supplies 'stay ahead' of what he calls its 'energy needs' (Samuelson: 1967c: 53). The reason is obvious: involved here are not energy *needs* at all but energy *wants*. This distinction between needs and wants is extremely important and has long been maintained by the economists themselves. But it has been virtually abolished by Samuelson and those cast in his ideological mould. Still, it assumes unmitigable significance in a situation in which the limits and the limitations of the Earth system are becoming ever more glaring. For needs being almost biologically self-contained can hardly do much violence to the Earth system. But wants, being prone to artificial stimulation by corporations in pursuit of profit and accumulation, become a major source of planetary dysfunction.

This is the grim meaning *in our time* of what Karl Polanyi once described as the great transformation. Over most of the human time on Earth, as he put it, the economy remained firmly embedded in society and conservation a basic, even existential, norm. Indeed, in pre-market communities, that is, communities in which the market may well be present but never dominant, 'the idea of [unbridled] profit is barred; higgling and haggling is decried; giving freely is acclaimed as a virtue; the supposed propensity to barter, truck, and exchange does not appear. The economic system is, in effect, a mere function of social organization' (Polanyi 1968: 49). In a situation like this, the economy is no more than a societally subordinate device for social provisioning and as such is informed by the prepotent norm of enoughness. In a situation like this, moreover, basic needs may not all be satisfied and poverty may well happen to be fairly tenacious. But the great transformation in more recent times inheres in the emergence and ascendancy of what in earlier times would have been a scandal: the idea of more and more and more—more and more of accumulation, more and more of consumption. In sum, the idea of the overkill. This seems to me to be exceedingly 'worser' than what Keynes (K-XXVIII: 344) once described as 'one of the worser crimes of present-day capitalism'.

But in terms of the human time on Earth this kind of overkill is an extremely recent phenomenon. For had it been otherwise, we would have long devoured the Earth and also disappeared as a species. Indeed, it is only under capitalism, and in particular under modern capitalism, that satiety becomes, in Joseph Schumpeter's telling phrase (1961: 131), 'a flying goal'. **But while earlier on, a goal like this would provide expanding markets for capitalism to thrive in, in our own times, it generates pollution for capitalism to writhe in.**

This can only be explained by the military-industrial man refusing to see right from wrong and destroying those socio-psychic norms which would be so essential to the integrity of the human habitat. We find here a complete collapse of what used to be, in Goethe's terms, 'a perfect correspondence between the inner nature of man and the basic structure of [the] external reality, between the soul and the world' (Worster 1985: 89). For the ever-expanding soul, incarnated in the reckless drives and urges of the military-industrial man, has become its own negation which cannot but cripple the already shrinking world. What confronts us here is nothing less than an exceedingly profound existential contradiction: *'the expanding anti-soul' continuing to escalate its energy 'needs', and the shrinking world continuing to lose its power to meet them.* Indeed, it is not just a shrinking world but one which, thanks to the rampant nuclearism of our time, is getting ever more dangerous to live in. Consider, for instance, the precipitation of what is known as the 'Gardner Effect'. This is the name given to Martin Gardner's finding that children whose fathers received, while working at the Sellafield nuclear plant in England, a total radiation dose of 100 mSv or a dose of 10mSv during the six months before the children got conceived, are *seven to eight* times more likely to get leukaemia than children whose fathers were not so irradiated (Aldhous 1990: 508).

This is the situation, then, in which Samuelson sanguinely expects an unending series of technofixes to continue to be available so as to make energy supplies always 'stay ahead' of the so-called 'energy needs' of the military-industrial civilization. But in invoking one of these technofixes which involves the 'extraction' of syncrude from the oceans and the atmosphere, Samuelson calls to mind a scientist who, according to Gulliver, 'had been eight years upon a project for extracting sunbeams out of cucumbers, which were to be put into vials hermetically sealed, and let out to warm the air in raw inclement summers' (Swift 1976: 223). I am not saying that from a purely technical point of view, the gaseous synthesis which Samuelson has proposed is as incredible as the extraction of sunbeams out of cucumbers. On the contrary, I do not disallow the possibility of its realization some day. But what merits attention is something entirely different. The plan to extract sunbeams out of cucumbers, no matter how comical, did take cognizance of a genuine contingency or need. In contrast, the plan to produce syncrude out of the oceans and the atmosphere, even if it turns out to be technically feasible, is meant only to help in the chase of a flying and therefore, in principle, an inaccessible goal. Besides, in place of manifesting a dynamized market economy, as such a chase would have done in the past, it would now produce an unacceptably polluted and contaminated environment.

In particular, if the chase came to take the nuclear rout. But since Professor Samuelson is convinced that we must ultimately take this rout, let us see the kind of a blind alley which he in fact is enamoured of. Let us assume, to begin with, that there never will be a nuclear accident again. That is, let us assume for the sake of argument that the world will for ever be spared a Chernobyl or even a Three Mile Island kind of disaster. Still, a nuclear programme entirely free of accidents, or what the nuclear lobby prefers to call 'incidents', cannot but spell an unmitigable environmental disaster. There are at least three good reasons why this must perforce be so.

1. *Thermal Pollution*: Nuclear power has been described as a kind of a thermodynamic overkill. For, all that a power plant needs is high-pressure steam to drive the generator. To be performed with thermodynamic efficiency, this task requires temperatures in the range of 1,000–2,000 degrees F. But the energy associated with the nuclear fission process is in the range of a million degrees F. Therefore, the use of nuclear radiation 'for the relatively mild task of boiling water violates the familiar caution against attacking a fly with a cannon'.

The fly could well be killed, 'but at the cost of considerable unnecessary damage' (Commoner 1976: 98–99). But as it is, cooling must become a necessary part of the process of nuclear power generation. 'One nuclear plant alone', Georgescu-Roegen (1976: 14) has written, 'may heat up the water in the Hudson River by as much as 7°F. Then again, the sorry plight of where to build the next plant, and the next, is a formidable problem'. One may cite here the specific instance of the nuclear power plant A at Sizewell in the UK which uses *400 million litres of water per hour for cooling purposes* (Caufield 1981: 464). This is cited from a *New Scientist* article with a very telling title: 'Can Britain Find Room for Nuclear Power?' The answer not only for Britain but also for the world as a whole is, No. Indeed, the Earth is too small a planet for nuclear power. For with nuclear power plants continuing to proliferate, it would become an over-heated planet which would have to face all the dire consequences of global warming. Therefore, those who recommend nuclear power as an antidote to global warming caused by thermal power plants would do well to note the following: The displacement of coal alone would require on a world scale 'the construction of a new nuclear plant every two or three days for nearly four decades'. Besides, even then the increasing consumption of oil and natural gas would be enough to keep the emissions of carbon dioxide at or above the present levels until supplies get exhausted (Keepin 1990: 302).

2. *Nuclear Waste*: Worldwide, there are about 400 nuclear power plants in existence these days. But in spite of Edward Teller's claim that the disposal of nuclear waste 'is no problem at all', there is still not available a *single* long-term waste disposal programme anywhere (Keepin 1990: 312–13). *In fact, the problem is fairly widely recognized to be unsolvable in principle.* Therefore, the continuing accumulation of radioactive waste produced by military and civilian reactors cannot but spell untold environmental hazards, including those which could lead to a variety of cancers. Increasing public opposition to nuclear power should, therefore, be easy to understand. It was this opposition, for instance, which resulted in the decision to dismantle the Shoreham, Long Island, nuclear power plant in the USA. Built at a cost of $5.3 billion to the complete satisfaction of the US Nuclear Regulatory Commission and even licensed to begin operations, it remained stalled under public pressure (Commoner 1990: 88). The opposition to this plant, to be sure, was based largely on the gross impracticality of evacuating people from its vicinity in case of an

accident. But there also has been mounting public opposition in both New Mexico and Nevada to the creation of long-term waste storage facilities there. The Office of Technology Assessment of the US Congress has reported that to clean up the nuclear waste produced by decades of military programmes will 'require yet unavailable technologies'. It should be no less true of the plans to clean up the radioactive waste which has been produced in the civilian sector. One of the technologies being considered these days involves the transmutation of waste into forms which would remain radioactive, 'but only for a few centuries'. Besides, such transmutation would take decades to be effected 'and consume tremendous amounts of energy', creating as many problems as it might solve. Surely, $2.5 million worth of energy which the transmutation of just one kilogram of waste might require does not argue a very encouraging prospect (Gibson 1991: 13, 16). So much, then, for Professor Samuelson's technofixes designed to keep energy supplies 'stay ahead' of energy needs. Still, one would do well to remind him of what the poet William Empson wrote in a different context some sixty years ago: 'The waste remains, the waste remains and kills'.

3. *Radioactive Tombs*: A nuclear reactor may be operated only for thirty years or so. But, given the intense radioactivity of its 'remains', it cannot possibly be abandoned even after it has been decommissioned. Nor can much be done about it. For instance, the Pacific Gas & Electric Co. shut down its Humboldt Bay nuclear reactor in California in 1976 and it was only in 1983 that it decided that 'the best action was to delay action'. Ironically, over decades into the nuclear power age, 'questions of how best to dismantle and dispose of a nuclear power plant remain largely unanswered' (Fischetti 1986: 28). Workers engaged to dismantle and decontaminate a plant immediately after it has been retired would be exposed to maximum radiation. But if the plant be 'mothballed' for thirty to fifty years, the risk of radiation may be reduced though the costs of decommissioning would mount. And they would mount still further if the reactor vessel and other components were to be 'entombed', that is, filled with concrete or some other high-integrity material, in the expectation that most radioactive elements would have decayed sufficiently over 100–150 years so as to allow the demolition of the plant. From decommissioning to demolition, then, it must perforce be a very costly process though estimates range from $50 million to $3,000 million per plant (Pollock 1986: 119).

Given such dimensions of a nuclear energy programme which may otherwise be presumed to be functioning perfectly well, the growing unpopularity of the so-called nuclear option, almost all the world over, is easy to understand. Indeed, it seems more or less certain now that, Professor Samuelson's sanguine expectations to the contrary notwithstanding, the unleashed power of the atom is *not* going to make energy supplies 'stay ahead' of the misperceived energy needs. In need of re-examination and redefinition, therefore, are these needs. For a reckless preoccupation with supplies *per se*, that is, a preoccupation which leaves the misuses of energy entirely out of account, cannot but imperil our very existence as a species.

But as far as Professor Samuelson (1983: 150) can see, 'Suddenly out of belated concern over ecology, we've made it difficult (1) to carry through our planned programme for nuclear-energy installations; (2) to expand coal mining, strip and otherwise; (3) to build long-overdue power-generating stations [thermal or nuclear].' Only, a reassessment, no matter how long-overdue, of the so-called energy 'needs' Samuelson does not find to be worth undertaking.

In evidence here is what one would like to call a single-issue imagination—that is, imagination produced by a reductionist, unholistic and uncritical world-view. 'Your typhoid is my typhoid', Professor Samuelson (1983: 55) has written, 'and we are all, so to speak, citizens of the same Hiroshima'. But even this powerful insight doesn't help him see that the Concordes, the Cadillacs, the car races and rallies and indeed all of the energy-devouring military and civilian obsessions of our time are but so many raging pathologies which must destroy both the rich and the poor. Besides, since over 82,000 people are guesstimated to be dying every day of sheer hunger and other poverty-produced diseases, Hiroshima is the most telling if hideous metaphor one can possibly think of. But such is 'the comic tragedy', as Whitehead (Georgescu-Roegen 1974: 41) might have said, of the self-confident scholars today that even thoughts of Hiroshima do not make them see that it would be utterly futile to try to keep energy supplies 'stay ahead' of the so-called energy needs.

But it is reductionism, taken as a deliberate suppression of the more daunting of the elements of the prevailing reality, which persuades the learned ideologues of the powers that be to continue to declare that all is for the best in the best of all possible worlds. In other words, whether it is a Keynes who refuses to consider even the possibility of misemployment or whether it is a Samuelson who insists that *some technofix or other* would always be available, reductionism and bestism can only be two sides of the same coin—ESCAPISM.

5   Confound Interest

> To Aristotle a usurer was a person beneath contempt. Today, even
> the Vice-Chancellors of the ancient Universities, which purport
> to hold up to reverence Greek thought and culture, are as
> enamoured as anyone of the excellence of compound interest.
>
> Frederick Soddy (1922: 26)

Misplaced Concreteness

Alfred North Whitehead once (1975: 68) made the point that the 'error
of mistaking the abstract for the concrete' was 'merely accidental'.
For it was really 'not necessary for the intellect to fall into the trap'.
Nevertheless, he must have thought that even if purely accidental, the
error was serious enough to merit a name; and the one he gave it was
the 'fallacy of misplaced concreteness'. This fallacy, he warned, 'is
the occasion of great confusion in philosophy'.

However, as far as economics is concerned, the error of mistaking
the abstract for the concrete is by no means 'merely accidental'.
Rather, it is built by actual design into the very structure—the over-
reduced structure—of this academic aberration. For, considered as a
mere method rather than a doctrine, as an apparatus of the mind and
a technique of thinking, it could not but be given to over-abstraction.

This alone should explain why theoretical economists who manage
to remain focused on the problem of *resource-allocation in the abstract* manage also to shy away from a *widespread resource-misallo-
cation in the concrete*. All *things excluded*—or *omnibus exclusis*—is
the formula which informs economic theorizing; and thus alone does
it get reduced to an exercise in the manipulation of arbitrarily chosen

symbols. Which, to borrow a telling phrase from Fritz Machlup (1974: 892), may also be described as 'proxies and dummies'.

Far would it be from an economics thus designed to assign any place whatsoever, let alone the pride of place, to the concrete. No wonder that while the economists have been busy playing with symbols, the world, almost unnoticed by them, has gotten into the throes of a historically unprecedented existential crisis. This is the reason why the fallacy of misplaced concreteness has been the occasion of exceedingly greater confusion in economics than in any of the social or natural sciences.

But *within economics*, by far the most ludicrous manifestation of the fallacy of misplaced concreteness are the kindergarten lullabies which the economists continue to sing in praise of what Keynes once (K-II: 13) called 'the dizzy virtues of compound interest'.

However, these virtues, whatever their worth, must perforce continue to dizzy, that is, confuse, the economists who are given by training to mistaking a mere paper-and-pencil operation for a material force of elemental power. Indeed, to adapt a telling phrase from Jonathan Swift, they are *so* dextrous upon sheer pieces of paper that they have managed to build not just a perpetual motion but a perpetual *growth* machine: a machine, moreover, which is powered by unabashed scientism on the one hand and an abstraction called compound interest on the other. This, to my mind, is the meaning, in effect, of Keynes's belief, cited later too, that science and compound interest will together win *an unlimited leisure for the human race*.

But consider an illustration which Frederick Soddy (1924: 17) gave to manifest the power of compound interest as a paper-and-pencil operation. Just *one* pound, he said, if Jesus had put it in a savings bank account bearing a compound interest rate of a little over five per cent, would in the early twenties be worth one octillion—one million raised to the power 8 or one followed by as many 48 zeros. A claim like this, Soddy added, could not be honoured by the entire human race even if it were to colonize the whole of the stellar universe. No wonder that he found the consequences of such thinking as was fixated on compound interest to lie 'beyond the legitimate bounds of the most extravagant comic opera'. This reminds one of the late Kenneth Boulding's description of 'mere economics' as something fit only 'for the comics' (Constanza 1991: xv).

In our own time, Garrett Hardin (1993: 61–65) has worked out an even more telling example. To begin with, he cites one of the Rothschilds as having made the following remark: 'Compound interest is the eighth wonder of the world'. Then, he goes on to suggest that if the thirty pieces of silver or *just two grams of gold* for which Judas had betrayed Jesus were to be deposited with the People's Perpetual Gold Bank of Jerusalem to earn compound interest at 5 per cent per year for two thousand years, it would grow to 8×10^{14} Earths made of solid gold. *In other words, by the year 2026 each member of the human race*, assuming the world population would have settled at only five billion, would be entitled to a share of as many as 160,000 Earths of solid gold! Considering that *Homo sapiens* is said to be some 40,000 years old, the period of 2,000 years selected for this exercise is really not impossibly long. Besides, says Hardin, since no gold vault on Earth could conceivably contain 8×10^{14} Earths of gold, compound interest is really not *a wonder of the world* but *a wonder out of this world*. [Implicit even in this paper exercise, as also in Soddy's, is the assumption of people—on Earth or in outer space— eager to continue to borrow from the bank with which the deposit had been made.]

But let us get back to the 1920s and note that Soddy (1922: 29) had critiqued Keynes himself for harping on 'the dizzy virtues of usury' as also for failing to tell an increment of debt from an increment of wealth. I do not know if Keynes was aware of what Soddy was saying about the economystic fixation on compound interest. But even if he were, he seems to have remained singularly unbothered. For according to him, 'As houses and equipment of every kind increase in quantity we ought to be growing richer on the principle of compound interest' (K-XIII: 366). Indeed, in his unholistic perspective, savings having become at once the 'duty and delight' of a large class were 'seldom drawn on and, accumulating at compound interest, made possible the material triumphs which we now all take for granted' (K-IX: 62). As far as I know, only on two occasions did he feel somewhat unsure of the charms of compound interest. On one of these he said: 'We used to think that private ambition and compound interest would between them carry us to paradise. Our material conditions seemed to be on the up-grade. Now we are fully content if we can prevent them from deteriorating... We no longer have sufficient confidence in the future to be satisfied with the present' (K-XIX: 641).

Keynes made these remarks in January 1927. But by 1928 he began again to be so 'satisfied with the present' as to be able once again to invoke the powers of compound interest. It didn't take long for the invocation to get congealed into a 1930 essay on the 'Economic Possibilities for our Grandchildren'. Every single pound, he said, which Francis Drake stole from Spain and brought into England in 1580 had by 1930 become 100,000 pounds. Such was the staggering power of compound interest as he found it (K-IX: 323–24).

But given his non-comprehensive, that is, unholistic, imagination, Keynes may not have even stopped to consider a vital implication of this explosion: the rentiers of England or of any other country could certainly have their claims continue to explode exponentially, *but mankind as a whole couldn't have any exploding or even linearly rising claims*. Instead, it could only get into an exploding *debt* to nature. I do not think that Keynes could have taken this kind of debt very seriously. Which is why he did not just come to suggest a four to eight times improvement in one hundred years in the living standards of what he called the progressive countries. Rather, he also insisted that, thanks to the power of compound interest, *mankind as a whole* would come to solve its economic problem. And that, too, to the point that men would hardly be able to find work for more than three hours a day (K-IX: 329).

Even so, he advised 'human beings in the aggregate' to continue to *pretend* that fair is foul and foul is fair and to continue to worship avarice and usury for at least one hundred years more. 'For only they can lead us out of the tunnel of economic necessity into daylight' (K-IX: 331). *Only, he did not make it clear as to how each one of 'us' could continue to worship avarice and usury even for a moment, let alone one hundred years*. For most of 'us' would have to be at the receiving end of the exploitation unleashed by the avaricious and the usurious. There was a third god, too, which Keynes said, 'we' must continue to worship along with avarice and usury: precaution. But, then, it is *not precaution but recklessness* which goes with avarice and usury. This alone should be the reason why we have been led not into daylight at all but into a fouler and fouler environment.

So much, then, for Keynes's dream that 'for the first time since his creation' would Man have to learn to occupy the kind of almost unlimited leisure 'which science and compound interest will have won for him'. What we find instead is a situation much worse than the one in which the 'love of money as a possession' could be counted as 'one of those semi-criminal, semi-pathological propensities which one hands over with a shudder to the specialists in mental disease' (K-IX: 328–29). Only if Keynes had designated this particular propensity as *hyper*-criminal and *hyper*-pathological, he could well have been speaking of the Keatings and the Milkens of our own time and, of course, of the Hindujas and the Mehtas, too. For as a money-maker, who could be more 'strenuous' and more 'purposeful' than these celebrities?

Be that as it may, in getting ecstatic over the charms of compound interest and at the same time in refusing to cognize the escalating consumption of the terrestrial capital, Keynes manifests the utter one-dimensionality of his thought and therefore its abiding untenability as well.

Indeed, with the benefit of hindsight though, we now know Keynes's advice to have been an illusion engendered only by one-dimensional thought. However, this one-dimensionality did not stop him from getting disillusioned with the charms of compound interest once again. In an August 1936 article which appeared in the BBC *Listener*, he spoke of the utilitarian and economic or rather financial ideal which had become 'the sole respectable purpose of the community as a whole'. This, to him, was possibly 'the most dreadful heresy' which had 'ever gained the ear of a civilized people'. He saw little point in continuing *ad infinitum* to accumulate wealth at compound interest: bread, that is wealth, and 'nothing but bread, and not even bread, and bread accumulating at compound interest until it has turned into a [*sic*] stone' (K-XXVIII: 342). Remarkably, included here is the phrase 'and not even bread', and this seems to suggest that at least at that moment, Keynes was persuaded of the utter futility of remorseless accumulation.

But unfortunately, since economic thinking continues to be as one-dimensional as ever, economists in our own time too refuse to be disenthralled by the charms of compound interest. Paul Samuelson (1967a: 88), for one, echoing without naming the Rothschild money-minter cited above, considers compound interest to be nothing less than the eighth wonder of the world. But while he is eager to celebrate exponential growth as an eighth wondrous phenomenon, he is not willing to look at depletion and pollution as but manifestations of the same eighth wonder working in an exponential reverse gear. Conceivably the most reductionist imagination, this. For while it can exult in looking at one side of the coin, it manages somehow not to see the other side. In other words, it can take what Keynes called 'the material triumphs' for granted all right, but refuses to take cognizance of the concomitant planetary exhaustion and devitalization. **But paradoxically,** exponential growth is *both* the *sine qua non* and what may be called the *cum qua non* of capitalism. As the *sine qua non*—literally, 'without which not'—growth is the source of profits and accumulation and provides capitalism with nothing less than its existential dynamics. But as the *cum qua non*—literally, *'with which not'*—growth entails an inexorable consumption of the planetary capital and spells nothing less than the relentless shrivelling of the very innards of capitalism. This bespeaks a profound and inherently paralysing contradiction which capitalism as a system can do not a thing to free itself from.

Let us recall in this connection A.N. Whitehead's warning about the fallacy of misplaced concreteness being the occasion of great confusion in philosophy. It seems to me that at least in economics, this fallacy has been and continues to be the occasion not just of confusion but of actual mischief. For in assigning to an abstraction like compound interest properties which it cannot possibly have, economists manage completely to displace the concrete itself from what they intend to perceive. The consequences of a displacement of this kind can be exceedingly dangerous: in particular, in our own time when the concrete being displaced is congealed in reckless depletion and pollution and is thus menacing in the extreme.

Displaced Concreteness

Just after designating compound interest as the eighth wonder of the world, Professor Samuelson says that 'A growing nation is the greatest Ponzi game ever contrived.' Now, Charles Ponzi, after whom this 'game' is named, was a most notorious American swindler who baited his potential victims with quick returns on initial investments and lured them into taking much bigger risks. So, if economic growth is the greatest Ponzi game ever contrived, it is not clear as to how it could remain unbusted 'for as far ahead as the eye cannot see'. But already, what the economystic eye, no matter how trained, *cannot* see happens, according to Jose Lutzenberger (McCuen 1993: 11), to be the 'the biggest holocaust in the history of life'. For that is what the destruction of the Amazonian rainforest, in effect, means: a holocaust which threatens nothing less than the viability of the human habitat itself.

In insisting that growth must remain unbusted for an unlimited kind of a time span, therefore, Professor Samuelson is only being dizzied by the abstract power of compound interest to the point that he begins to see it as a veritable force of nature—inexorable and untameable. Only, its inexorability and untameability disappear from the typical mainline economist's purview altogether when it comes to the destruction of resources. Which only means that in a perspective like this, the relentless devitalization of the Earth itself caused by the military-industrialism of our time can find no place. But such effective elision of the fate of the Earth and therefore of the fate of our species as well is the natural product of what is no more than an incorrigibly reductionist intellection. Which can be seen to have untold 'gnosticidal' power: that is, untold power to murder knowledge.

However, reductionist thought feeds on what Whitehead once called 'chill abstractions, divorced from aesthetic content'. And one can do little better than to confront such abstractions with the very concrete and grim existential specificities of our own time. Which is to say that economic growth could continue to be the greatest unbustable Ponzi game ever contrived *if and only if* one continued to dwell in a world of chill abstractions. On the other hand, if one did not fail to focus on its specific constituents such as the PCBs, CFCs, motor vehicles, Concordes and the rest—in sum, all the embodiments of latter-day progress—one would perforce come to see what passes for economic growth these days to be an untenable Ponzi: that is, an unsustainable swindle.

Not just a swindle, perhaps, but, as Walter Schwarz (1989: 11), for one, sees it, 'a cancer destroying the planet'. For, according to him: 'Every percentage point of economic growth adds hundreds of thousands of centrally heated homes, cars, supermarkets and washing machines; more roads, more acres of fields under concrete'. And, as he could well have added, more millions of tons of topsoil washed away. There must be something sickening about a situation, as Schwarz suggests, in which supermarkets offer not wholesome food in three varieties but industrialized food in 300, as also 52 brands of shampoo and innumerable kinds of cheese.

But the embodiment 'par unexcellence' of economic growth understood as Ponzi pure and simple is the motor car. The reason is simple and is best stated in an adaptation of Ivan Illich's words (1974: 15): High quanta of energy congealed in the car degrade social relations just as inevitably as they destroy the physical milieu. In other words, the auto owner inflicts a Ponzi both on the car-less and on the environment—and, thus, of course, on himself as well. On the car-less, because cars are not buses; which means that people without cars are not only denied adequate means of public transport but are also made to suffer the consequences of all the traffic congestion and atmospheric pollution caused by the motor car. On the environment, because of the intensely toxic emissions of his vehicle. And on himself, too, because he cannot avoid breathing the air polluted by motor cars, other people's *and his own*. In a word, the car is the occasion not just of mounting economic inequity—of an increasing and impassable chasm between the 'carred' and the 'uncarred'—but of mounting *environmental iniquity* as well.

Worldwide, there are reported to be more than 500 million cars and trucks in existence now—most of them cars. This is over sixteen times larger than the world's vehicle population in 1930. But while a three-fold increase in the human population since that year has aroused a great deal of very legitimate concern, the much larger and still more catastrophic and unsustainable compound interest increase in the world's car population is being accepted more or less cheerfully as a necessary concomitance of economic growth and progress.

But we would do well to remember that motor vehicles generate more air pollution than any other single human activity. More specifically, a recent study of tunnel workers in New York City has revealed that 'exposure to vehicular exhaust, in combination with underlying heart disease or other cardiovascular risk factors could be responsible for a very large number of preventable deaths'. [Remember Professor Samuelson's claim about the ten million New Yorkers continuing to sleep easily at night?] Overall, motor vehicle emissions are a major source of climate modification and health problems caused by environmental pollution (Walsh 1990: 260, 267, 293).

All this argues a civilization of inverted priorities—a civilization which is hell-bent, in Paul Ehrlich's words (1989: 10), on squandering a one-time inheritance and also on severely damaging the biospheric apparatus which supplies mankind with its *only* source of daily income. In other words, what is taking place is, on the one hand, an escalating consumption of the terrestrial *capital* and, on the other, a relentless diminution of the terrestrial *income* caused by a disruption of the processes which capture the incoming solar energy.

But the economists, unconcerned alike with the consumption of capital and the concomitant diminution of the current planetary income, manage somehow to see nothing but the inexorability of an exponential economic growth. As they see it, moreover, no amount of prodigality can deter such growth. Indeed, so inverted or even perverted are the priorities of military-industrialism that ignoring the urgency of the need for civilian reconstruction altogether, it can spend billions on, say, a manned flight to the moon. Incidentally, President Kennedy's own scientific adviser, Jerome Wiesner, dismissed this venture as a 'distraction' which only the sci-fi crowd of deluded dreamers could take seriously (Young 1989: 11). Needless to say, for a distraction like this only the poor and the destitute, going without homes and other basic necessities even in the United States, have to pay. Even so, 'growth' is still taken to be the Open Sesame to the Promised Land, little thought being given to the utter amorphousness of the GNP which it is supposed to be the growth of. But this unconcern with the precise composition of the GNP is so misleading that Oskar Morgenstern himself once (1972: 1185) described it as a concept fit for the Dark Ages. His specific objection was that the GNP, as defined by the economists, continues inexorably to increase *pari passu* with such wasteful consumption of fuel as takes place during, say, the endemic traffic jams. Which only means that, more generally, the economist's GNP is nothing but an amalgam of utter incompatibles, of goods and bads, of say, not just clothing and shelter but of clothing, shelter and the CFCs and as such it cannot but be conceptually unavailing. Verily, it is an abstraction which has little regard for the nature of the specific components of economic activity.

Only an abstraction like the GNP could be married with an abstraction like compound interest and an illusion called growth generated. No wonder that the period after the Second World War, during which an Earthwide ecological crisis began precipitating, is taken even by Robert Heilbroner (1993: 126) to be an 'era of transformational change'. Of change so positive, moreover, that the 'discouraged tone' of *The General Theory* would have vanished if only it had been written during this period. As against this, it seems fairly reasonable to argue that if only its author had been able to internalize the long-term ecological and societal implications of the post-war economic celebrations, the tone of *The General Theory* could well have become still more discouraged.

In particular, if Keynes had been endowed with a vision basically historical in nature. For he would then have seen that 'the industrial and demographic growth rates experienced during the last two centuries represent a transient and ephemeral epoch in the longer span of human history' (Hubbert 1987: 76). Transient and ephemeral and therefore unrepeatable.

In sum, the very concept of growth which requires a prodigal consumption of the terrestrial capital and which at the same time fails to cognize the concomitant diminution of the terrestrial income must perforce be rooted in *some* fallacy. The one involved here entails, to my mind, removing or displacing the concrete itself from the focus of attention. So let us call it the Fallacy of Displaced Concreteness.

6   Prevarication Pur Sang

For the next twenty-five years, in my belief, economists, at present the most incompetent, will be nevertheless the most important, group of scientists in the world. And it is to be hoped—if they are successful—that after that they will never be important again.

John Maynard Keynes in 1932 (K-XXI: 37)

[Economists] ... are the trustees, not of civilization, but of the possibility of civilization.

John Maynard Keynes in 1945 (Harrod 1951: 194)

When a Royal Commission solicits opinions from five economists, they get six answers—two from Mr. Keynes.

Anonymous (Samuelson 1986: 275)

Keynes and Marshall

What Professor Paul Samuelson half-heartedly calls Keynes's 'lifetime variability' is not easy to explain. Half heartedly, because the 'desultory study' he says he once made of Keynes's variability did not lead him to discover anything which he would have to 'rationalize or apologize for'. Even so, Keynes's own 'defence of being protean' is not very convincing, much less 'impeccable', which Samuelson thinks it is: 'When my information changes, I alter my conclusions. What do you do, sir?'

But if this indeed were so, Samuelson or anyone else for that matter would be hard put to it to explain the 'lifetime variability' of the way Keynes looked at none other than Alfred Marshall himself. For with respect to Marshall, at least, his information was not likely to change, much less keep changing. But consider the following three samples: 1. In a 1906 letter to R.H. Dundas which appears in Roy Harrod (1951: 117), Keynes wrote: 'Amusing that you have met Marshall. A very great man, but I suppose rather a silly one in his private character. Mrs. is charming, isn't she?' In the accompanying footnote, Harrod has this to say: 'I do not rely on this letter as sole evidence for [Keynes's] feeling about Marshall as a man. On more than one occasion in private conversation, when I assumed a tone of reverence due to a great one in speaking of Marshall, Maynard seemed anxious to correct my misapprehension. "He was an utterly absurd person, you know."' I do not know what impelled Keynes to dismiss Marshall as rather silly in private character or what aspect of Marshall as a person he was feeling so unhappy about as to describe him as an utterly absurd person. But given his own notoriously abnormal impulses, which Harrod (ibid.: 182) also alludes to, his dismissal of Marshall can hardly be taken very seriously. In particular, because Marshall's 'impulses' are not known to have been other than perfectly 'straight-forward'. Besides, Marshall seems to have been a lot more generous than Keynes, to whose father he once wrote as follows: 'Among your many honours, there is perhaps none greater than that of being the father of J.M. Keynes' (ibid.: 157).
2. Be that as it may, the Memoir of Alfred Marshall that Keynes published in the September 1924 issue of The Economic Journal is anything but a relegation. On the contrary, it is an extremely glowing tribute. But, then, only Keynes, having dismissed him as someone rather silly in *private character*, and whom he would later describe as utterly absurd, could find it so easy to declare that 'Marshall belonged to the tribe of sages and pastors'. The point must be made, too, that no one—just no one—could possibly belong to the tribe of sages and pastors unless he had personal qualities of the very highest order. And, as Keynes put it *this time*, the sage in Marshall, though not particularly superior to other sages, was strong enough to be superordinate to the economist in him—no matter if the latter was 'the greatest in the world for a hundred years' (K-X: 173). Marshall, thus elevated, became 'the first great economist *pur sang* that there ever was; the first who devoted his life to building up the subject

matter as a separate science, standing on its own foundations, with as high standards of scientific accuracy as the physical or the biological sciences' (K-X: 222).

3. But there was going to be one more turnabout. For Marshall's *Principles of Economics* which in 1924 Keynes described as 'that rounded globe of knowledge' (K-X: 212) became before long a book 'void of content' (Harrod 1983: 81). I am not saying that Keynes had no right to chide Harrod for having failed to make the 'discovery' which he himself had made. What I wish to manifest instead is the very distinct possibility that there was nothing to stop a man like Keynes to come to rediscover Marshall's *Principles* as a globe of knowledge as rounded as ever before.

Incidentally, Keynes thought it to have been a 'fatal decision' on the part of Alfred Marshall to abandon his first intention of separate independent monographs in favour of a great treatise'. Economists, he added, 'must leave to Adam Smith alone the glory of the quarto, must pluck the day, fling pamphlets into the wind, write always *sub species temporis*, and achieve immortality by accident, if at all' (K-X: 197–99). Its eloquence or perhaps bombast notwithstanding, all that this sentence says is that the economists have little better to do than to indulge themselves with a peculiar brand of journalism—by definition the antithesis of theory. But a claim like this could possibly be born only out of an implicit conviction that the status quo, being eternal and hence immune to any irreversible and irreparable damage, could at the most come to face merely transient and perhaps even unrelated problems.

In other words, the economists who must write always *sub species temporis*, that is, in the light of time, must also take care *always* to see the prevailing order itself *sub species aeternitatis*, that is, in the light of eternity. This only means that having put the prevailing order itself far outside the pale of examination, they must remain confined to the world of technomanic trivialities and non-issues.

But there is also something more to this dictum about the quarto than that. For it is one of those totally misleading statements which Keynes could manage somehow to sell as nothing less than the most sagacious of profundities. Verily, the choice is not and could not have been between the quarto and the pamphlet but between an apology of the status quo and a critique of it. A *magnum opus* can be as much of an apology as a pamphlet and a pamphlet can be as much of a withering critique as a *magnum opus*. In writing A *Modest Proposal*, that ultimate exemplar of what a value-free or rather an ethically disoriented economic calculus could turn out to be, Jonathan Swift became entitled to much greater glory than would come the way of the authors of several quartos put together. And yet he took just about 3,300 *words* to compose it. It follows that if one chose to write only apologies, no matter how big or how small, one could only produce 'that flavour of final purposelessness [and] inner irresponsibility' which Keynes once found Lloyd George for one to be an embodiment of. This means that coming only to defend the prevailing order or to take it for granted, the economists would cease to use their critical faculties and become as 'void and contentless' as Lloyd George could ever have been (K-X: 23–24) and could well come to produce truly large quantities of footloose, that is, inherently inconsistent and trivial, verbosity.

Remorseless Variability

Be that as it may, Keynes seems never to have tired of prevaricating. Indeed, he seems to have been a compulsive prevaricator if ever there was one. Whatever the psychological reasons which kept pushing him this way and that and which I am in no position to go into, he appears to have been very firmly resolved to continue to stay very much within what Edmund Burke (1884: 417) would call a veritable 'dyke of prevarication'. As he himself once put it: 'But alas I scarcely know where I stand. Somewhere, I suppose between Liberal and Labour, though in some respects to the left of the latter, not feeling that anyone just now really represents my strongest convictions' (K-XXI: 372–73). But a choice between Liberal and Labour was not his only vexation. For he seems not to have known where exactly he stood nor what his strongest convictions were with respect to quite a wide range of issues.

Thus, in October 1925, he spoke of 'the turbid rubbish of the Red bookshops' [in Moscow?] and referred to Karl Marx's *Capital* as 'an obsolete economic textbook' which was 'not only scientifically erroneous but without interest or application for the modern world' (K-IX: 258). After the collapse of the Soviet Union, this remark certainly merits serious attention. But what matters in the present context is something different. Which is that less than eight months after having spoken of 'the turbid rubbish of the Red bookshops', Keynes told Albert Einstein in Berlin 'of a kind of sympathy that he had for

Communism' (K-X: 383). Further, and less than four years later, he would be writing on the manifesto of the redoubtable Sir Oswald Mosley who in turn would before long be founding the British Union of Fascists. He, that is, Keynes, found the manifesto's promises to the producer rather weak and those to the consumer rather wild. But it was 'the spirit' informing the document which he liked: its rejection of the idea of natural forces using an invisible hand to bring about economic harmonies: its power to shock those with '*laissez-faire* in their craniums, their consciences, and their bones:' its promise of combining 'liberal humanitarianism, big-business psychology, and the tradition of public service' to produce a specifically British variety of socialism—yes, socialism: and, finally, the 'boyish ebullience of its author' (K-XX: 473–76).

Having given this testimonial to Oswald Mosley, Keynes came to give one to Albert Einstein, too, and described him as a double symbol —'a symbol of the mind travelling in the cold regions of space, and a symbol of the brave and generous outcast, pure in heart and cheerful in spirit'. So it was no accident he said that Einstein was so detested by the Nazi lads whom he also called nasty lads (K-XXVIII: 21–22). Yet, what Keynes managed to forget altogether was that Mosley's lads were no less nasty than those of the 'original' Nazis.

Little wonder that Keynes has been described as 'a swinging weather-vane of a man', a cartoonist's dream, a boneless human who could turn his back on himself and be 'both right and wrong' at the same time (Johnson 1973: 12). For such a one as this, it would hardly be a problem to declare in one breath that a *class war* would necessarily find him 'on the side of the educated *bourgeoisie*' and claim in another breath taken barely six months later that the republic of his imagination was to be found 'on the extreme left of [the] celestial space' (K-IX: 297, 309). But to him being on the 'extreme left' meant being less conservative in his inclinations than the average Labour voter and also playing in his mind with the possibilities of greater social changes than those which came within the philosophy of, say, Sidney Webb.

One may refer here to a point he made in the preface to the French edition of *The General Theory*. He had grown accustomed to his new skin, he said, and had almost forgotten the smell of his old one (K-VII: xxxi). Which only means that his conceptual novelties were quite literally skin-deep or superficial. Verily and in substance, his economics was no less reductionist and over-mechanistic than the economics he was trying to get away from. But in the present context, it is a different kind of a Keynesian 'skin problem' I wish to draw attention to. For Keynes could manage to change his skin so fast that at least on some occasions the lingering smell of the old wouldn't let him recognize that of the new. Little wonder that the sentence *immediately following* the pronunciamento about 'the extreme left of [the] celestial space' marks a swing *back* to the camp of 'the educated *bourgeoisie*': 'Yet—all the same—I feel that my true home, so long as they offer a roof and a floor, is still with the Liberals.'

But as the first two quotes given at the head of this chapter show, Keynes reserved his most amusing or rather ludicrous turnabout for the economists themselves. Thus, at one point, he could wish and hope that after a horrid interval of twenty-five years, they would for ever cease to have any significant role to play in the world, and barely thirteen years later he came to consider them to be the trustees of the possibility of civilization itself. However, each one of these assertions can easily be seen to have been an exceedingly wayward mental transience—each of them being as meaningless as the other. For, it just cannot be clear as to how extreme professional importance sustained for twenty-five years by incompetence could give way to complete unimportance sustained for ever after by competence. Nor is it clear as to how the economists fully co-opted into an orgiastic civilization could redeem it from self-destruction merely if they were told that they were the trustees of it.

This verdict about the economists being the trustees of the possibility of civilization Keynes pronounced at the end of a speech he gave at a dinner meeting held on 21 June 1945 to commemorate his resignation from the editorship of *The Economic Journal*. A brief account of this meeting appears in the Current Topics section of the issue of the *Journal* for June-September 1945 (pp. 298–300). But it makes no mention of all the champagne which, according to Roy Harrod, Keynes had been deliberately made to imbibe.

I do not know if this champagne had anything to do with the verdict he gave. But we know from Harrod's testimony that he took a little time before handing over the possibility of civilization to the custody of the economists. Perhaps the hesitation had at least something to do with an earlier remark of his that it would be splendid if 'economists could manage to get themselves thought of as humble, competent people, on a level with dentists' (K-IX: 332). But he was too much of a prevaricator to have been daunted for long by this distraction. So he went ahead and turned over the possibility of civilization, that is, the human future itself, to the care of the economists.

In any case, the audience that night, all men and women of high learning, seems to have swallowed the trusteeship idea hook, line and sinker. In fact, *The Economic Journal* write-up just referred to speaks of it as 'an exordium upon economists'. Which means that if one wants to know something about economics, one must *begin* with the presumption that the economists are the guardians of the future of civilization. Harrod has also written that what Keynes said was true, 'not something slipshod, which might pass muster on such an occasion, but an accurate description, which would bear the test of close scrutiny in the clear light of day. And it did full justice to economics'.

Full justice, indeed! And that too in the form of a compliment which happened to be just one of those compulsive and irritating turnabouts which Keynes was so helplessly and hopelessly given to, and which, moreover, could hardly mean a thing; much less bear the test of close scrutiny. In particular, because exactly a month-and-a-half after Keynes had designated the economists as the trustees of the possibility of civilization, Hiroshima came to be razed to the ground. And with that, civilization, or rather the very possibility of civilization, began its relentless and historically unprecedented recession. Keynes didn't live long after Hiroshima and may not have found much time to dwell on its implications. But nothing but sheer professional insensitivity must have prevented Harrod from seeing what had happened. 'The unleashed power of the atom,' in Einstein's unforgettable phrase, had changed everything save people's modes of thinking and had therefore failed to blast any of the ivory towers housing hordes of economists. No wonder that they continued to perceive as the possibility of civilization what in fact was, as Einstein (1960: 376) put it, a drift towards 'unparalleled catastrophe'.

The explanation lies in the cussed commitment to the status quo which, in spite of all the hazards and irrationalities it congeals, continues to determine the priorities and inform the pursuits of the economics profession. Far would it be from it therefore to see the massive and remorseless misemployment of men and materials brought about by the historically unprecedented consumerist orgies and weapons mania of our time. Besides, and in conclusion, this refusal to consider (K-VII: 379) even the possibility of misemployment, that is, of an egregious misdirection of economic activity, was the one immutable fixation of John Maynard Keynes, irrespective of how wild his variability might otherwise happen to be. Hardly surprising, this. For an implicit and unquestioning presumption of the legitimacy of the prevailing order, no matter how grim its crisis of legitimation, was the one fixed point of reference from which his thought never could deviate. In other words, his prevarication, even if pathological and exasperating, could touch anything under the Sun but *never* the status quo itself. For he seems to have taken it to be nothing less than a sacred cow, the basic anatomy of which could not be brought under examination under any circumstances whatsoever. For only then would he be spared the urge to prevaricate back into singing paeans to it.

Part Three: Samuelson— And Some Other Problems of Our Age

Mankind is distinguished from animal life by its emphasis on abstractions. The degeneracy of mankind is distinguished from its uprise by the dominance of chill abstractions, divorced from aesthetic content.

Alfred North Whitehead (1968: 123)

When something is foolish, let it be called foolish, as when something is viciously cruel, let it be called viciously cruel.

John Kenneth Galbraith (1993: 3)

The Illusion of Choice*

> The last five or six decades have seen American economics come
> of age and then become the dominant centre of world political
> economy.
>
> Paul A. Samuelson (1986: 797)

> Will economics never come of age?
>
> Joseph A. Schumpeter (1961: 115n)

Milton and Shakespeare

Thanks to their woefully reduced—that is, oversimplified—modes of
perception, mainline economists manage always to invert the meaning
of the existential reality. But at least some of them manage also to
invert the meanings of what the very great in literature have said.
John Hicks, for instance, has thus inverted the meaning of a famous
phrase from Milton's *Paradise Lost* and Paul Samuelson, of a line
from Shakespeare's *King Lear*. Besides, needless to say, in each case,
the Nobel Laureate in question has managed also to reduce the sublime
to the ridiculous. This becomes clear the moment we return the
citations to their respective contexts. For it is only by removing them
from their contexts, in the first instance, that Hicks and Samuelson
have been able to assign to them meanings which have nothing to do
with the meanings which Milton and Shakespeare themselves had
respectively given them.

* An earlier version of this chapter appeared in the September/December 1994 issue
of *Lokayan*.

Consider the Milton quote which appears as an epigraph at the very beginning of Hicks's *Value and Capital* (1972: 9): 'reason also is choice'. It is the parenthetical part of line 108 of Book III of *Paradise Lost* and carries a message also contained in *Areopagitica*, a powerful pamphlet Milton wrote against state censorship and in defence of 'domestic or private liberty': 'When God gave [Man] reason, He gave him freedom to choose, for reason is but choosing ...' But such reason, said Milton, could be exercised *only* under conditions of freedom. For what could virtue be under conditions of 'prescription and compulsion' but a word, a mere name? And 'what gramercy' —what thanks—would be due to enforced sobriety or continence? But freedom can have problems, too. For men do not just have the faculty of reason which makes them choose but also 'minds that can wander beyond all limits and satiety' (Milton 1958: 163–64).

This argues nothing less than an existential dilemma which Milton traces in *Paradise Lost* (Line 99, Book III) to the very nature of Man whom he sees as both 'sufficient to have stood' and 'free to fall'. But 'falling' is much easier than 'standing' so that Man would very likely 'hearken' to his satanic tempter's 'glozing lies' and thus slide towards error. After all, 'True freedom must include the freedom to err' (Bush 1983: 259n). Even so, Milton (1958: 181) seems to have been certain that 'Truth is strong, next only to the Almighty'. So strong, indeed, that she 'needs no policies, nor stratagems, nor licensings' to become victorious over Error—if only ultimately. For these policies and licensings are 'the shifts and the defences' which 'Error uses against her power'. In a word, given a regime devoid of censorship, Truth must prevail.

But with the benefit of hindsight, though, we do not find Truth to have been 'sufficient to have stood' its ground. In other words, it has not been able to resist, much less overwhelm, Error. Else, we would not as a race be facing the kind of predicament we now are. No wonder. For blatant censorship has been replaced by relatively subtle but no less effective manipulation. Perhaps, on this account alone, would Milton be a sorely disappointed and disillusioned man today and as worried about human survival as we are.

Be that as it may, it is easy to see that Milton's assertion that 'reason is but choosing' has nothing whatever to do with Hicks's identification of reason with choice. For Milton is concerned with fundamental questions of human existence, of human ontology—indeed, with questions of the very viability of Man as *a responsible species*. This is the Miltonian Sublime I alluded to a little earlier. In contrast, all that Hicks's reason-as-choice consists in is the substitution of one ethereal symbol X for another ethereal symbol Y, each of them called a commodity (Hicks 1972: 20–21). But we cannot afford to be so non-specific particularly when we know that it is not X and Y which are, say, destroying the ozone layer and blighting life in the oceans but CFCs in one case and PCBs in the other. In the circumstances, what Hicks calls the Marginal Rate of Substitution [MRS] cannot but be a mere sterilized technicality incapable of promoting *relevance* to a horrid reality which happens to be both explosive and involuting. For it is an amalgam of exploding hazards and a shrinking Earth-system. Whitehead himself who found human degeneracy to be rooted in chill abstractions would be hard put to it to find a chiller abstraction than Hicks's MRS.

Here, let us recall the extinction of meaning which Samuelson's concept of the Production-Possibility Frontier suffered when, in Chapter 2, we put it in confrontation with Whitehead's point about the senselessness of a durationless instant of time even in the abstract and with Schrödinger's point concerning the impossibility of reversal in real-life situations. It seems obvious that in a similar confrontation, Hicks's MRS would also suffer a complete extinction of meaning. This is the reason why a fantasy like this would have nothing to do with, say, Milton using his reason to choose Truth but not Error, Right but not Wrong, Responsibility but not Irresponsibility and so on. What the MRS boils down to, then, is what I alluded to a little earlier as the Hicksian Ridiculous.

But why just the Hicksian Ridiculous? Why not the Economystic Ridiculous? Consider, for instance, the way that Kenneth Boulding once (1965: 139) saw the Economic Man: 'a generalized chooser and decision-maker' who in order to maximize something or other has to sacrifice 'a little ham for a little more eggs in a breakfast', or 'a little justice for a little more progress in a policy' or even 'a little red for a little more green in a painting'. Professor Boulding wrote this when he was still an inmate of the Neoclassical Prison House and would probably have made poor Rembrandt turn violently in his grave. No wonder that having escaped out of there, he got concerned in the last years of his life with issues of an altogether different import.

But not many economists have been lucky enough to experience the intellectual ecstasy of a jail-break of this kind. No wonder that they continue to be focused on abstract choice, on 'economizing', and remain totally impervious to the sheer bizarrerie of what happens when these abstractions are dragged into the world of reality. As Edwin Cannan once (1932: 425) put it a little impishly, an unscrupulous house-owner who had decided to put his house to fire so as to be able to cheat the fire-insurance company must still take care not to 'use more matches than necessary'. But this is not known to have moved his pupil Lionel Robbins, according to whom: 'There are only twenty-four hours in the day [so that we] have to choose between the different uses to which they may be put.' With Robbins, in fact, even 'hired love' comes to have 'an economic aspect'. Therefore, the economist, being unable to do a thing in the situation, becomes 'a true tragedian' (Robbins 1949: 15, 28, 30).

Evidently, no human activity can possibly be excluded from the purview of such non-specific choice-making with the result that Raymond Firth (1971: 130), for instance, says that every 'sex congress', even if maritally legitimated, must entail a sacrifice—an 'opportunity cost'—'in time and in energy'. Such indeed cannot be the intimations of a social science in full bloom but must instead be those of economics as *the* Dismal Science: a Casanova of today or of any other time would, in order to be able to avail himself of one 'opportunity', *have* to bear the cost in terms of some other. This bespeaks the very ultimate in suffering to which Man must forever remain condemned. For confined to a 24-hour regimen, he can't get all the love, hired and unhired, which he would like to have. Only, Professor Robbins never made it clear what conceptual difference would it make if the Earth had a 240-hour or even a 2,400-hour long day.

This, then, is the kind of light which economics, understood as 'the logic of choice' (Hicks 1983: 289), throws on the existential reality. For whatever else it may do, and no matter how thoroughly mathematized it may well be, being 'nothing else but pure technics', it cannot possibly distinguish between, say, the specific kind of reason-and-choice dynamizing a man like Chico Mendes and that dynamizing those who killed him in December 1988. Ecological stability of the Amazonian rainforest was the one *consuming* passion which informed the way that *he* reasoned and decided the choices that *he* made. But the sheerly reckless profiteering which entails the destruction of the rainforest was the passion, no less consuming, of his assassins whose reasoning it informed and whose choices or mischoices it decided.

To lump Chico's reasoning and choices with the reasoning and mischoices of his killers would be the very ultimate act of economystic folly inspired directly by the reductionist formula which Rene Descartes (1985: 140) enunciated a long time ago: 'Reason is a universal instrument which can be used in all kinds of situations'. To my mind, this oft-cited Cartesian utterance is an unrectifiable and hopeless oversimplification. For it ignores the menace of Unreason which with the passage of time has continued only to become ever more virulent. Which means that in getting hooked on a conceptual holdall called the 'logic of choice', the economists must perforce remain entirely insensitive to the gravity of the consequences of the mischoices which those in power make in the world of reality, not just in the world of abstractions.

But such mischoices cannot but destroy opportunities for the underlying multitudes who as a result are left with no *choice* but to suffer. Marie Antoinette's 'Let them eat cake' is but a classic manifestation of the cynicism which the comfortable tend normally to cultivate in response to human suffering. In our own time, embodying such cynicism is Ronald Reagan [who else?]. For according to him, the homeless are 'homeless by choice' (Wright 1989: 46). It seems to me that what Hicks calls 'the logic of choice'—that is, economics itself—is but an academic surrogate for such cynicism of the comfortable.

Nor is Samuelson's definition of economics as the 'science of choice' (Samuelson and Nordhaus 1992: 3) in any way more humane and illumining than Hicks's definition of it as the logic of choice. For the scientist is as insensitive as the logician was to the sustained and tendentious destruction of human autonomy through remorseless manipulation. Which in turn must make them both completely insensitive to the widespread mutilation of human ability itself to make well-reasoned choices. It is precisely this ability which is sought to be destroyed through a Pavlovian conditioning and sustained persuasion—most of it hidden—of ordinary people. With vast multitudes thus manipulated and, in Paulo Freire's terms, even domesticated, choice can mean not a thing except in the distracting pages of glossy textbooks.

Consider, for instance, the way that Samuelson and Nordhaus (1989: 26) dismiss the phenomenon of consumer manipulation. They claim on the one hand that 'economics describes and analyses how different societies cope with limited resources' and insist on the other that it 'must reckon with consumer wants and needs whether they are genuine or contrived'. But if coping—yes, *coping*—with limited resources is the principal economic problem which we face, it cannot possibly be a matter of indifference *as to whether the wants are genuine or contrived.* For they have to be genuine.

Indeed, contrived wants must perforce spell nothing but ecological catastrophe and therefore the very ultimate economic calamity as well —sooner rather than later. In other words, it would be an act of exceeding intellectual irresponsibility even to suggest, let alone assert, that economics must focus on how limited goods *get rationed among whatever wants a society generates.* For if 'society'—or rather the Madison Avenue—continues to generate *whatever* wants it likes to, economics cannot in principle be concerned with anything like rationing or allocation—indeed, even with 'free' market allocation. On the contrary, it could only be rationalizing and legitimizing relentless *misallocation.* Remember Joseph Schumpeter's point about satiety becoming a flying goal under capitalism? Little that they may see it, the word *whatever* spells the complete undoing of 'the science of choice' which Samuelson and Nordhaus, among others, seek to sell. Therefore, in invoking Shakespeare in their support, they cannot but look pathetically supine.

In particular, because in removing the *King Lear* line—'reason not the need'—from its context and assigning a whimsical meaning of their own to it, they have managed only to get Shakespeare 180 degrees wrong.

For, what we see in their formulation, to begin with, is a complete extinction of the fundamental distinction between absolute needs and the needs of the second class which Keynes (K-IX: 326) himself once made. In the terminology of our own time, absolute needs would be known as basic needs or just *needs* and the needs of the second class as *wants.* Now, even if we agree that Lear is in fact saying what Samuelson and Nordhaus imagine he is, he should have said: 'Reason not the *wants*'. But he *could not possibly have said that.* For, needs may well be beyond examination, beyond reason, but wants cannot be. And it is in refusing to question the validity of wants which the Madison Avenue generates and transforms into veritable needs that the mainline economists of our time come *nolens volens* to serve as the apologists of the status quo.

But Samuelson and Nordhaus's 'Shakespeare Problem' lies essentially in taking a line from the very beginning of a Lear speech *and then in making it support a thesis which the speech itself is in fact meant only to question.* In support of this claim, one may refer to the explanation which Kenneth Muir (1967: 98–99) gives in the Arden Shakespeare *King Lear*. Two of Lear's daughters, Goneril and Regan, are telling him that he really doesn't *need* a large number of attendants and the speech which he makes in response opens with an explosive 'O! reason not the need'. Evidently, the word 'need' as used here has nothing to do with 'ends' in the abstract which the economists like to take for granted. Rather, it refers to Lear's specific need, the need of a king, for servants and it is this *particular* need which he does not want Regan to reason. Besides, even the basest of beggars, he says, no matter how little they possess, may have something more than what is necessary for bare existence. Evidently, this refers to the poor of Shakespeare's England, not to those of the India of our own time.

Being all tensed up because of the refusal of his daughters to allow him all the servants he thinks he as a king needs, he does reason —does question—does argue about—Regan's *specific* need for the fashionably scanty dress she is wearing. That is, in suggesting that she is herself violating the canon of need, he is, in effect, suggesting only that his need for servants is none of her business. Still, Samuelson and Nordhaus take his 'reason not the need' as a veritable injunction against examining wants *per se*. In fact, they seem to suggest that in making Lear refuse to allow anyone to reason his need for servants, Shakespeare was in effect laying the very foundations of the mainline economics of today. For this economics also refuses to reason any needs or wants whether genuine or contrived. But Samuelson and his co-author would be hard put to it to explain Lear's determination to reason some of his daughter Regan's needs. A few lines later in the speech, Lear is about to explain the difference between *true need* and *the perverted needs* of fashionable women, when he breaks off to pray for his own chief need at the moment—patience or fortitude. Later, in Act IV, Sc. I, we find Shakespeare using Gloucester to lambast 'the superfluous and lust-dieted man' and to plead that 'distribution should undo excess, and each man have enough'.

I am not suggesting that Shakespeare was a full-fledged or even a Fabian socialist. But nor was he a proto-ideologue of consumerism and certainly not a potential copywriter for the Mughals of the Madison Avenue. Be that as it may, when I tried to draw Professor Samuelson's attention to the way he and Nordhaus had managed to misuse Shakespeare, he simply refused to take any note of what I was saying. Instead, he wrote something about 'children and non-dons' even enjoying being frightened into buying mouthwashes. I certainly admire his unmatched ability to respond even to relatively unknown people like me; and I do admire his ability, also unmatched, to refuse to take note of anything in which he perceives a lurking threat to his ideological predilections. Still, I am flattered not a little by his decision, apparently in response to my letter, to drop the *King Lear* line from the 1992 edition of *Economics*. Perhaps, he is not so unbelievably unpersuadable as I had thought him to be! But, more important, the reference to mouthwashes does not provide much of a defence to his ideological predilections. For what matters is not that 'children and non-dons' do in fact enjoy being frightened into buying mouthwashes. What matters rather is that a grown-up don, like Samuelson himself, is too frightened to have a full look at consumerism which happens to be a raging pathology of our time. No wonder. A close examination of consumerism could well come to sour his 'great romance' with 'the Keynesian revolution'.

Patriotic Housewives

For, after all, Maynard Keynes himself was an early harbinger of the resource-devouring existential menace which would soon become known as consumerism. In fact, in a January 1931 BBC broadcast entitled 'Saving and Spending', he rhetorized as follows: 'Therefore, O patriotic housewives sally out tomorrow early into the streets and go to the wonderful sales which are everywhere advertised. You will do yourselves good—for never were things so cheap, cheap beyond your dreams. Lay in a stock of household linen, of sheets and blankets to satisfy all your needs. And have the added joy that you are increasing employment adding to the wealth of the country because you are setting on foot useful activities bringing a chance and a hope to Lancashire, Yorkshire and Belfast.' And towards the end of the same broadcast came the following assertion: 'Be confident therefore that we are suffering from the growing pains of youth, not from the rheumatics of old age' (K-IX: 138, 141). But the reckless squandering of resources which his plea for an orgy of spending entailed could at best help attenuate or even dispel the problem of unemployment only for the time being. For the long-run consequences of a remorseless resource-destruction, as is becoming ever more evident now, could not be delayed indefinitely. In other words, what Keynes proposed as an antidote to 'the growing pains of youth' would itself precipitate 'the rheumatics of old age'. But it is easy to see, that the production of the rheumatics of old age caused by the treatment of the growing pains of youth which Keynes proposed could only be a case of economic iatrogenesis: *an economic pathology produced by the prescribed economic remedy itself.* Nevertheless, Keynes's advice to the patriotic housewives to sally out into the streets in search of sheets and blankets was little more ennobling intellectually than the one which *The Journal of Retailing* would be giving some years later. According to Vance Packard (1951: 59), this is what this journal said: 'Our enormously productive economy ... demands that we make consumption our way of life, that we convert the buying and use of goods into rituals, that we seek our spiritual satisfactions, our ego satisfactions, in consumption ... We need things consumed, burned up, worn out, replaced and discarded at an ever increasing rate'. All this, that is, what both Keynes and *The Journal of Retailing* said, seems to have come straight out of that [intellectual] underworld to which, we were once told (K-VII: 32), Karl Marx, Silvio Gessell and Major Douglas belonged.

However, what matters is to note that such pleas for orgiastic consumption, whether they came from the academic pulpit or from business journals, were not exceptions but the rule. For the abetment of such consumption was, as Jules Henry (1963: 19) once put it, the First Commandment of the capitalist era; and those who once bought full-page advertising space in *The New York Times* and other papers articulated this Commandment as follows:

CREATE
MORE
DESIRE

A remorseless and unending creation of such desire becomes breathtakingly easy in a situation in which the State is only too eager to provide almost free lunches to the corporate rich. I say 'almost free lunches' for the simple reason that, according to the economists, no completely free lunches are ever possible. Indeed, any mainline economist worth his reductionist salt, Milton Friedman for instance, would be only too glad to confirm the sheer impossibility of free lunches. But he would rather not talk about 'the almost free lunches' that I am referring to. For they embody and manifest a State-sponsored parasitism which the clinically tidy theories of economics could have nothing to do with. These are the 80 per cent tax-deductible expense account meals which are in effect a federal food-stamp programme for the highly contented and comfortable Americans.

No wonder that most of the corporate executives, lawyers and politicians who come to a place like Chicago's oak-panelled Metropolitan Club for its prime beef and the sixty-seventh-floor panorama of the city never forget to keep track of their receipts. Which help them virtually to write off their cocktails and gluttonous orgies as 'business expense' and thus to pass on the costs to ordinary taxpayers to whom no deductibles are ever available. C. Wright Mills once (1972: 161) spoke of people who are too rich to 'have to look at the right hand column of a menu'. But here is another reason why the right hand column of the menu card becomes virtually irrelevant: it is the State which will foot the bill—at least a major part of the bill. Needless to say, no economic theorist would be concerned with the revealed preferences of such people. Which, however, seem to have been quite obvious to a former waitress at the Metropolitan Club. Many of her customers, she recalls, 'think you're scum if you're on food stamps, but they're the first to cut corners. I'd see them writing off "business" dinners with their girlfriends or wives. I finally realized that they're on welfare just like me, only they don't call it that'.

However, expense-account orgies do not by themselves consumerism make. Also to be taken into account are, as we have seen earlier, the $200 billion a year tax subsidies given to the rich in the form of, say, home-mortgage and built-in sauna deductions. In fact, the rich do not even bother about high tax rates, which with the help of their lawyers and accountants, they can always dodge. But what they really care about are their deductions and entitlements to secure which they must spend, spend and spend. As Marx perhaps would have put it, 'Consume, consume! That is Moses and the prophets!'

The State, as we have just seen, is only too eager to help. No wonder that the most affluent 4 per cent of the American families with incomes of over $100,000 a year manage to collect over 8 per cent of all federal subsidies for retirement—some $30 billion a year. Nevertheless, President Clinton, like other politicians in either of the two factions of what C. Wright Mills used to call the 'property party' (Chomsky 1992: 176), finds it easier to cut into the $16 billion a year Aid to Families with Dependent Children than to 'dismantle the subsidies now taken for granted by campaign contributors and other members of the comfortable classes'. This has not been taken from a new New

Left handout but from a recent article on 'Welfare for the Well-Off' which has appeared in *Time* itself (Goodgame 1993: 36–37).

But unable to see all this, Professor Samuelson (1986: 998) remains focused on man's humanity to man now congealed according to him in the humane welfare state. Which he takes to be only a system of *mutual reinsurance arrangements for the transfer*—his italics—of 'incomes from us when we fare well in the market place to ourselves when our human needs exceed what we can earn'. To Samuelson (1979: 837), the 'we' becomes a single, seamless entity with no incompatibilities of interests, no contradictions, no exploitation—in sum, what he designates as 'WE, INC'. I cannot imagine a more cynical suppression of societal dichotomies, of iniquities and injustices informing a contemporary military-industrial state. Indeed, 'WE, INC' is almost a mental black hole into which Samuelson seems eager to dump anything and everything he doesn't want to think about— perhaps even the ninety-five million functionally illiterate Americans who constitute over one-half of the adult population of their country and who cannot follow simple written instructions (Sivard 1993: 39). Of these, some thirty million are guesstimated to be completely illiterate and as such cannot even read the warning on a can of pesticide. That is, a hefty one-sixth of the adult population of the United States has no choice—yes, *no choice*—but to sit frozen before the written word. Evidently, only in a highly clinical and sterilized universe of discourse may some meaning be assigned to Samuelson's 'us' and 'ourselves'. But in the world of murky reality, there simply is no way to impound the wretched and the contented together in the United States or anywhere else. There are, as we have seen earlier, some 37 million Americans who have no health insurance at all and many more millions who have too little of it. Melding them with expense account orgiasts could well yield an illusion of what Samuelson calls 'mutual reinsurance' all right but not the real thing.

Advertising

But, then, illusions *are* what iniquity requires; and it is only natural that, given its kind of commitment to Iniquity with a capital I, the United States should have a more highly developed industry manufacturing illusions than perhaps any other country in the world. This industry is called advertising. It is only natural, too, that an ideologist of the status quo like Paul Samuelson should have little to say about this industry by way of critique. No wonder that whatever he has written about advertising, at least to my knowledge, is nothing much to write home about.

For it is informed by a total lack of criticality. Indeed, even when some critical comment or other does manage to sneak in, it doesn't really belong to the text which remains entirely unaffected. Or, uncontaminated? Thus, in an earlier edition of *Economics* (1961: 137), we read about innuendo and not direct statement being a major weapon in the advertiser's armoury. And in a later edition (1976: 48) the following: 'But in actual life, as Galbraith never tires of pointing out, business firms spend much money on advertising to *shape*—and, some insist, *distort*—consumer demands. We are terrorized into buying deodorants; from childhood on, we are conditioned to desire what business wants to sell'. Further, and as a result, the sequence 'consumer demand → corporate prices and production' is often inverted to become 'corporate advertising → consumer demand → high prices and profit'.

Now, if taken at all seriously, this alone should be more than enough to dispel the hitherto tenacious illusion of consumer sovereignty. But with this doctrine gone, not much would be left of the very concept of rational resource allocation nor of mainline economics nor for that matter of *Economics* itself. That is why such statements were never meant to be taken more seriously than some wayward *obiter dicta*. Besides, when we come to the Nordhaused editions of *Economics* like the thirteenth (p. 605), even these *dicta* get expunged and replaced by a highly sterilized statement to the effect that concentrated industries tend to have much higher levels of advertising and R&D spending per unit of sales.

Incidentally, even before he gave his advice to the patriotic housewives, Keynes spoke of advertising having become 'a highly intellectual business' (K-XIX: 660). So, it should be perfectly in order to see some of the specific manifestations of this kind of intellectuality in our own time. In particular, because an understanding of this intellectuality alone can help us see how consumption and therefore a major component of what is known as the GNP comes actually to be manipulated in a modern ultra-industrial society.

In order to see what forms can such manipulation assume and how far it can go, one would do well to include various kinds of promotional practices under the generic term 'advertising'. To my mind, it is only through an examination of advertising that we may come to learn something about the role which plain fraud plays in the legitimization of the status quo. For, individual exercises in advertising may well be intended to sell some specific product or other. But advertising *per se* is meant only to sell a general idea: *the idea of the legitimacy and inviolability of the prevailing order*. That is what the 'intellectuality' of advertising is all about. Indeed, once, in Freirean terminology, the massification and domestication of people has taken place, that is, once they have been co-opted and even absorbed into the 'system', they can be made to buy anything, just anything. The power of the advertiser, then, begins to manifest itself not just in pushing the sales of, say, mere deodorants. Rather, what it manifests itself in are canned promotions by the pharmaceutical industry, for instance, of drugs which are not always very effective and instead may well be dangerous. For they may cause nasty, even life-threatening adverse reactions. Heavily paid and confidence inspiring physicians 'who tout drugs knowingly and glowingly' are an essential part of this 'slick, collaborative fakery' meant to manipulate the trusting and vulnerable TV viewers. All that has to be done is to slip into the regular newscasts such medical 'news' segments as have been prepared by the drug companies and are known as video news releases or VNRs (Taylor and Mintz 1991: 480–81). It follows that in the light of sales-promoting terror as blatant as this, no one can have the right to blow out of all proportion an abstract kind of a molehill: the idea of the rational rationing of limited goods in the market.

The point of it all is that we have no option but to take an unmitigably critical view of the role of advertising in the modern economy. By actively eliding this role, the economics profession only lays itself bare to the charge of intellectual irresponsibility. In particular, because the kind of *economic distortion* caused by advertising should hardly be a matter of total unconcern to the economists. This is why: an ever-increasing production and proliferation of self-consciously generated disinformation or what John Milton would have called 'glozing lies' must itself be a very costly exercise. And the costs must be recovered, in fact recovered several times over, from the consumers, of course.

Ironically, it is the pharmaceutical industry whose products are meant to relieve suffering which makes these 'recoveries' more effectively than just any other industry. No wonder. For its sales promotion techniques happen to be far more aggressive than those of the other industries. This alone should explain why in the United States, for example, profit margins reported by the drug companies routinely happen to be three times as large as those of the other Fortune 500. To cite a specific instance of the pharmaceutical industry's intense addiction to profits, Johnson & Johnson has taken over a $14 drug used in deworming sheep and is selling it for treating colon cancer in humans, but at a price nearly 100 times as high. It is hardly surprising, therefore, that drug manufacturers come to spend one billion dollars per year more on advertising and lobbying than they do on developing new and better medicines. Which excess should in turn explain why they have managed to raise the cost of immunizing American children by over 1,200 per cent between 1981 and 1991 and why roughly over the same period wholesale drug prices have risen *at nearly six times the inflation rate* (Levine and Silverstein 1993: 730).

Years ago, Ivan Illich (1977: 70–83) gave graphic details of the Pharmaceutical Invasion which has long been mounted by the drug companies and which has never been stemmed. To promote Valium, he wrote, Hoffman-LaRoche spent $200 million in ten years and engaged during the seventies some 200 doctors a year to write 'learned' papers about its properties.

Even earlier, during the mid-sixties, the advertising expenditure of the drug companies came to $33,000 per physician, and in the late-seventies, *The Journal of the American Medical Association* itself was grossing $7 million a year from advertising. No wonder that four out of the top five television advertisers happen to be drug companies. Indeed, so thoroughly are they conditioned by what Stanley Adams calls their profit addiction that not unoften they may even introduce such drugs as have never been tested for their efficacy or side-effects. The classic example is the introduction of the notorious drug called thalidomide. Meant to be a tranquillizer, it soon became known to be the cause of the 'seal limb' kind of birth defect. But ignoring the warnings, its German manufacturers continued to claim that it was perfectly safe even though tests to check its effects on the fetus *had simply never been done* (Adams 1985: 34).

Evidently, predatory pricing must necessarily be a defining feature of the kind of profit addiction which the drug companies are widely known to suffer from. No one, not even AIDS victims, can be allowed to escape the pricing wrath of the pharmaceutical giants. Consider, for example, the specific case of AZT. Scientists at America's National Cancer Institute developed it to fight malignancy. But instead they found it to be effective against the human AIDS virus. Burroughs Welcome, a leading pharmaceutical company in Britain, managed somehow to acquire the proprietary rights to this medicine and, claiming to have spent 'hundreds of millions of dollars' on its development, began in 1988 to sell it at $3 per capsule. Which meant an annual cost of some $10,000 to an average AIDS victim (Anderson 1991: 93).

Besides, drug companies keep sailing under various flags of convenience and manage to dump many drugs in Third World countries: even such drugs as are actually known in their home territories to be associated with serious side-effects. A particularly noxious case in point is a drug called Chloramphenicol. This is sold as Chloromycetin by Parke-Davis and is meant to fight typhoid. But so effective was the company's advertising that even in the United States, where typhoid is rather rare, it managed to earn during the 1960s about a third of its overall profits by selling this product alone. The reason: excessive over-prescription. Doctors used to prescribe it to some four million patients per year to cure them of even trifling ailments so that as many as 399 in every 400 patients hardly ever needed it. Besides, it had been known for years to induce aplastic anaemia, an incurable disease of the blood. Hundreds of those who had taken it died undiagnosed even in the United States. Parke-Davis was forced in due course to insert strict warnings of hazards and cautionary statements concerning this drug into every package offered for sale within the United States *but not abroad*. The drug continued to be promoted rather recklessly in the poor countries where a new drug-resistant strain of typhoid bacillus began to spread before long.

But fraudulent pharmaceutical research which Ivan Illich reported as having taken place in the sixties and seventies had not ceased or perhaps had not even abated by the late eighties. In fact, not very long ago, the Washington DC Bureau of *The Economist*, London, highlighted a number of instances of such research having been promoted very recently in the United States. One such involves *The Journal of the American Medical Association* itself. It carried an article claiming that a drug called Retin-A could erase wrinkles in the ageing skin. As a result, as many as one million tubes of it were sold in the month of February 1988 alone, and more would have been if only they had been available (*The Economist* 1990: 103). A Congressional committee found later that the authors of the article on Retin-A as also of the accompanying editorial had 'neglected' to mention their considerable financial interests in the firm making it. The committee also found the group of tests performed by the authors to belong to the ten most egregious instances of alleged or proven misconduct in biomedical research. Besides, a panel of independent experts selected by the National Institute of Health reported that the safety and effectiveness of Retin-A had not been established nor its role in preventing or promoting skin cancer otherwise induced by the Sun. In other words, it was at best a placebo and at worst a carcinogen, *but in each case a money-spinner for the manufacturers.*

But, then, the pharmaceutical industry does not just promote research which is fraudulent. It also impedes research which is authentic as, for example, Pfizer did in blocking the publication, in the *British Medical Journal* itself, of a paper manifesting a possibly high incidence of gastric ulcers associated with the use of its drug called piroxicam (Chetley 1990: 65). But such suppression of vital information concerning the side-effects of drugs seems to be quite common. Another instance: The Upjohn Co. has recently admitted having suppressed what it knew already in 1973 about such side effects as paranoia and memory loss associated with the world's leading sleep remedy and its prize product for raking in profits—Halcion (Cowley 1992a: 58).

In the light of all this, it is not much of a surprise to find a group of doctors from the UCLA School of Medicine reporting recently in the journal of the American College of Physicians that there is a 'marriage of mutual regard' between medical journals and drug advertisers. As a result, the pharmaceutical industry comes to exert 'enormous influence [even] over peer-reviewed medical journals' which cannot but 'lead to inappropriate prescribing practices' (Wilkes et al. 1992: 912, 918). The euphemism concerning the prescribing practices seems to merit some attention, please.

No less striking and tenacious is the promotional fraud associated with what are called 'protein-enriched' shampoos and hair conditioners. In particular, because none of these preparations can possibly contain any protein at all. For protein preparations can be stabilized and protected against putrefaction *if and only if* they are either carefully refrigerated or even deep frozen. This means that proper protein in a hair preparation would putrefy just as surely and quickly as a piece of raw mutton would if left on the table overnight, particularly during summer. What the hair preparations contain, then, is no protein at all but some hydrolysed animal material. It is this which is treated with hot acid and broken down into its amino acid subunits. There is not a biochemist around, Harold Morowitz (1979: 265) tells us, who would call this thing 'protein'. All that happens is that 'Amino acids go in the jar and "protein" goes on the label'. Besides, whatever their worth, the amino acids are meant only to be rinsed away. For if they stayed on the scalp, they would serve only as food for skin bacteria.

Morowitz analysed this protein-enriched fraud many years ago. But the products, the very possibility of whose existence he put out of the question, still continue to be remorselessly advertised and sold all the world over. Nor has any Congressional committee or panel of experts undertaken any investigation into this ongoing global swindle. What's more, even a critic of unethical advertising like Charles Medawar (1979: 73) could only find something decidedly 'sick' about advertising a protein-enriched hair cream in a poor country like India 'where protein-calorie malnutrition is rife'. He doesn't seem to have known that such a cream could not even be produced.

But the line between advertising which is based on plain fraud and advertising which is basically subliminal in nature is not possible to draw. In any case, what they have *in common* is a lot more important: making money, no matter how. No wonder that 'Revlon's glamorous campaigns with model Jerry Hall and actress Brooke Shields helped buoy operating profits from an estimated $80 million in 1985 to $225 million in 1988' (Pomice 1989: 45). Not to be left behind, Estee Lauder are reported to have paid a record $5 million to Paulina Porizkova, a sex bomb from what once was Czechoslovakia, to lend 'image' to their perfumes. As a result, the growth of Lauder's exports 'from being moribund for a long time, has really skyrocketed' (Chakravarty 1989: 128).

In the age of what is called 'mega marketing', advertisers keep devising wild and weird ways of selling and selling ever more. Consider, for instance, Reebok International's 1989 campaign slogan: 'Reeboks let U.B.U'. That is, 'Reeboks let You Be You'. This means that the problem of human becoming which the philosophers of all ages have struggled with has been reduced drastically to the acquisition of a pair of *shoes*. I say acquisition and not purchase because it is the acquisition which matters, not the mode of it. Not long ago, I saw a TV report about people being mugged and even killed so that their Reeboks could be removed. But not all those kids who actually buy these high-priced sneakers, certainly not all those inner-city kids who buy new pairs *every three weeks*, may have enough legally available money needed for the purpose. The only way for them to make the money, then, is to go into the drug trade (Barrett et al. 1989: 51). This cannot but threaten a shredding of the social fabric itself—sooner rather than later. But entirely oblivious of or unconcerned with such brutalization and criminalization actually promoted by sneaker advertisers, Richard D. O'Connor (1989: 583), himself a senior executive in this business, finds Reebok's campaign to have been a 'wildly imaginative' example of 'this type of creative work'.

A great deal of such creativity means the power to sell just anything, even junk, in fact even junk food—to children in particular. As Holly Hacker of the *Los Angeles Times* reported on 4 June 1991, nine out of ten commercials on Saturdays promote sugar-coated cereals, candy bars and other low-nutrition products which children would do well to avoid. Besides, the situation has worsened over the years. In 1976, advertisements for high-sugar cereals outnumbered those for low-sugar cereals 5 to 1. Now, the ratio has jumped to 17 to 1 and may be largely responsible for a reported 54 per cent increase in obesity among elementary school children. Way back in 1977, the Centre for Science in Public Interest and another private group called Action for Children's Television urged the Federal Trade Commission to halt such advertising. But the US Congress blocked reform efforts on the ground that such regulation was beyond the Commission's jurisdiction.

It should be obvious, then, that advertising cannot but bring about an egregious misallocation of resources. For, to alter a telling phrase from Paul Baran (1969: 30) people do not in fact need what they are made to want and are not allowed to want what they actually need. A transformation of this kind may not be very difficult to bring about but must still be quite expensive. Thus, in 1987, TV advertising was in the USA a $23.3 billion-a-year business and in 1985 the average thirty-second-long prime-time telecast would cost $100,000. And in 1987, a thirty-second announcement during the 'Super Bowl' telecast watched by an estimated 120 million people cost $600,000. The corresponding charges for a *ten-second* prime-time telecast in India vary between Rs. 90,000 and Rs. 1,60,000.

Little wonder that TV commercials are by and large not even meant to entertain or inform, much less to educate, the viewers. That is, TV does not even seek to sell any programmes to the viewers. **What it does seek to do** *is to sell the viewers to the advertisers* (Palmer

1988: 19, 23). Reduced to a state of captivity so thorough, the consumer wouldn't even know when to try to be on his guard. For as Marshall McLuhan used to say, even if the temperature of the bath water continues to rise by only one degree every ten minutes, how does the bather know when to scream? John Leo (1989: 71) has also written that the idea is to follow consumers everywhere and *nail them* when they least expect it. 'Even a stroll down a quiet urban street is now the equivalent of watching a Super Bowl's worth of commercials. There are ads on cabs, buses, public phones, trash baskets and "rolling billboards", trucks that drive around simply to be seen. Several cities are allowing ads on parking meters, which means that no pedestrian will ever be in danger of being more than ten feet from an ad'. An average American is said to be bombarded with some 2,000 advertising 'messages' every day so as to produce a condition best described as 'sell shock'.

All this must perforce produce a new variant of slavery which can hardly be less disgusting than the one which Abe Lincoln abolished. For, what defines the new slavery is a denial of the use of Reason and the concomitant attenuation of the very humanity of man. What is involved here is not *just* the promotion of specific products. Far more important, what is involved here is the mutilation of Reason so thorough and thus the cultivation of Instinct so assiduous, that people, having become mere denizens, can come never to question the legitimacy of the status quo, no matter how dysfunctional it may have become. I am not saying that the art of what Walter Lippmann (Chomsky 1984: 21) once called 'the manufacture of consent' cannot be further refined. Indeed, with so many critics of the 'system' still around, the consent is far from complete. Which means that the process of the manufacture of consent cannot be said to have come to a close.

But, still, the crucial question is the following: Can people, sucked into a state of psychic thraldom, ever make a free, informed choice? Can they ever be taken to embody what is called consumer sovereignty in *any* non-trivial sense? To Kenneth Boulding (1969: 513), there should have been no problem about what he once called 'virtuous advertising' which is something purely informative in nature. In fact, such advertising has a positive and necessary role to perform. But he was not concerned with the kind of socio-economic pathologies which 'non-virtuous' advertising must perforce promote. For it involves, as we have seen, much, much more than persuading people to buy

'Bumpo rather than Bango'. Which, according to him, was non-virtuous advertising all about. Also unacceptable is his argument that advertising, no matter how non-virtuous, has in itself 'an entertainment and cultural value, and that it promotes mass communication in the form of cheaper magazines, newspapers, radio and television'. But his position simply would not wash. One has only to focus on the kind of internalization of the values and mores of an exceedingly iniquitous socio-economic order which these magazines, even if not entirely in the *Playboy* mould, are known to promote. Nor must one ignore the kind of ecological devastation through remorseless deforestation which they wreak.

But Kenneth Boulding was not the only economist to turn a Nelson eye to the exceedingly baleful and socially disruptive role of advertising. Indeed, advertising is one of the defining unconcerns of the economics profession. Which, focused though on consumer sovereignty, remains nevertheless blind to a consumer having to pay not just for the product but also for the disinformation—*in other words, for being made a fool of*. Besides, what one pays for one's own disorientation may often be many times larger than what one pays for the product itself. What Douglas Dowd (1989: 65) calls 'the contrived and massive inefficiency' of contemporary capitalism is manifest even in toothpaste, more than 90 per cent of whose price in the United States consists of marketing, not production, expenses. Nor is this a very recent phenomenon. For even in 1939, a Chevrolet which General Motors (GM) used to sell for $950 cost them no more than $150.

Over the years, sales prices of GM and of other motor car manufacturers as well must necessarily have risen far more rapidly than production costs. For given the increasingly subliminal nature of advertising as a whole and of TV advertising in particular, car corporations must necessarily have been able to push their prices much beyond what they would otherwise be charging. GM's Chevrolet, for example, is sold as the Heartbeat of America (O'Connor 1989: 583); and not a few of the over-rich and under-critical Americans must be only too keen to pay whatever the manufacturers demand just in order to be able to hear the heartbeat of a motor car. That is, just in order to be able to partake of, or to be seen to embody that lifestyle with which the Chevy and, in particular, the more expensive GM models, are associated.

This also goes for the high-priced Reeboks. 'Here, the only way to be a big kid on the block is to dress flashily. And the shoe manufacturers are just cashing in' (Barrett et al. 1989: 51). Only naturally, frenzied advertising is a most indispensable part of their plans to cash in. Advertising is not meant just to persuade people to buy *but to buy at higher prices*. Else, who would touch a $200 pair of sneakers?

What we have in advertising, then, is a veritable engine of inflation. No wonder. For advertisers come necessarily to create a situation in which they can charge the prices *they like*; and the prices must be high enough to let them recover their promotional expenses many times over. **In other words, the more effective it is,** *the smaller* **must be the percentage of the national product which advertising can be made to account for.**

This formulation flies in the face of the standard economystic position to the effect that since, say, in the United States, spending on advertising in recent years has been just above 2 per cent of the gross domestic product, it may not be a very important determinant of consumer behaviour (Schmalensee 1987: 35). The figures may not be exactly comparable. But according to the two Pauls, Baran and Sweezy (1969: 225), all kinds of advertising and market research expenditure during the early sixties came to about 6 per cent of the US national income. Which is *some* evidence at least in support of my view that in an inflationary situation for which effective advertising itself is very largely responsible, it can come only to constitute a *relatively smaller*, not larger, share of the national product, howsoever conceived.

Besides, as to Schmalensee's view enshrined in *The New Palgrave* itself that advertising does not mean much for consumer behaviour, we have only to remind ourselves of the resounding consequences of the glamour campaigns mounted in recent years by Revlon and Estee Lauder and of the pathologies generated by the manufacturers of Reebok sneakers. In any case, what do tobacco advertisements do but produce addictions and thousands of deaths from lung cancer every year? According to an Associated Press release of 22 June 1992, 3,000 American children take to smoking every day, 90 per cent of these having been influenced by the advertising campaigns of R.J. Reynolds, makers of the Camel brand juvenile cigarettes.

Besides, with tobacco sales within the metropoles such as the USA and Britain very likely to decline ever more rapidly because of a steadily growing health consciousness, British American Tobacco [BAT] has focused its sales promotion drives on Africa and, as per press reports, has converted that continent into a veritable ash tray.

No wonder that in 1989, in spite of a 3 per cent decline in US production, US manufacturers did manage to export 100 billion cigarettes—more than twice as many as in 1983. Even Dan Quayle, when still in office, managed to muster sufficient brain power to be able to say: 'Tobacco exports should be expanded aggressively because Americans are smoking less'. This should explain why by the 2020s, about 70 per cent of more than ten million of tobacco deaths per year worldwide will take place in the Third World (Mintz 1991: 24, 28).

Incidentally, as one of the immediate consequences of the victory of 'free-market' capitalism over socialism, eastern Europe has become veritably 'an open playing field' for the American cigarette companies. For, there being little awareness of health and environmental issues, say, in Hungary, tobacco companies expect that there won't be any interference for about ten years in their plans to carry out what Noam Chomsky (1993: 58) calls 'lucrative mass murder'.

It follows that, as Ezra Mishan (1981: 241) puts it, consumers' tastes can be formed, unformed and possibly deformed by advertising. Therefore, and in his words, 'a respectable case for commercial advertising does not look to be possible'. Would that he had also emphasized the apparent paradox that it is precisely because of its aggressiveness and effectiveness that commercial advertising *could* well come to account for a *smaller, not larger*, share of economic activity. That is a point, moreover, in cognizing which mainline economics would cease to be a sustained exercise in the cultivation and promotion of uncriticality. Instead, it would become a potent solvent of the glosses which its ideologues like to cover the status quo with.

8   The Uncold War

> SHIRLEY (*angrily*): Who made your millions for you? Me and
> my like. Whats kep us poor? Keepin you rich. I wouldnt have
> your conscience, not for all your income.
>
> George Bernard Shaw (1962a: 380)

> According to the conventional picture, the US has won the Cold
> War. Righteousness has triumphed over evil with the victory of
> democracy, free-market capitalism, justice and human rights.
>
> Noam Chomsky (1991: 215)

The Belindia Syndrome

But according to the *unconventional* view which I prefer to profess,
there is another war which continues to rage unabated all the world
over and within the United States, too. I call it the Uncold War.
Uncold, because in spite of its exceeding virulence, it is not a hot
war in the formal sense: no armies need receive marching orders,
no battleships need be launched, no missiles fired. But it still is
hot enough to singe all except those who happen to be afflicted
with incurable smugness. Once we cognize its reality, therefore, we
cannot but see that this is a war which the United States has *not* won
so far. Indeed, this is a war which it will not win, cannot
win—*wouldn't even want to win*—as long as it remains a sort of
unrelenting Belindia.

'Belindia' is a nickname which Brazil, with its economy booming
and the income gaps widening came to acquire in the seventies; and what

it signifies is a compact and prosperous 'Belgium' surrounded by a vast and poverty-stricken 'India' (*The Economist* 1993: 33). But to my mind what matters far more than the image of an island of prosperity being surrounded by an ocean of poverty is the sheer coexistence of reckless abundance and unremitting poverty *within* a country like the United States itself. As such, what really matters is the possibility—indeed, the inevitability—of affluence and indigence coexisting as mutually reinforcing processes within the same country: a truth which is incarnated in the inimitable Shavian quote given above. No wonder that even the United States has got what Noam Chomsky calls its own Third World at home. Thus considered, the United States is as much of a Belindia as Brazil or any other country in the world today. In fact, the world itself is nothing but a Belindia—a Belindia which is heavy with the seeds of its own destruction.

But let us get back to the original Belindia. According to the Brazilian correspondent of *The Economist*, things are much worse now than they used to be during the seventies. Thirty-two million people, more than a fifth of the total population, have incomes below \$120 a year: enough to buy basic foods but no clothes, medicines and so on. So, to be able to buy some of these things, they have to go hungry. About 15 million receive no more than \$60 a year and five million work for no money at all but just for food, shelter or hand-outs. In the meantime, the country's richest 20 per cent earn 32 times as much as what the poorest 20 per cent do, a multiple which is very close to the UNDP's 26 (Haq 1993: 17). This bespeaks an inequality which is even greater than that which is rampant in Bangladesh. With the cruzeiro losing about one per cent of its value every 36 hours, things continue to become much worse for the poor but not for the rich who buy financial instruments which enable them to have their assets revalued every 24 hours. In other words, inflation continues to wreak havoc on the poorest 20 per cent of the Brazilian population but leaves the richest 20 per cent entirely untouched.

No wonder that in Brazil, by far the wealthiest Third World country, two out of three people go hungry and as many as 1,000 children are guesstimated to die of hunger-related diseases *every day* (Steingraber and Hurley 1993: 101). However, the way Professor Samuelson—naturally—'cynicizes' the poorest 20 per cent of the population is worth noting. Affirming that when 'the whole nation becomes more affluent', the minimum standards deemed necessary 'for a decent life' also rise, he says: 'We shall always have a lowest 20 per cent of the population with us ... [But informed humanitarians tell us that an] affluent society can afford to provide a decent minimum for all its members' (Samuelson 1973: 802). However, he forgets that 'the whole nation', even if it happens to be the United States of America, cannot and will not become more affluent. No wonder that not a few Americans have to huddle in the open against the cold, wait for food at soup kitchens, seek shelter in phone booths and warmth over open air grates (Alter 1984: 20–23). To all these people, the minimum standards deemed necessary for a decent life would mean not a thing. In any case, if *the whole nation*—that is, not only the Other than the Other America but the Other America, too—became more affluent, Samuelson's informed humanitarians wouldn't have a thing to worry about and accordingly his reference to them would ·be entirely pointless. Besides, what really matters is *not* that 'we shall always have a lowest 20 per cent of the population with us'. For what matters instead is the assault of the over-consuming top 20 per cent upon the global ecosystem and upon the poor.

One may refer here to the alternative state-of-the-Union address which Roosevelt Jones, himself a black homeless activist, delivered on the steps of the Capitol in faltering, earnest tones just as Ronald Reagan was delivering the official version late in January 1983. As *The Financial Times*, London, reported on 8 February that year, Jones, addressing an audience of some 300 protesters, declared: 'As I look across America, I see one-fifth of a nation ill-housed, ill-clad, ill-nourished. That is the state of the Union. Millions of us are homeless. That is the state of the Union. Millions are out of work, out of hope and out of choices. That is the state of the Union. Millions of Americans are groaning under the weight of economic adversity. That is the state of the Union'.

Therefore, nothing but stark cynicism could have made George Bush, for instance, want to send experts to the late Soviet Union to help solve its housing problem and at the same time forget all about the millions of homeless in his own country. But John Kenneth Galbraith (1990: 51), for one, would never advise anyone to move from East Berlin to the South Bronx—not even in search of liberty. For 'nothing so represses freedom as an effective absence of money, food, and a place to live'.

Besides, the whole [American] nation may or may not be getting more and more affluent but it certainly *is* getting more and more *aeffluent*. I have coined this term to be able to focus on the human body itself getting contaminated with toxic products as also with the effluents generated by an affluent society like the United States. Evidently, this has had consequences entirely unexpected and unsuspected by the economics profession. Recent tests conducted by the US Environmental Protection Agency's National Human Adipose Survey show that most Americans could well be having toxic compounds stored in their fatty tissues. In fact, *one hundred per cent of human tissue samples* in a recent test contained several compounds known or suspected to cause cancer, birth defects and other health problems. This cannot but be a direct consequence of the breathtaking expansion of the petrochemical industry in the United States over the last few decades. From just one million tons in 1940, its output grew to 125 million tons in 1987—an increase equal to 12,500 per cent (Newman 1992: 56–57). What we see here, then, is a high probability of most, if not all, Americans as also others having had their fatty tissues laced with dangerously toxic organic compounds during the period beginning with the forties. But consider, in this light, Professor Samuelson's claim noted earlier that for the world as a whole the third quarter of the twentieth century 'outshone any epoch in the annals of economic history' and also that we may never see the like of it again. Let us hope that we do not. But evidently the captains of the petrochemical industry need to be warned of the threat to their own fatty tissues. Which being as fatty as those of ordinary mortals would have no protection against the toxicity produced by their corporations. This fate is similar to that of a nuclear aggressor nation coming to produce a nuclear winter and therefore its own unintended mirror destruction.

In the circumstances, the assurance which Samuelson gave in 1973 on behalf of the 'informed humanitarians' would be a bit difficult to take seriously. In fact, according to Noam Chomsky (1993: 51), already in 1971, that is, two years prior to Samuelson's assurance, there 'was a rapid intensification of the class war that is waged with unceasing dedication by the corporate sector, its political agents, and ideological servants. The years that followed [Nixon's New Economic Policy] saw an attack on real wages, social services, and unions.... The ideological component of the offensive sought to strengthen authority and habits of obedience, to diminish social consciousness and such human frailties as concern for others, and to instruct young people that they [would better be] confirmed narcissists'.

The class war which Noam Chomsky talks about is not a topic fit for polite company; and for this reason alone, one should take all the care to bring and keep it under the focus of discussion. One and perhaps the most important form it takes in the United States as elsewhere is Deprivation—of course, with a capital D. We have already seen that 37 million Americans have no medical insurance at all. We would do well to know, too, that of these 23 million are below the age of 35 and further that only one out of every eight benefit dollars reaches Americans in poverty (Howe and Longman: 88, 90). Since the early seventies, unemployment has gone up by nearly 50 per cent in black Los Angeles—'a city that spends *nothing* on social programmes for the poor'. Moreover, since 1972, Aid to Families with Dependent Children has actually *declined* by 20 per cent and since 1981, federal housing assistance has been slashed by 70 per cent (Leonard 1993: 124). No wonder that shanty towns and refugee camps for the homeless in, say, San Francisco have been attracting busloads of photo-snapping foreign tourists (Gibbs 1990: 20).

Most of the homeless have drifted well past the limits of respectability and many have moved deep into alcoholism or mental illness. '[The] bruised and broken woman who slept in the gutters of medieval Paris now beds down in a cardboard box in a vest-pocket park in New York City ... The tattered ranks of America's homeless are swelling [but during subfreezing temperatures they have had to do without] even a lump of coal'. Further: 'In Detroit, auto sales are stronger, but the city estimates homelessness is up by 50 per cent .... Because they live without addresses, the homeless are unable to receive food stamps and welfare in most states [and remain] invisible in unemployment statistics and impossible to count' (Alter 1984: 20–21). But ironically, some ten million adult Americans who do have addresses, who do figure *as fully employed* in the statistics and two-thirds of whom are high school or college educated still remain desperately poor. For poverty 'in the United States is a problem of low-wage jobs far more than it is of welfare dependency, lack of education or work inexperience' (Schwarz and Volgy 1993: 192).

Evidently, when it comes actually to *running* the largest aeffluent society the world has ever known, the military-industrial powers that be have ideas very different from those of Samuelson's informed humanitarians: they are in no hurry to banish poverty no matter how well they can afford to do so. For such a society can simply not come 'to provide a decent minimum for all its members'. On the contrary, it is structured *only* to deprive the underclass of any access to a decent minimum. 'Unto every one that hath shall be given, and he shall have abundance: but from him that hath not, shall be taken away even that which he hath.' (St Matthew, ch. 25, v. 29). What this suggests in our context is that the development of overdevelopment at the top and the development of underdevelopment at the bottom are but conjoint products of the same relentless pathology: the illimitable greed of those who have. However, with our ecological host having come under mounting stress, this kind of an arrangement cannot continue to hold much longer, let alone indefinitely.

It follows that military-industrial inexorability which cannot but entail an escalating and eco-disruptive *pre-emption* of resources by and for the overlying minorities must perforce generate penury for the underclass. The pre-emption of resources effected through a gross misuse of power, that is, through outright corruption and inflation, is, indeed, the principal weapon in the armoury of the oligarchs of our time. As Noam Chomsky (1993: 17) puts it: 'State power has not only been exercised to enable some to reap wealth beyond the dreams of avarice while devastating subject societies abroad, but has also played a critical role in entrenching private privilege at home'. *But necessarily concomitant with the entrenchment of private privilege at home is the entrenchment of private suffering at home: suffering too profound for the comfortable to comprehend.* Jonathan Kozol (1993: 10–11), for instance, speaking of 'the savage inequalities of education in America', tells us of a neighbourhood of the South Bronx in New York City where life expectancy today is lower than that in Bangladesh. Further: 'In East St. Louis, the saddest place I have seen outside of Haiti, an all-black city is buried in the toxic smoke of one of the largest waste incinerators in the Midwest, a huge sewage treatment plant, and two huge chemical plants. At night, the plants are illuminated, and it's like a scene out of Dante's Inferno. The air is so toxic that the city has the highest rate of fetal death in Illinois, the highest rate of child asthma in America. The city is so poor that at the time I visited, there had been no municipal garbage pickup for four years. Heaps of garbage piled in the backyards of the children's homes. In a city poisoned by two chemical plants, the chemistry teacher had no chemicals the week I visited. The physics teacher had no water in his lab'.

But given the ascendant logic of abstract and therefore insatiable greed, such immiseration will not abate even in the United States, its riches notwithstanding. Or, rather, because of its ersatz riches. **For,** on the one hand, the oligarchs cannot help creating the immiseration and, on the other, they cannot help preserving it. Else, it would have been eradicated long ago.

One cannot be sure. But in order perhaps to alleviate such immiseration, Lawrence Summers of Harvard, the chief economist of the World Bank at the time, proposed in December 1991 that 'the dirty industries' of the West be shifted to the Third World. *The Economist* of 8 February 1992 (p. 62) carried a summary of an internal World Bank memo which Summers had prepared in this connection a little earlier. It began as follows: 'Just between you and me, shouldn't the World Bank be encouraging *more* migration of the dirty industries to the LDCs?'

In support of this grand proposal, he said that 'a given amount of health-impairing pollution should be done in the country with the lowest cost, which will be the country with the lowest wages'. For in such a country, the earnings forgone from increased morbidity and mortality would be the lowest. But that in effect would spell lowest costs and maximum profits for the multinationals concerned. Only, Summers did not make this point explicitly—at least not in *The Economist*'s summary of his memo which was also silent on such minor details as the sovereignty of the country or countries which would be made to accept the dirty industries.

However, in response to the outcry which the leakage of this memo provoked the world over, Summers (1992: 4) recanted his thesis as follows: 'It is not my view, the World Bank's view, or that of any sane person that pollution should be encouraged anywhere, or that the dumping of untreated toxic wastes near the homes of poor people is morally or economically defensible'.

But given this very considered concern for morality, it is surprising in the extreme that 'one of America's best economists', as the World Bank described Summers (*The Economist* 1992: 16), failed to say a thing on a profound immorality informing the American economy itself: an immorality which impels it to dump toxic wastes *mostly* in poorer locations—at home and abroad. In fact, as *Time* itself reported not long ago, three out of every five black and Hispanic Americans live in areas with uncontrolled toxic-waste sites. It referred specifically to a black ghetto in Chicago called Altgeld Gardens. Which, its name notwithstanding, is, in fact, a housing project built atop a former landfill whose fetid odours still rise from the basements after more than sixty years of existence. Likewise, in New York, not far from the notorious Love Canal, there is a trailer-park settlement called Forest Glen. It has been built on heaps of foul-smelling hazardous waste which the Environmental Protection Agency says may contain as many as 150 toxic compounds. The *Time* write-up continues as follows: 'Tens of thousands of impoverished people—many blacks and other minorities—living in the countless Altgeld Gardens and Forest Glens in the inner cities and rural pockets of the nation are the victims of what critics call environmental racism' (Elson 1990: 46).

It is no accident, according to Penny Newman, that toxic-waste dumps, incinerators and other dangerous installations are located in the poor, rural areas of the United States. The economics of it is simple enough. When an industrial plant moves into a community, those who can afford to do so move out. It is only the poor who are forced to remain behind. Which also goes for dumps and incinerators. Besides, there is evidence to suggest that the choice of locations for dumps and incinerators is very largely determined by ethnic considerations. No wonder that as much as 40 per cent of America's landfill capacity is concentrated in only three communities with very large minority populations: Emelle, Alabama—78.9 per cent black; Scotlandville, Louisiana—93 per cent black; and Kettleman City, California—78.4 per cent Hispanic (Newman 1992: 59–60). Evidently, Disraeli's point about 'two nations' acquires an extremely sinister meaning.

According to the Environmental Defence Fund of the United States, as a nation, Americans throw away enough iron and steel to continue to meet the requirements of domestic auto-makers without any break; enough glass to fill the twin towers of New York City's World Trade Centre every two weeks; enough aluminium to rebuild the entire commercial air fleet of their country every three months; and enough office and writing paper to build a twelve-foot Great Wall coast to coast every year (Hightower 1989: xvi).

Hazardous wastes would be in addition to this relatively innocuous inventory, and the costs of managing them staggering. Specifically, the *cost* of landfilling hazardous wastes in the United States soared from $15 per metric ton in 1980 to $250 in 1989 while the *amount* of such wastes leapt from 9 million tons in 1970 to 238 million in 1990 (Puckett 1994: 53).

Symbolizing the enormity and gravity of the *crisis* of garbage accumulation 'bedevilling a nature-hostile consumer society like the United States of today is Fresh Kills, a 130 fetid feet high garbage dump sitting over a 3,000 acre site in Staten Island, New York. Already

the largest accumulation of refuse in the world, it continues to grow
unabated (Young 1992: 44) and, if cleared, could fill the Panama Canal
twice over (Grossman and Shulman 1990: 38). According to the
Environmental Protection Agency, the United States generated in 1990
some 195 million tons of municipal solid waste (MSW)—over four
pounds per head per day (Delong 1994: 35). No wonder that a convoy
of ten-ton garbage trucks carrying America's annual waste would
reach halfway to the moon (Grossman and Shulman 1990). That was
in 1990. But by now, the garbage convoy should be getting a little
closer to the destination. Incidentally, this is a kind of 'moon landing'
the distinct possibility of which has not sent the American powers
that be into a state of ecstasy so far.

Evidently, generating an output of which so much can be just thrown
away would require astronomical amounts of mineral resources. No
wonder that the United States *alone* consumed more of minerals from
1940 to 1976 *than all of humanity till 1940*. But minerals have to be
mined and mining in itself produces enormous quantities of waste—
incomparably greater than mere municipal garbage. Thus, in the United
States, non-fuel mining creates about 1,300 million tons of waste each
year. Which is about seven times as large as the amount of garbage
being produced at the same time. Much of the mining waste is inert
though it can still clog the streams and becloud the air. But a good
deal of such waste contains environmental contaminants which wind
and water can carry far beyond the mine itself (Young 1992: 45).

This has a most serious implication which seems to have been
completely lost on Keynes and the Keynesians. To them, consumption
is no more than a quantity, innocuous in itself and symbolized by a
capital C: a single-dimensional figure, changes in which become
changes in the GNP. But, in fact, consumption has become an orgy
bounded by swelling streams of garbage on the one side and turgid
rivers of mining waste on the other. Of these, the disposal of mining
waste doesn't seem to be possible and the disposal of garbage alone
is a messy $80 billion a year business in the United States—or at least
was in 1990 (Wilson and Rathje 1990: 54). By the mid-nineties, it
could well have crossed the $100 billion mark which is more than a
third of the Pentagon budget. Besides, the garbage, no matter how
much be spent on its 'disposal', never can disappear. It just gathers
and gathers. To repeat, with William Empson, the waste remains, the
waste remains and kills. Fresh Kills! What a name!

All this bespeaks a veritable war on the Earth as also on those who have to suffer all sorts of deprivations in a modern military-industrial society like the United States. But entirely unmindful of the reality of this war and of its grim implications, even Professor Galbraith (1994: 240–41) has come to claim that 'established capitalism' as it exists, say, in Europe and the United States, is 'essentially a peaceful system'. For the rich or even 'the merely affluent' have something to lose if war comes. But if this indeed were so, what would Lockheed Martin, for one, be in aid of? Besides, given the ongoing war on the Earth, the rich and even the merely affluent have a great deal to lose, may be not right now but certainly not much later. We would therefore have no option but to reject the Galbraith thesis. Respectfully, of course.

For we also have no option but to focus on the precipitation of a crisis of untold gravity. Shall we call it the 'fourth crisis'? Perhaps, Keynes himself could be advising the patriotic housewives of our own time and everyone else *not* to sally out into the streets nor to be taken in by the distracting sales everywhere advertised. For they would be doing themselves and all of us good to refuse to ape a society which can discard every year 220 million tyres, 1.6 billion pens, use up 18 billion disposable diapers (Grossman and Shulman 1990) and so on and on. This reminds one of E.F. Schumacker, an eminent pupil of Keynes's own, who used to advise people to seek 'the maximum of well-being with the minimum of consumption'.

Be that as it may, numerous municipalities and states of America, particularly those with heavier concentrations of industry and greater urban density, have attempted to send their wastes to less dense, often poorer areas. This has led to a veritable 'garbage war among the states'. California seeks to unload garbage in Arizona, New York looks to Vermont and so on (Blumberg and Gottlieb 1989: 3).

This explains why the dumping of waste abroad has emerged as a most lucrative new industry. One wonders how Joseph Schumpeter would designate this phenomenon—as an instance of creative destruction or one of destructive destruction only? For the risks involved for countries which get persuaded to accept the waste range from paralyzed ecosystems, polluted aquifers and blighted crops to congenital deformities and cancers. Indeed, heavy metal residues, chemical wastes, pharmaceutical refuse, municipal sludge and incinerator ash being unloaded on the recipients could promise little else.

Exporters of such waste often display remarkable business acumen. For instance, Jack and Charles Colbert who were making big money as toxic-waste exporters once relabelled a shipment of their merchandise as 'pure dry cleaning solvent' and managed to sell it to a company in Zimbabwe which, to make the payment, obtained funds from the US Agency for International Development. In due course, the Colberts came to be prosecuted for fraud and were put behind the bars, too. But they are reported to be running their business actively from within the prison walls, using the phones available there (Weir and Porterfield 1989: 27–29).

I do not know if Summers's confidential World Bank memo includes a specific list of the dirty industries of America which would need to be dismantled so that they could 'migrate' to the Third World. But if such a list were indeed to be prepared, the automobile industry would have to be at the very top of it. For, as we have noted earlier, motor vehicles generate more air pollution than any other single human activity. But what happens to the rest of the industrial structure of America once the automobile industry has thus got ready for migration could be anybody's guess. Besides, would Summers still allow the United States, with its automobile industry having emigrated to Third World countries, to import the carbon monoxide spitting automobiles?

This *reductio ad absurdum* follows directly and naturally from Summers's original ignorance of or unconcern with the American exports of exceedingly toxic wastes to the Third World. Concomitant with this ignorance or unconcern is his naive though unstated assumption that once a few dirty industries have migrated to the poorest of the poor countries, America would become a land of ecological bliss, and perhaps the rest of the world, too. But much more than a few individual industries being dirty, that is, environment-contaminating, it is an energy-guzzling *culture* which is ecologically 'dirty' and which is already metastasizing throughout the world. Therefore, the suggestion that some dirty industries be encouraged to migrate to the Third World and the recantation of the idea on some supposedly moral grounds would *both* be meaningless.

For the Third World has already been assigned a new service function. Which is the acceptance and absorption of sheer filth from the First. In fact, after the disintegration of the Soviet Union, Russia also is taking on this service function like any other well-behaved Third World country. It is receiving Canadian, German and other

Western European toxic and hazardous waste sometimes disguised as building materials, fuel or dyes (Vidal 1993: 24). Therefore, those who question the morality of the Third World being made to accept dangerous garbage would have no option but to examine the ecological credentials of the First.

In sum, and putting it a bit schematically, the Belindia Syndrome spells an exceedingly sinister existential predicament: the First World or the 'Belgian' part of Belindia not only continues to wallow in waste and in the process to consume the terrestrial capital but also to unload a good part of the resulting effluence on the Third World or the 'Indian' part of Belindia. Just between you and me, Professor Summers, shouldn't all this be raising what Schumpeter would have called the question of [your] sincerity? More so, because we as a race have also to thank the rulers of your First World for another existential menace— the nuclear menace? And this is a menace which is as much an integral part of the culture of disruption—that is, as much an integral part of the basic strategy of the Uncold War—as your dirty industries.

Keynes and the Nuclear Menace

E.F. Schumacher (1976: 39) once wrote about the 'cheerful brutality' of Keynes's oft-cited view, examined earlier, that in the long run we are all dead. But he could well have noted, too, that starting from around the time of Keynes's own death, the brutality had ceased to be cheerful any more and had instead become sinister in the extreme.

But only someone who was either not aware of, or was not concerned with, the developments taking place in some of the hard sciences of his own time could have persisted in his indifference towards the extreme criticality of the evolving human predicament. Keynes was one such. Indeed, starting from around the time of his youth, such developments would, by the time of his death, make the removal of our race from the face of the Earth at least technically possible.

But conspicuous as these menacing developments were, Keynes does not appear to have been much distracted by them. Little wonder. For, as George Orwell (1968: 125) has written, 'To see what is in front of one's nose needs a constant struggle'. But coerced as he must have been by 'the tyranny of the here and the now', Keynes was in no position to have engaged himself in that kind of struggle. And yet, as Bertrand Russell once (1956: 162) wrote, emancipation from that specific tyranny contains nothing less than the very essence of wisdom.

Far would it be from Keynes, then, to perceive the essential gravity of the evolving situation. Even so, given his perception of himself as a veritable Cassandra, he was under a *professional obligation* to see what was happening. But, then, his unconcern with the mounting gravity of the situation would before long manifest itself in the complete obsoletion of his own work as also that of the other social scientists, both mainline and branch-line. For this work used to be done in a situation in which the continuation of the human race was just taken for granted and to the point, too, that it would have made no sense and could well have looked ridiculous for anyone actually to say that it was being taken for granted. But a situation would soon precipitate in which the continuation of our species could not be taken for granted any more. As Arthur Koestler once (1981: 35) put it, the cosmic catastrophe precipitated by the Hiroshima bomb 'pulverized the assumption on which all philosophy, from Socrates onward, was based: the potential immortality of our species.' This only means that most, if not all, of social science which belonged to the earlier situation would lose all meaning in the later. The only way to arrest what Einstein described as the drift towards unparalleled catastrophe would then be to rethink our modes of thinking, our perceptions and our conceptions, which the unleashed power of the atom had failed altogether to alter. This argues the need for that constant intellectual struggle, that relentless praxis, without which we would fail even to see all the existential perils lying right in front of Mankind's Nose.

In fact, the sheer awesomeness and the tenacity of the impact of the Hiroshima explosion made Arthur Koestler propose in a 1960 BBC broadcast that 6 August 1945 mark the beginning of a second calendar. As he elaborated some years later, this was by far the most important date in human history. His reason was simple: 'From the dawn of consciousness until 6 August 1945, man had to live with the prospect of his death as an individual; since the day when the first atomic bomb outshone the Sun over Hiroshima, Mankind as a whole has had to live with the prospect of its extinction as a species'. The sheer novelty of it all, he added, must oblige us to revise our axioms, the first of these being the implicit presumption of the potential immortality of the human race (Koestler 1980: 507; 1981: 33). *In sum, our race as a whole happens now to be exposed to mortality.*

But we anticipate. Let us get back to the year 1898 when with the discovery of radium by Marie and Pierre Curie probably the first decisive step towards our predicament today came to be taken. In fact, the dangers inherent in radioactivity were soon recognized by Pierre Curie himself. More or less consumed by the penetrating rays emanating from his own discovery, he became increasingly ill and desperate. So it was only in June 1905 that he could go to Stockholm to receive his 1903 Nobel Prize and to give vent to his anxiety in his acceptance speech. It was at the end of it that the concerned scientist in him spoke out: 'It is possible to conceive that in criminal hands radium might prove very dangerous, and the question therefore arises whether it be to the advantage of humanity to know the secrets of nature, whether we be sufficiently mature to profit by them, or whether that knowledge may not prove harmful'. Even so, he brushed aside the worries and concluded with the following remark: 'I am among those who believe with Nobel that humanity will obtain more good than evil from future discoveries' (Easlea 1983: 46). One can't help wondering what would he be saying today.

Frederick Soddy, another major scientist of a generation later, was not so sure of Mankind obtaining more good than evil from the discoveries then taking place, given in particular all sorts of inequities and iniquities which reigned in the world then and which continue to reign today. It was he who initiated the process which would ultimately cause the Atomic Era or the era of the 'not divisible' to be replaced by what he called the Tomic Era or the era of the divisible (Soddy 1953: 123). One of the foremost radiochemists that ever were, he won the 1921 Nobel Prize in chemistry with Einstein winning the physics prize for that year. But already in 1912, Soddy was warning against 'ransacking' the globe of the stores which had required geological epochs of the past to lay down and which science itself would be powerless to replace. The more spectacular the achievements, he said, 'the more swift and sure will be the decline'. He was still hoping that the controlled release of atomic energy, or what he would have preferred to call 'tomic energy', would provide the only answer known to science to the problem of the inevitable and ultimately crippling shortages. To be sure, he was not unaware of the difficulties involved in effecting nuclear fission and it would take thirty years of concerted scientific or rather scientistic effort before Enrico Fermi and his group could demonstrate in 1942 what Soddy had imagined in 1912.

Besides, to Soddy, the whole destiny of the race—spiritual, intellectual and aesthetic as well as physical or material—appeared to hang upon the possibility of transmutation or what would now be called nuclear fission. For as he saw it, if fission remained unrealized as a source of unlimited energy, human civilization would be forced 'back into its former physical condition of hand to mouth existence [dependent] upon the daily supply of solar radiation'.

Unfortunately, Soddy went *completely* wrong—both with respect to the way he grossly underestimated the potential of solar energy and to the way that he grossly overestimated the potential of atomic energy. What he dismissed as mere hand to mouth existence associated with a complete dependence on solar energy could in fact be a fairly sumptuous fare. For as Barry Commoner (1976: 128) reminds us, solar energy is by far the *richest* resource available on the Earth *and the least used*. Indeed, if all of it were to be converted into electricity and then sold, it would be worth more than $500 billion per day. This computation was made many years ago, so the figure now would be much higher. Of course, the whole of the solar energy coming to the Earth *cannot* be converted into electricity but a great deal more of it can still be. Certainly, there is no reason why we should use no more than a *few* hundredths of just one per cent of the incoming solar energy. As Commoner has pointed out more recently (1990: 96), fairly cost-effective and environmentally benign technologies are already available to tap this huge resource. Photovoltaic cells, for instance. They not only convert sunlight directly into electricity but also permit maximum decentralization of the electric power system. Which in turn would ensure a considerable reduction, even elimination, of transmission costs and losses as also the kind of health hazards which power lines are now known to give rise to. Besides, as with the passage of time, fossil fuels get run down relentlessly and thus become increasingly expensive, these advantages of solar energy must perforce become ever more pronounced. Which means that if in the meantime, the military-industrial civilization of our time does not manage to commit some sort of a nuclear or ecological hara-kiri, *it could perhaps cease to be fossil-foolish and become solar-sensible instead.*

But a great mind that he was, Frederick Soddy failed woefully to perceive the potential bounties of the Sun. Not only that, he failed also to see the fell hazards of fission. Thus, he seems to have had little idea of the inherently intractable and tenacious problem of radioactive and therefore intensely toxic waste which science would inevitably give rise to in passing what he thought was the very 'ultimate test'. Nor does he seem to have foreseen the truly vast amounts of waste heat which even controlled fission would produce. But as we have seen already, nuclear power is conceivably the very ultimate example *yet* of thermodynamic overkill and therefore of waste. 'Yet', because fusion power if ever realized would be still more so.

But we again anticipate. For we have yet to take note of Frederick Soddy's *fright* of nuclear power, his enthusiasm for it notwithstanding. His traumatic experience of what we now call the First World War added an entirely new dimension to his perception of the question of nuclear fission. What warned him of the extreme dangers that could lie ahead was the wartime misuse of the relatively innocuous process of nitrogen fixation for making explosives.

In comparison, as he began to see it at the time, the misuse of nuclear fission by the military could be infinitely more dangerous. Therefore, it could well be a curse rather than a blessing. Deciding that man was not yet ready for it, Soddy came fervently to hope that the control of atomic energy could actually be *postponed* till such time as it would be safe enough to have it. 'Imagine, if you can, what the present war would be like', he wrote in 1915, 'if the [nuclear] explosive had actually been discovered instead of being still in the keeping of the future. Yet it is a discovery that conceivably might be made tomorrow, in time for its development and perfection for the use or destruction, let us say, of the next generation, and which, it is pretty certain, will be made by science sooner or later. Surely it will not need this last actual demonstration to convince the world that it is doomed, if it fools with the achievements of science as it has fooled for too long in the past.'*

Two years later, that is, long before the First World War was over, Soddy was even more specific about the kind of perils which would be involved in nuclear warfare: 'War, unless in the meantime man had found a better use for the gifts of science, would not be the lingering agony it is today. Any selected section of the world, or the whole of it ... could be depopulated with a swiftness and dispatch that would leave nothing to be desired'. Even so, it seems difficult to accept Thaddeus Trenn's view (1979: 267) that, in anticipation of atomic

* This and the other Soddy quotes used here are, unless otherwise stated, taken from Thaddeus J. Trenn: 1979.

fission which would be made possible before long, Soddy began to drag his scientific feet. For to my mind, Soddy's sustained involvement in questions of the scientist's social responsibility argued no more than a sharp distinction between science proper on the one hand and mere scientism on the other. Which in turn would argue a self-consciously prescribed *direction* for one's *scientific feet* and equally self-consciously designed shackles for what in effect could be no more than *scientistic feet*.

Frederick Soddy was certainly not in a minority of one. But only a few, like H.G. Wells for instance, seemed to be concerned with the reckless and entirely unshackled movement of untold pairs of scientistic feet. No wonder that a potentially terminal crisis has continued to become ever more menacing from the very beginning of this century.

But the economists almost without exception have remained totally unbothered by or perhaps even unaware of the exceeding gravity of the long precipitating predicament. From this point of view, at least, the somewhat dubious pride of place belongs to John Maynard Keynes. This is not a little surprising. For it was in 1931 that he wrote about his Cassandra Complex, so one could reasonably expect that he would also have 'croaked' about a major peril which civilization would before long have to contend with: which had been taking shape for years: and which not a few had been talking about already. But all that he could perceive in 1919 (K-II: 1–3) were some nondescript rumblings of a heaving Earth which everyone in continental Europe but no one in England and America was aware of.

Only naturally therefore what Keynes came to describe as 'the fearful convulsions of a dying civilization' or as 'Europe's voiceless tremors' did not mean much more than the impossibility of 'a return to the comforts of 1914'. Hardly anyone in England, he said in 1919, seemed 'to feel or realize in the least that an age is over'. What he was proclaiming here was of course the end of the age of *laissez-faire*. But what he failed completely to see was that the 'sandy and false foundation' of 'the intensely unusual, unstable, complicated, unreliable, temporary nature of the economic organization by which Western Europe has lived for the last half century' would with the passage of time continue to become 'sandier and falser'. He did talk of a sense of the impending catastrophe which overhung the frivolous air and even 'of events marching on to their fated conclusion uninfluenced and unaffected by the cerebrations of statesmen in council'. But he failed altogether to see that the futility and smallness of 'Man' would perforce continue to become ever more pronounced with the passage of time. This becomes clear the moment we speak not of any ahistorical and abstract creature called 'Man' but of a historical and Earth-eating military-industrial Man. In the modern scientific Man, as Julian Huxley once put it, 'evolution was at last becoming conscious of itself' (Huxley 1959: 20). But then it is in the modern military-industrial Man that *Homo sapiens*, the conscious component of evolution, has already become its exact opposite *Homo insipiens*. And this for the simple reason that it can be seen to have precipitated the possibility of its own extinction. 'The great events' in confrontation with which Keynes saw Man to have become rather futile and small can then be seen already to have become exceedingly horrendous developments, which in our own time promise nothing less than the extinction of the race either through a relatively lingering ecological paralysis or in a more or less sudden nuclear combustion.

But what Keynes could well have called 'the cerebrations of the orthodox economists' were and could be of no avail in comprehending the manifestly multiplying malevolences of the time. For the economists could at the most see mere symptomatic vagaries of the military-industrial order but *not* any inexorable recklessness, any prepotent hamartia, any uncontrollable hubris which had been virtually programmed into its structure since its very inception. Little wonder that they took its abiding durability, even legitimacy, for granted and would have found it hard to believe that anyone could be so perverse as to question its essential validity on any ground whatsoever.

Human Expendability

Nevertheless, there was at least one malady which Keynes, for one, did try to draw attention to: of course, with his much-wonted ambivalence thrown in.

As he put it (K-IX: 325): 'We are being afflicted with a new disease of which some readers may not yet have heard the name, but of which they will hear a great deal in the years to come—namely, *technological unemployment*. This means unemployment due to our discovery of means of economizing the use of labour outrunning the pace at which we can find new uses for labour'. But the 'new disease' came before long to be seen as 'only a temporary phase of maladjustment' and even as the key to the ultimate solution of Mankind's—yes, *Mankind's*—economic problem. And this in the sense of *both* ensuring material abundance and eliminating the very need to do much work. In fact, as Keynes claimed, for many ages to come, 'the old Adam in us' would have to satisfy his urge to do *some* work with no more than three-hour shifts (K-IX: 328–29).

But while taking such 'wings into the future', he failed to see or at least to say that the destruction of work was nothing less than one of the inexorable and indeed defining impellers of the industrial age itself. For what he called the discovery of the means of economizing labour had always been and would always be outrunning the pace at which the industrial age could find new uses for labour. In other words, the destruction of work or of something which Keynes himself considered to be a most essential source of human contentment was quite literally built into the very structure of the industrial civilization. Besides, with the passage of time and the relentless sophistication of technology, such destruction of work could only be expected to intensify. This tendency in our own time has been compounded by a runaway kind of military spending which continues to pre-empt such resources as could otherwise be available for creating authentic employment opportunities.

But what matters is to note that the process of economic disfranchisement *as an integral component of the economic process itself* started fairly early in the industrial age. In fact, delivering his maiden speech in the House of Lords, Byron argued that it was only 'in the blindness of their ignorance' that the Luddites had failed to rejoice at the technical improvements 'so beneficial to Mankind' and had instead, conceived themselves to be sacrificed to them (Leontief 1982: 188).

But many tried to persuade the workers that their woes could be no more than temporary. For the introduction of new machinery could, if indirectly, bring about considerable increases in the demand for labour. For a country like England, the industrial pioneer in an unindustrial world, this was evidently not untrue—at least to begin with. Indeed, given the relative *ease* with which British exports could enter the more or less captive colonial markets, the apparently endless expansion would *necessarily* come to create more numerous job opportunities than those destroyed by the ongoing technical innovations.

This means that as long as economic expansion continued, unemployment could perhaps be *expected* to remain no more than a mere spectre. But no. For according to Leontief (1982: 188) there are signs today 'that past experience cannot serve as a reliable guide for the future of technological change. With the advent of solid state electronics, machines that have been displacing human muscle from the production of goods are being succeeded by machines that take over the function of the human nervous system not only in production but in the service industries as well'.

What we have here is a major source of human redundancy in the modern world. 'Using a somewhat shocking but essentially appropriate analogy', Wassily Leontief (1983: 405) has written, 'one might say that the process by which progressive introduction of new computerized, automated, and robotized equipment can be expected to reduce the role of labour is similar to the process by which the introduction of tractors and other machinery first reduced and then completely eliminated horses and other draft animals in agriculture'.

Still, all this is no reason why Leontief (1982: 192) or anyone else for that matter should insist that 'The history of technological progress over the past 200 years is essentially the story of the human species working its way slowly and steadily back into Paradise'.

So: Maynard Keynes taking wings into the future in 1930 exulted in the eventual dawn of an El Dorado of economic bliss so fabulous that the struggle for subsistence would disappear forever; and Wassily Leontief insisted in 1982 that the human species, by doing away with the very need to do work, was moving slowly and steadily back into Paradise. But each, conditioned by the reductionist lore of his profession, managed to ignore all that we must actually take care to focus on.

Let us recall that science and compound interest together served as Keynes's vehicles for translating Mankind into a state of absolute economic bliss. But, of these, his science was entirely innocent of an awareness of the existential constraints imposed by the entropy law and his fixation on compound interest was rooted in the twin fallacies of misplaced and displaced concreteness. Keynes's vision of the future therefore does not appear to be very promising.

Nor does Wassily Leontief's. But for a very different reason, though. *His* hobby-horse for carrying *Mankind* back into Paradise is made of solid-state electronics and involves reasoning which is dubious through and through. Embedded in this reasoning are two unstated assumptions which are not easy to swallow. One, that the advancing

destruction of work caused by automation in a few highly industrialized countries does indeed mean the eventual extinction of work for
Mankind as a whole. And, two, that a state of worklessness so
thorough could somehow be taken to be a defining feature of Paradise.
But it stands to reason that a situation so crazy, even if it ever came
to pass, would spell not Paradise but Hell. Indeed, as George Bernard
Shaw put it once: 'A perpetual holiday is a good working definition
of hell.' Besides, there is a famous passage in *Man and Superman*
which he uses to make the same point: 'Here there is no hope, and
consequently no duty, no work, nothing to be gained by praying,
nothing to be lost by doing what you like. Hell, in short, is a place
where you have nothing to do but amuse yourself' (1962b: 610). But
the desire for unending amusement is the defining mark of a Philistine
who manages to be insensitive to everything but his own obsessions.
Besides, only a Philistine could try to seek in amusement an escape
from unrelenting boredom which a state of unending idleness must
necessarily produce. Besides, what Shaw says earlier in the same play
(*ibid.*: 527) about a lifetime of *happiness* could well be said, and with
much greater justification, about a lifetime of *idleness*: 'No Man alive
could bear it: it would be hell on Earth.'

It follows that one could *not* assume, even for the sake of argument,
that life without work would be a tolerable, much less a pleasant,
experience; nor that automation would ever be available to more than
truly microscopic minorities of the human race. In any case, Leontief's
hobby-horse of solid-state electronics is taking even such people *as
it can carry not into Paradise at all but actually into pockets of the
cancer-promoting electromagnetic hell.*

Substantial evidence to this effect is already available though most
people do not yet appear to be willing to take it seriously. Ironically,
the victims themselves do not seem eager to recognize the possibility
that their health might be threatened by the invisible emanations
coming from power lines and video-display terminals—VDTs for
short. In consequence, very few of the millions who use the VDTs
may be concerned about the potentially harmful magnetic fields which
these machines emit. The damage that those exposed may suffer ranges
from cataracts and cancers to reproductive disorders. Increased rates
of leukaemia have also been found among power-station operators,
telephone linemen and others who are chronically exposed to electric
and magnetic fields. Microwave radiation may not *initiate* the cancers,
perhaps, but once some cancer cells get going, it is likely to promote

the growth of tumours. There have been some twenty investigations around the world which show a link between exposure to electric and magnetic fields and the development of cancer, especially brain cancer and leukaemia (Brodeur 1989: 309). Thus, the US Office of Technology Assessment *itself* has come round to the view that the emerging evidence no longer allows one to assert categorically that there are no risks. Indeed, there appears a parallel between the kind of correlation between smoking and lung cancer which began to be recognized some thirty years ago and between electromagnetic fields and brain cancer (Kirkpatrick 1990: 80).

No one claims to know exactly how electromagnetic fields might cause cancer though studies suggestive of a causal relationship are available. Besides, as the *Harvard Medical School Health Letter* for March 1990 reported, office workers who use VDTs for more than twenty hours a week during the first three months of pregnancy have more miscarriages than those who do not use these terminals. But lack of firm knowledge about *how* electromagnetic fields *may* cause cancer and other problems cannot justify any complacency towards them. *For that amounts to saying that if scientists cannot explain how something is happening, it cannot be happening.* Paul Brodeur (1990: 145) makes a telling point in this connection: Scientists do not still know exactly how inhaled asbestos fibres act to cause cancer; yet everyone knows that asbestos causes cancer, and only fools would willingly expose themselves to asbestos.

Unmindful of such considerations, however, the Establishment, the scientific establishment included, has sought only to gag such research as promised to highlight the hazards involved. An important target of such gagging has been Dr Robert Becker, an orthopaedic surgeon and research scientist at the Veterans Administration Hospital in Syracuse, New York. He became convinced of the serious threat to human health posed by the electromagnetic fields emanating from power lines. Soon enough, his application for a five-year renewal of his medical investigatorship came to be deferred and his research grant from the National Institute of Health discontinued on account of his determination to look into a yet insidious threat to nothing but national health itself. By 1980, all his Veterans Administration grants were terminated and he was thus forced to retire. Little wonder that many scientists and researchers who know better find it prudent to keep quiet for they know that their silence would help them get the grants (Brodeur 1989: 53, 303).

But such silence imposed by the corporations and the rest of the Establishment must by and large expose to the risks of radiation not the very poor who have been forced to the margins of the American economy but mainly those who happen to be active at the very centre of its centre. In other words, when it comes to protecting the vast corporate investments, no matter how ill-conceived and ill-directed, no one, just no one, is unexpendable. That is, everyone is at least potentially expendable. The essential gravity of the problem of human redundancy, therefore, is *not* indicated by the prevailing rates of formal unemployment but is a function instead of the inherent and unavoidable *expendability* of Man himself under capitalism. 'A Study of Economics as if People Mattered' was the subtitle which E.F. Schumacher gave to his evocative *Small is Beautiful*. It seems that every economics textbook writer, if he is at all honest, would do well to use the following as a subtitle: 'A Study of the Economy as if People were all Expendable'.

Let us see how, for instance, Manville, the asbestos giant used to treat men as entirely expendable. It was contended at a damages trial in the early eighties that the company had known of the dangers of asbestos for *at least forty years* but had deliberately concealed the information from the workers. Giving evidence in support, Charles Roemer, a prominent attorney, said that in the early forties, he had discussed the question with some company executives. One of them, Vandiver Brown, according to Roemer, did admit that the company's physical examination programme had produced X-ray evidence of asbestos disease among the workers exposed to asbestos, and that it was the company's *policy* not to tell the employees anything. For, 'it would be foolish for us to be concerned'. At a subsequent deposition taken in April 1984, Roemer recalled that he had said, 'Mr. Brown, do you mean to tell me you would let them work until they dropped dead?' and that Brown had replied, 'Yes, we save a lot of money that way' (Brodeur 1985: 276–77).

Not surprisingly, that still is the way corporations think. In support, one may refer to two internal corporate memos which appear in Newman (1992: 57). One of these is from the Occidental Petroleum Corporation and outlines its attitude on the manufacture of DBCP, a product known to promote sterility and cancer among those exposed to it during manufacture, transportation, distribution and use. Estimates of damages likely to be claimed with legal fees added, the memo insists, must be prepared. 'Should this product still show an adequate profit, meeting corporate investment criteria, the project should be considered further'. The other memo was from a vice-president of the Gulf Resources and Chemical Corporation. It was concerned with the amount Gulf would have to pay if it continued to expose children in the town of Kellog to lead-contaminated smoke. For poisoning 500 children it put the liability at six to seven million dollars. Accordingly, Gulf *increased* the emissions from the smelter to cash in on the high lead prices of 1974 and the children of Kellog suffered the consequences. According to an EPA report, the blood-lead levels were the highest ever recorded. Of the 179 children living within one mile of the smelter, 99 per cent had blood-lead level over four times as high, and of these 41 eight times as high, as the current norms accepted as safe.

In addition to all this, and according to a study released by the Economic Policy Institute on Labour Day 1992, most Americans are working for longer hours and for lower wages and considerably less security. Besides, poverty rates are high by historic standards and 'those in poverty in 1989 were significantly poorer than the poor in 1979' (Chomsky 1993: 280). Even so, poverty is not a central issue in economics. Indeed, with economists tending generally to avoid 'the more messy problems of their profession', the poor 'do not get many pages in the college textbooks nor much attention in the scholarly journals' (Galbraith 1994: 180). Besides, given a 'deeply ingrained, even theological, opposition to providing income to the poor' (*ibid.:* 183) policy makers remain by and large unconcerned with what *The New Republic* described editorially on 14 November 1994 as a basic issue: 'an erosion of wages and a growing number of people who work full time yet can't keep a family of four afloat'. Incidentally, the same day, *The Nation* also carried an article about the poor getting poorer: Even with the latest [1991] increase in the minimum wage, it said, 'the rate is almost 20 per cent lower in uninflated dollars than it was ten years ago' (McDermott 1994: 579). Indeed, about the same time, the *Business Week* itself spoke about the blue-collar set 'singing the blues' with a 7 per cent decline in real wages within six years since 1988 (Bernstein 1994: 123). And, finally, as a professor of economics at Harvard, James Medoff (1994: 78) reminds us, the Supreme Court has now made it possible for US corporations to fire older workers well in time for them to be denied their full retirement benefits.

So much, then, for Leontief's vision of Mankind moving back into Paradise. It seems to be at least as eccentric as Teilhard de Chardin's idea of the noosphere defined as 'a sphere of reflection, of conscious invention, a felt union of souls' (Huxley 1959: 14n). Indeed, even in 1925, when Teilhard de Chardin began talking of the 'felt union of souls', he could well have considered the implications of the trauma of the First World War. But perhaps he couldn't have. For he seems to have been given to a veritable urge to invert reality. An extremely ludicrous instance of this 'inversion complex' is his perception of the promise of the Bikini explosions: 'For all their military trappings, the recent explosions at Bikini herald the birth into the world of a Mankind both inwardly and outwardly pacified. They proclaim the coming of the *Spirit of the Earth*' (Teilhard de Chardin 1969: 152). This first appeared in September 1946 and cannot be dismissed even as theological mysticism run wild. For it could only have been some private idiosyncrasy which had nothing to do with his Jesuit background but which nevertheless impelled him to get into a state of Nero-like ecstasy whenever he came to contemplate death and destruction.

In 1983, the World Council of Churches itself published a report entitled *Marshall Islands: 37 Years Later* which in no way suggested 'the birth into the world of a Mankind both inwardly and outwardly pacified'. On the contrary, what we read is a horror story beyond the powers of a Hitchcock to pack into a movie. As many as sixty-six atomic and hydrogen bombs were exploded over the Marshalls —forty-three over Enewetok and twenty-three over Bikini. The combined 'yield' of these explosions must have been many hundreds of times as high as the yield of explosives expended during *any war in history*, including the Second World War and the Vietnam War. No wonder that during the testing, as many as six islands simply disappeared from the face of the Earth.

Nor should we ignore the incalculable and long-lasting 'collateral' damage caused by ionizing radiation: cancers, cataracts and reproductive disorders manifested in miscarriages, stillbirths and 'jellyfish' babies—short-lived lumps of jelly born sometimes with horns (Keju-Johnson 1983: 31–33). One cannot be sure whether it is the Marshallese or the survivors of Hiroshima and Nagasaki who should be taken to have been more unfortunate. But there simply is no reason why or how the explosions over the Marshalls could be taken to argue a Mankind both inwardly and outwardly *pacified*: unless by 'pacified' we mean a Mankind completely resigned to its threatened extinction.

It follows that the very concept of the noosphere as Teilhard de Chardin came to articulate it, *is a hotchpotch of a whimsical physics and an equally whimsical biology.* Whimsical physics, because in getting ecstatic over the idea of the noosphere, Teilhard de Chardin showed scant concern for the constraints entailed by the second law of thermodynamics; and whimsical biology because instead of getting concerned over the continuing destruction of biodiversity, he was actually looking forward to 'the day when [Mankind] will have abolished or domesticated all other forms of animal and even plant life' (Teilhard de Chardin 1969: 162).

Teilhard de Chardin may not have known it but we certainly know that in coming to abolish other forms of animal and plant life, Mankind cannot but abolish the chances of its own survival. Whether it happens to abolish these life forms by design or by accident hardly matters. For in either case, its own fate as a species would be quite effectively sealed. Therefore, his claim that outside and above the biosphere is the noosphere merits nothing but rejection. Equally worthy of rejection is the assertion that the noosphere is really a new layer, 'the thinking layer', that is, 'another membrane in the majestic assembly of telluric layers'. All this is mysticism of a very private kind run riot and authentic science could hardly avoid dismissing a formulation like the following: 'This sudden deluge of cerebralization, this biological invasion of a new animal type which gradually eliminates or subjects all forms of life that are not human, this irresistible tide of fields and factories, this immense and growing edifice of matter and ideas—all these signs that we look at, day in and day out —seem to proclaim that there has been a change on the Earth and a change of planetary magnitude' (Teilhard de Chardin 1959: 183, 182). Not surprisingly, he was *so* carried away by his own eloquence that he once described the noosphere as a 'stupendous thinking machine' and then a little later made the following declaration: 'Only by reaching to the heart of the Noosphere [we see it more clearly today] can we hope, and indeed be sure, of finding, all of us together and each of us separately, the fullness of our humanity' (Teilhard de Chardin 1969: 191, 180). Indeed, even after Hiroshima, he managed to 'see it more clearly' than ever before nothing less than 'the fullness of our humanity'. Only someone without any power to see reality as a whole could exult in the elimination or subjugation of 'all forms of life that are not human' and see it as a positive transformation of 'planetary magnitude'.

Here, then, is the Uncold War which Privilege has unleashed against the Earth and against the race: a war which is getting ever more intense with the passage of time: a war which demands recognition as being by far the grimmest existential peril we have known since the beginning of our time on Earth. And here too are veritable hordes of scholarly Panglosses who continue to assure us that nothing is wrong with the best of all possible worlds: that we as a race will come before long to solve the economic problem for all time to come: that we are moving back towards Paradise: that the noosphere spells the eventual domestication and even abolition of all other forms of animal and even plant life to the everlasting glory of Man. The nature of the existential reality on the one hand and of the scholarly misperceptions of it on the other couldn't possibly be more mismatched than this.

9   Economics Against Life*

> Finally we shall place the Sun himself at the centre of the Universe. All this is suggested by the systematic procession of events and the harmony of the whole Universe, if only we face the facts, as they say, 'with both eyes open'.
>
> Nicolaus Copernicus (Kuhn 1981: 154)

The Gaian Perspective

But, alas, mainline economists or rather economysticians take all the care in the world not to keep both eyes open. Indeed, the very mythos of their profession requires them to put only one eye to any use at all. Which they do. Even so, they remain convinced of the *full employment* of their powers of perception and also of the extreme rigour of their cerebrations. However, with one of the eyes so firmly shut, the other also cannot but fail to function properly so that they cannot even see some of the most obvious and overarching verities of life. Which only means that they cannot but continue to produce an unending series of misconceptions and misperceptions.

But the situation is not entirely hopeless in that a most effective antidote to economystic one-eyedism is now available in the form of what may be called the Gaian perspective. This is a perspective, moreover, which once internalized can help us see as nothing else can the fell perils which the military-industrial civilization of our time happens to congeal and its inherent unsustainability, too. This is a perspective, therefore, which can help us dispel, as nothing else can, all the laboured rationalizations fabricated no end in the service of this civilization by the economics profession.

* See Herman E. Daly's (1968: July) paper entitled 'On Economics as a Life Science'.

The ancient Greeks gave two names to their Earth goddess, and each one of them has become part of the vocabulary of science. The more popular of the two was Ge which happens to be the root from which a variety of sciences such as geometry, geography, geology and many others derive their names. And now James Lovelock, a leading life-scientist of our time, has assigned the other and the more evocative name, Gaia, to the unending interaction between life and non-life taking place around the Earth. He views Gaia as a planet-sized living organism having properties which cannot be predicted from those of its parts. To my mind, what we have in his conception is the soaring of science to the peaks of poetry in the very important sense that it would take nothing less than a leap of the poetic imagination to recognize as *One* what has long been segmented into myriads of bits and pieces, both in theory and in practice. Evidently, one couldn't possibly overemphasize the need for a synthetic view of this kind. For most of the perils that we happen to be confronted with today flow out of a mania for analysis which conditions the modern military-industrial man. 'One of the most highly developed skills in contemporary Western civilization is dissection: the split-up of problems into their smallest possible components. We are good at it. So good, we often forget to put the pieces back together again' (Toffler 1984: xi). Besides, ecosystems for instance, having been ripped apart, cannot even be put back together. Deforestation, we are told, is for ever.

Given such threats to the viability of the biosphere, at least for purposes of human habitation, the so-called biological analogies of Alfred Marshall (Pigou 1966: 314–15) look somewhat simple-minded—at least in retrospect. Consider, for instance, his well-known analogy between the way that trees grow and die in a forest and the way business firms do so in the economy (Marshall 1974: 263–64). Young trees, he says, struggle through the benumbing shade of their older *rivals* with many succumbing on the way. Those which survive and grow taller come to tower above their neighbours and get a larger share of light and air. But sooner or later age tells on them all and one after another they give place to others which have on their side the vigour of youth. And so, too, with the growth and death of business firms except joint-stock companies which may begin to stagnate all right but do not come readily to die. Still, even a joint-stock company, Marshall says in conclusion, is likely to have lost so much of its elasticity and progressive force that the advantages are no longer exclusively on its side in its competition with younger and smaller rivals.

However, if Marshall's purpose was to establish what Bacon would call 'the resemblances of things', he could not possibly have failed more resoundingly than he did in this particular case. This is easy to see. A forest is not just a simple collection of trees, fighting for light and air, growing and dying, but otherwise uninteracting. It is a living ecosystem buzzing with a diversity of plant and animal life which happens to be absolutely essential to the stability and viability of the human habitat. Therefore, no matter how rivalrous, trees have a positive role to perform. Which business firms, even if entirely 'unrivalrous' *may not necessarily do*. In fact, not a few of them have a distinctly *negative* role to perform. Therefore, one would do well *not* to be distracted by a superficial similarity between the life cycle of a tree and that of a business firm and to focus instead on the inherent dissimilarity between the role of the one and that of the other.

For, in our own time it is not very important to see a firm growing to its prime like a tree and then dying. What we need to see instead is its impact on the global ecosystem. Du Pont is an obvious example. It would be misleading in the extreme to compare its growth pattern with that of a tree which plays only a beneficial role in the ecosystem. As against this, in releasing a vast variety of dangerous chemicals, Du Pont has long been directly responsible for several environmental ailments including ozone depletion. In other words, what matters is *not* its comparison with a *single* growing and naturally dying tree but its role in promoting ozone depletion worldwide. Besides, and thanks largely to veritable hordes of profiteers making inroads into, say, the Amazonia, a holocaust of trees and therefore of life is taking place there. Consider, for instance, the specific case of a logging consortium called the Barama Company Ltd. It is owned by a South Korean trading giant, Sung Kyong [20 per cent] and a Sarawak logger, Samling Timbers [80 per cent] and has obtained a logging concession for the exploitation of a part of the Guyanese Amazonia. Even the royalty payments it has to make for a twenty-year period to the government of Guyana have been fixed in terms of the local dollar. Which is very much of a 'gift' it has managed to get from Guyana whose weak currency can continue only to become weaker and weaker (Colchester 1994: 46). This is just one of the numerous instances of what is being sold as South-South cooperation: *a grabbing firm thriving in a dying Amazonia*. Evidently, what we see here is nothing like Marshall's analogical 'fit' between a decaying tree and a dying firm. Rather, what we have to bracket together is a dying *forest* and the 'youthful' firms which are, no matter for what reasons, clearing and burning it. Arthur Schopenhauer once described himself as a mortal leaf on an immortal tree. With the forests being destroyed recklessly, he would be hard put to it to justify that analogy today.

Be that as it may, only an indifference towards the laws of thermodynamics could have persuaded Marshall to expect better analogies from biology than from physics. But even a rudimentary concern for this important branch of science would have made him adopt a self-consciously *biophysical* approach towards economics. Biophysics would then have become the Mecca of the economist and the wind would have been taken out of neoclassicism's sails.

Let us get back to Gaia which Lovelock (1987: 11) defines as being 'a complex entity involving the Earth's biosphere, atmosphere, oceans and soil'. The biosphere, being the most active and indeed the prepotent constituent of Gaia, has to be treated differently from all the rest which may together be taken to constitute the Earth's 'chemosphere'. This term is mine, not Lovelock's. But what needs to be articulated here is the hypothesis to the effect that Gaia as a whole constitutes 'a feedback or cybernetic system which seeks an optimal physical and chemical environment for life on this planet' (*ibid.*) Since Lovelock is concerned primarily with the way that the living matter around the Earth manages to manipulate the non-living matter, it is but natural that he should recognize the biosphere to be only one of the constituents of Gaia, the other being the chemosphere.

However, for reasons to be explained a little later, I do not find it necessary to assign a separate identity to the chemosphere and consider it instead to be a part of the biosphere itself. In other words, as far as I am concerned, the biosphere alone constitutes Gaia. But, for the present, let us have a closer look at Lovelock's Gaia. Being primarily a cybernetic system which seeks to keep itself in a constant state, it [or she] is presumed to possess a kind of intelligence which all cybernetic systems, say, the thermostat of an electric oven, must possess. So, according to Lovelock (1987: 146): 'If Gaia exists, then she is without doubt intelligent in this limited sense at least.' She uses this intelligence, he says, to select and to maintain the optimal conditions for her health and continued existence and thus has the power to keep the Earth a fit place for life. That is, for herself. This power manifests itself in a variety of ways, one of these being a regulated chemical composition of the atmosphere. 'Thus the atmospheric concentration of gases such as oxygen and ammonia is found to be kept at an optimum value from which even small departures could have disastrous consequences for life' (*ibid.*: 10). Similarly, temperature regulation is an important Gaian function and so is the control of the salinity of the oceans. But if we are to go by the extreme complexity of the way that the human body, for instance, regulates its own temperature or the way that the kidneys regulate the salinity of our blood, we may not find it easy to solve the profound mystery of these basic Gaian functions (*ibid.*: 57). Under the circumstances, we are left with no option but to presume that life manages somehow to maintain the conditions it needs. At least intuitively, this presumption seems to be perfectly legitimate. Indeed, in Lovelock's own telling formulation: 'No amount of insulating clothing will indefinitely protect a stone statue from winter cold or summer heat' (*ibid.*: 20). In other words, it is the human body which actively helps clothing to help itself. Putting it a little differently, if a bicycle and the cyclist riding it be taken as a unit, then it is the cyclist who keeps the unit going.

However, all this, simple and self-evident though it seems, is anathema to the mainstream biologists. Reporting on a March 1988 conference on Gaia which was sponsored by the American Geophysical Union, Richard Kerr (1988: 393–95) says that a number of those attending the conference severely criticized Lovelock for having propounded a kind of hypothesis which could never be tested. But Lovelock had never claimed in the first instance that it *could* be tested. In fact, he had actually said that it could not be: 'Yet this *feeling,* however strong, does not prove that Mother Earth lives. Like a religious belief, [the hypothesis] is *scientifically* untestable and therefore incapable in its own context of further rationalization' (Lovelock 1987: ix; emphasis mine). Still, eager now to speak not 'poetically but more scientifically', he began to think in terms of a weaker version of Gaia which, however, he has yet to articulate in print.

Since I am not a biologist nor any kind of a hard scientist, I am not in a position to say anything on the nature of the technical issues which the conference was trying to settle. Still, from a strictly *human* point of view, they do not appear to have been very significant. And, as far as I am concerned, that is what matters. My concern, therefore, is not with the way that life *per se* interacts with non-life. It is rather with the way that our race interacts with its environment, living and non-living. I do not think that the self-proclaimed anthropocentricity of this position need cause one any embarrassment. For, in a situation in which we as a species are facing the threat of extinction, we cannot even afford the luxury of an utterly non-anthropocentric intellection. This only means that 'anthropocentrism', as understood here, has nothing whatsoever to do with the traditional meaning of the term. For, I do not put Man at the centre of the universe nor do I allow him the right to conquer and to destroy nature. Therefore, as I use this word, it signifies nothing but the affirmation of the inviolability of the right of mankind to continue as a species. This is an affirmation which, I insist, can be in need of no justification whatsoever. In other words, anthropocentrism in *this* sense is nothing less than a fundamental value premise which argues not a conquest of nature but a necessary adjustment to it.

That apart, I should like also to submit that, to my mind, the non-human reality itself begins to acquire meaning if and only if human beings are there to *assign* meaning to it. Otherwise, it would have no more than a chaotic and therefore meaningless existence— if existence it could still be called. For, matter, inchoate and physical, lies in a darkened existence apart, until Man's consciousness illumines it and invests it with meaning. To cite Rabindranath Tagore,

> Only the colour of my consciousness
>   has tinted the emerald green
> And the ruby red ...

I know this affirmation raises a question which has long been debated and I do not hope to be able to settle it here. In fact, *merely* because I do not expect to settle it, I find it necessary at least to affirm the imperative role of a sentient species—our own—in the *articulation* of reality.

Besides, I can seek some support in what a great scientist, Niels Bohr, told another great scientist, Werner Heisenberg, when the two, having a walking tour, came to the Kronberg Castle: 'Isn't it strange how this castle changes as soon as one imagines that Hamlet lived here? As scientists we believe that a castle consists only of stones, and admire the way the architect put them together. The stones, the green roof with its patina, the wood carvings in the church, constitute the whole castle. None of this should be changed by the fact that Hamlet lived here, and yet it is changed completely. Suddenly the walls and the ramparts [begin to] speak a different language' (Prigogine 1984: 37). In other words, the castle gets transformed beyond recognition the moment it is 'Hamletized' or rather humanized.

In order to see what all this has to do with Gaia, let us substitute the Earth system for the Kronberg Castle and mankind as a whole for Hamlet. Evidently, as an event, the coming of a sentient species to a planet cannot but be infinitely more important than the coming of an individual to a man-made castle. But the point I wish to emphasize here is the following: While the walls and the ramparts of the Kronberg Castle began merely to speak a *different language* the moment Bohr recalled that Hamlet had once lived there, the Earth, already a living planet no doubt, comes to acquire the faculty of speech itself the very moment that Man appears on the scene and becomes a dumb planet once again the moment he disappears. The 'different language' which Bohr was referring to could only be taken to signify the much greater significance with which Hamlet had invested the Kronberg Castle. This means that the Earth's loss of speech, which I am talking about, can only mean the complete destruction of the very meaning of reality which the extinction of our species must necessarily cause. Since I am not a philosopher, I do not know how those who are would react to what I am saying. But I think it should pass muster at least in terms of what G.E. Moore used to call the Common Sense views of the world.

Even so, one may refer here to a celebrated conversation on the nature of reality which Albert Einstein and Rabindranath Tagore had way back in 1930 at the former's residence. Neither could *prove* what he was saying to the satisfaction of the other. But each still held on to his own position. Einstein stated his as follows: 'I cannot prove that scientific truth must be conceived as a truth that is valid independent of humanity, but I believe it firmly. I believe, for instance, that the Pythagorean theorem in geometry states something that is approximately true, independent of the existence of Man'. In contrast, Tagore took the stand that the world does not exist apart from us and that if there were no human beings, the Apollo of Belvedere would no longer be beautiful (Prigogine 1984: 61–62).

Einstein's insistence that the Pythagorean theorem is independent of the existence of human beings seems unacceptable for the simple reason that the least it would need in order to be articulated was a Pythagoras. For this theorem, or any other, could not just be floating in the air. On the other hand, Tagore's view that the world does not exist apart from us could mean something if and only if 'existence' were taken to mean 'significance'. For, in the raw, *material and physical* sense, the world obviously does exist; and if it did not, we would not even have evolved as a species. What I am trying to do here, from a Common Sense point of view, is to 'sell' a world-view which is self-consciously anthropocentric, holistic and critical in orientation and which recognizes the *Idea of Survival* as a necessary part of our defence against Extinction. For, nothing but plain Common Sense suggests that reality to be *significant and meaningful*, must necessarily be a human reality and a human reality *alone*. But, as Tagore too would not have failed to emphasize, it is a kind of reality which Man himself has now converted into something utterly chaotic and meaningless: in sum, a nightmare.

The point of it all is that there is little point in talking of Gaia except from a specifically human point of view. And this is a point of view which Professor Lovelock does not consider to be worth bothering much about in what he calls the Gaian context. It may well be, he tells us, 'that the white hot rash of our technology will in the end prove destructive and painful for our species' but it is not likely to 'endanger the life of Gaia as a whole' (1987: 107–08). He is concerned primarily with the well-being of a large range of micro-organisms or the anaerobes which can only grow in the absence of oxygen and, thanks to Lynn Margulis, does not consider it unlikely that 'large mammals including ourselves serve mainly to provide them with their anaerobic environment' (*ibid.*: 109).

I cannot but dismiss such a formulation as a manifestation of desiccated scientism. Still, I find it necessary to submit that, from a specifically human point of view, even a planet-sized super-organism like Gaia can be seen to have turned out to be an exceedingly fragile and vulnerable system. Since I am concerned primarily with the way that the *human* segment of living matter may and in fact does impair the self-renewability of the totality of its own environment, it is natural that I should simply ignore the distinction between the living and non-living parts of Gaia. In other words, it is only natural that, persuaded as I am of the prepotency of the biosphere, I should prefer to consider it alone as Gaia. In any case, Lovelock himself thinks that the atmosphere, for example, could well be a mere adjunct of the biosphere: 'not living, but like a cat's fur, a bird's feathers, or the paper of a wasp's nest, an *extension* of the living system designed to maintain a chosen environment' (*ibid.*: 10; emphasis mine). Besides, he does not always make a distinction between Gaia and the biosphere. Indeed, while making a formal statement of the Gaia hypothesis in the preface to the book I am referring to, he speaks of the *biosphere* as 'a self-regulating entity with the capacity to keep our planet healthy by controlling the chemical and physical environment' (*ibid.*: xii).

Therefore, from the *human* point of view, I consider it more convenient to treat the biosphere by itself as being Gaia. But irrespective of whether we assign to the chemosphere a separate identity of its own, as Lovelock does, or merge it completely with the biosphere as I do, Gaia continues to remain a cybernetic system which seeks to keep itself in a constant state. But there is a radical and therefore irreconcilable difference, too. Lovelock's Gaia cannot but dismiss the intensifying petrochemical pollution and even a nuclear holocaust as no more than minor episodes occurring during the course of an aeons-long existence. Indeed, as he puts it, the very concept of pollution is anthropocentric in nature and 'it may even be irrelevant in the Gaian context' (*ibid.*: 110). Also, citing a 1975 report of the United States National Academy of Sciences, he says that a war in which about 5,000 megatons of nuclear bombs were exploded would cause no more than local, even if catastrophic, devastation to the aggressor and victim nations. But 'areas remote from the battle and, especially important in the biosphere, marine and coastal ecosystems would be minimally disturbed' (*ibid.*: 41). But this, in the light of the Nuclear Winter theory, may well be dismissed as a woefully untenable claim—perhaps even from a 'Gaian point of view', which, in any case, I am not much bothered about. But from a human point of view, which alone can or should matter, a nuclear holocaust of this order would be an unmitigable disaster. There would, in the first instance, be no 'areas remote from the battle' and more people would die in, say, India or China than in the US and the former USSR put together for the simple reason that far more people happen to be 'available' in India or China for this purpose.

Let us therefore put aside as completely pointless the notion of a trans-human Gaia which may continue to live for another hundred million years or perhaps even for a much longer period but which can only distract attention from human problems of unexceedable urgency. Let us instead focus on a Gaia which, from a human point of view, happens to be stricken with mortal dysfunction caused primarily by human misdeed, which may before long be crippled beyond recovery, and towards whose ill-health we cannot afford to be indifferent.

Extensive contamination of the globe with a variety of toxic and biologically non-degradable products and wastes is one form that this ill-health takes. Indeed, it has now become possible with the help of a sensitive invention of Professor Lovelock's own to detect pesticide residues in organic matter throughout the globe, from the milk of nursing mothers in the United States to the flesh of penguins in Antarctica (*ibid.*: x) *and thus to see even intuitively that the world is an organic unity*. Only someone completely unaware of the very existence of Gaia could propose as Lawrence Summers did that the World Bank should encourage the migration of dirty industries to Third World countries. Incidentally, the DDT contamination of the milk of nursing mothers in the United States was once found to be so intense that 'it would have been declared illegal in interstate commerce if it were sold as cow's milk' (Ehrlich and Ehrlich 1970: 129). *This means that environmental malpractices anywhere must be of concern to people everywhere*. For the sheer range of modern technology is so vast that there can hardly be such a thing as a more or less localized environmental insult. Plans for 'security' or those for 'prosperity' prepared by, say, the US Establishment, should therefore be of great concern to people everywhere. Taking a very specific example, the world as a whole and therefore Russia itself, no matter how liberalized, should feel threatened by the *Russian* ships dumping hundreds of thousands of gallons of radioactive waste into the Sea of Japan. Likewise, in banning the use of some of the most lethal, carcinogenic and neurotoxic chemicals for agricultural purposes inside its own borders but in allowing them to be exported to Third World countries, the USA doesn't cease to be exposed to their effects. For it happens to be one of the world's largest food importers and therefore cannot escape the hazardous chemicals simply by banning their use within its own borders. This has been described as the pesticide boomerang of the USA (Weir and Schapiro 1981: 121). And, then, there are the residues of exported pesticides which would come back to America through Gaian cycles as well.

However, as far as conventional economics is concerned, Gaia or the biosphere, or for that matter, nature *per se* is not much of a factor worth considering even today. Marston Bates, a leading biologist of yesteryear, once accused the economists of pretending that nature does not exist (Daly 1968: 399). At the general level, this refusal to cognize the existence of nature bespeaks, as George Orwell would perhaps have put it, 'the completest indifference' to the laws of thermodynamics. The economystic preoccupation with everlasting exponential growth is a most telling manifestation of such indifference. For evidently, Samuelson's claim about compound interest growth continuing to take place 'for as far ahead as the eye cannot see' could be sustained *only* in a world which had repealed the laws of thermodynamics. But as it is, the very idea of growth is a resounding contradiction of this fundamental branch of physics.

Here, one may take note of Georgescu-Roegen's (1983: 427–28) extension of thermodynamics from energy to matter. As he has argued, just like energy, matter too can neither be created nor destroyed; and just like energy, again, available or utilizable matter continues to become unavailable or unutilizable matter. For instance, there simply is no way in which matter eroded by friction like tyre rubber may ever be recovered.

But undaunted by the law of conservation and the law of entropy *both*, the theory of economic growth continues *implicitly* to assume that matter-energy can be created *ad infinitum* and also that by a transformation of disorder into order, the Arrow of Time reversed. However, as Professor Lovelock has put it evocatively in one of his letters to me, 'We do not in any way reverse the Arrow of Time. We are like the eddies which form in the wake of its travel.'

Besides, as Georgescu-Roegen (1983) has taken care to emphasize, the science of thermodynamics is necessarily anthropomorphic in nature. Indeed, all concepts thought up by the human mind—and we do not know of any other—have to be unavoidably anthropomorphic. That is, it is from the human point of view *alone* that utilizable matter-energy continues to become unutilizable matter-energy. This only means that the basic thermodynamical distinction between 'available' matter-energy which is capable of serving human ends and 'unavailable' matter-energy which is not, is 'far more anthropomorphic than any other scientific concept' and is at the same time 'the root of the most stringent form of scarcity' that men face.

Still, finding out exactly when, say, the oil bonanza will end—for end it must—is really not very important. Nor very important, therefore, is what Georgescu-Roegen (*ibid.*: 431) calls 'dancing around the computers' to seek an answer to this question. Instead, really important would it be to know the kind of damage which the reckless dissipation of matter-energy is doing to the biosphere. For, Man happens to be an integral part of this complex system of interacting life-forms which he needs to sustain him. Therefore, the economists can no longer pretend that the biosphere doesn't exist.

Granted, then, that a biospheric orientation of economic inquiry is basic to its relevance, how does one try to bring it about? Obviously, by focusing on the extreme and entirely unprecedented matter-energy-intensity of the fires of both consumerism and militarism which are now raging the world over. The moment we state this, the depletory impact of the contemporary civilization on the biosphere becomes evident, and thus its own unsustainability also. For to be maintained at all, it requires massive minima of matter-energy inputs; and as such, the privileged and rather small minorities which manage to live in style and the security managers who divert billions towards 'defence' today impose severe and increasing penalties on ordinary people and also on the integrity of Gaia.

In other words, to Gaia or the biosphere come large doses of degraded matter-energy and toxic wastes and to the 'socio-sphere' come a variety of crippling iniquities. For, as the biospheric base shrinks, the costs involved in meeting the elite privileges and in buying ever more of 'national security' get inevitably and relentlessly shifted on to the underclass by way of inflation, for example. Jumbos do not fly on biogas; and the minuscule minorities which alone may manage to use them do not necessarily have to pay for their services either. Which also goes for company Cadillacs and most of Five-Star hospi-tality. In fact, the matter-energy-intensity of *unpaid for luxury* is a major source of ecological disruption today.

What all this means is that runaway consumerism and unbridled militarism are both extremely matter-energy-intensive and bio-disruptive forms of waste. But what this *also* means is that matter-energy-intensity on the one hand and social-inequity on the other go together, and together must they cause the biosphere to become increasingly hostile to Man himself; and together, too, must they engender new and disabling tensions for human society to contend with. The focus on matter-energy-intensity, therefore, leads naturally to an analysis of nothing less than the defining limitation of the prevailing socio-economic world order. In order to be pertinent and non-spurious, therefore, economics would do well to make such an analysis one of its basic concerns. It seems perfectly reasonable to demand, then, that it shed its wonted fads and fears and assign top priority to a study of the interactions of the biosphere and the socio-sphere.

In other words, and in a self-consciously Gaian perspective, an analysis of the orgies of militarism and consumerism today ought to be a central concern of economics and yet it is not one which could be called even peripheral. That is reason enough to presume that economic orthodoxy is in effect an exercise in the legitimation of the prevailing culture of disruption.

It is in this specific sense, then, that economic orthodoxy becomes very much of a celebration of the destruction of life. Would that Herman Daly had used the following as the title of his paper referred to earlier: 'On Economics as an Anti-Life Science'. Be that as it may, we ought never to forget that, at least from a human point of view, Gaia is only partially an open system. It does receive its 'food'—solar energy—from a source external to it all right, but it cannot expel the military-industrial waste into an environment external to it. To be able to appreciate this point, one has merely to remember that the human body, for instance, is not a closed system at all. It receives its food from, and at the same time excretes its wastes into, an environment external to it. That is to say, as an open-ended thermodynamic system it inhales and it exhales; it ingests and it egests. But Gaia is virtually sealed as far as excretion is concerned. No wonder that we have to live with a garbage dump like Fresh Kills. Still, what ought to matter from our point of view is Gaia's inability to do away with the intensely toxic petrochemical, nuclear and the rest of the military and industrial wastes. *Which, therefore, cannot but continue to accumulate within itself.* Professor Lovelock once wrote to me to say that Gaia is not as constipated as I think she is. But whatever the merits of his view that from her own point of view Gaia is very much of an open system, from our own she is not. Indeed, she cannot even fart which the ruminant animals, for example, do to get rid of the methane their systems produce. The point of it all is that, at least for purposes of human habitation, Gaia suffers from a built-in and a very serious limitation which we could ignore only at our peril. Had it been otherwise, we might never have heard of the problem called pollution.

However, pollution is but man-made entropy, that is, man-made acceleration of the degeneration of order into disorder. This argues qualitative changes taking place simultaneously in the Earth's crust because of the relentless extraction of minerals and in its biosphere because of the injections of toxic effluents.

Evidently, this is something which economics cannot afford to ignore, but which it still manages to ignore. The reason lies in the misperception of our irredeemably dissipative habitat as a veritable cornucopia so that compound interest growth can continue to take place for far into the unforeseeable future. This bespeaks a gross unconcern for, if not an ignorance of, the entropy law. In fact, judging by what Samuelson at least has actually *written* about it, the economics profession hardly even knows what entropy is all about. Which means that the standard economist cannot possibly be aware of, much less concerned with, economics being a counter-entropic, counter-factual, counter-existential and, possibly, counter-intellectual orchestration.

Samuelson and Entropy

With A.N. Whitehead (1964: 40), for one, it was nothing less than 'an axiom that science is not a fairy tale'. But with Professor Samuelson, in contrast, *science is nothing but a fairy tale*. For as he (1980: 747) put it once, science can help us turn the hourglass over so that we can stop the sands from falling at least now and then. Which is a claim to the effect that science can help us stop and even reverse the thermodynamic Arrow of Time itself. This, I contend, is neither science nor sense. Rather, it is nothing less than an instance of the murder of knowledge—of 'gnosticide'. Or, shall we call it an instance of the entropy of reason? For to suggest that the Arrow of Time can be stopped or reversed is to claim in effect that entropy itself can be stopped or reversed. Which could well mean that the Sun itself could stop radiating energy through its own dissipation and instead could well begin receiving energy from its environment and thus let all life be destroyed. Some of the earlier editions of Professor Samuelson's *Economics* (e.g., 1961: 9) used to carry the following eminently quotable assertion: 'Where it is a duty to worship the Sun, the laws of heat will be poorly understood'. I do not know why he decided to drop this dictum from the later editions. But it could better be read in the reverse also. Which means that a widespread and poor understanding of, say, the law of entropy by the mainline economists could only argue their unquestioning acceptance of the legitimacy of the prevailing military-industrial order: an order which they only worship, but do not critically examine.

Be that as it may, Samuelson has managed only to put the entropy law on its head. But once we become aware of the economystic inversion of an irreversibly dissipating entropic reality into something which is taken to be a mechanism utterly immune to the ravages of time, we are left with no option but to deny to mainline economics its basic validity.

This is easy to justify. The entropy law is a schematized recognition of the relentless and literally universal and spontaneous dissipation of order into disorder and therefore of the inexorable devitalization of our habitat as well. Which means that it is not just 'our most powerful scientific insight into how nature works', as Barry Commoner (1976: 28) describes it. More important, it is conceivably the most strident warning that we as a race can get of the egregiously precipitating existential crisis of our time. In other words, the entropy law is overarchingly important, in fact more important than just any other scientific law, not merely because it is a major and integral constituent of classical thermodynamics: the only physical theory of universal content which, according to Albert Einstein (1949: 33) himself, 'will never be overthrown'. It is overarchingly important also because it tells us that any civilization which remains unconcerned about the entropic nature of reality and becomes instead an exercise in the reckless *destruction of low-entropy reserves* is only getting ready for being overthrown before long. Just after this had been written came a letter from Paul Ehrlich saying that a major environmental catastrophe could occur by the year 2050—'indeed much sooner than that if we are unlucky'. *What we are facing as a race, then, is a catastrophically intensifying existential emergency.* In order to appreciate the exceeding gravity of this emergency, we can do little better than to put it in the context of the entropy law. For no attempt to understand reality can afford to ignore what James Lovelock (1989: 22) describes as 'the most fundamental and unchallenged law of the Universe'.

This only means that its glamour and apparently spectacular performance notwithstanding, the military-industrial civilization of our time is an obvious recipe for disaster. Which could come sooner rather than later and on thermodynamic grounds alone. In the United States, for instance, it takes many more than ten kilo calories of energy inputs to provide just one kilo calorie worth of food on the dinner table. A large part of the explanation lies in the ascendancy of chemical agriculture to the concomitant demise of organic agriculture—in the movement, in other words, 'from soil to oil'. But very largely, too, the phenomenon is explained by the ascendancy of increasing commercialization of the food sector of the economy and therefore by the emergence of food processing as an industry in itself. Indeed, in the

United States, this industry happens to be the fourth largest energy consumer (Steinhart and Steinhart 1974: 307–08). To the unwary, industrialized food coming quite literally in hundreds of varieties, all aggressively advertised and not necessarily wholesome, would argue expanding choice and unending progress. But it is easy to see that such heavily processed food can only be a major source of accelerated and unsustainable thermodynamic deficits and therefore of an actual and ultimate attenuation of choice. In a word, while such deficits happen in fact to *define* our existential situation, so that we cannot even hope ever to be able to balance our matter-energy budget, tenacious illusions of growth and maximization continue to inform or rather transfix the economystic imagination.

This is something which professional economists with rare exceptions such as Nicholas Georgescu-Roegen, Kenneth Boulding and Herman Daly do not care to bother about. Little wonder that instead of being informed by the entropic and life-sustaining quintessence of the existential reality, economics has turned out to be only a sustained apology of an entropy-insensitive, life-threatening and therefore ultimately self-defeating world order. It follows that what John Maynard Keynes (K-XIII: 489) once called the powerful and mighty 'citadel' of economic orthodoxy has always been a perceptual and conceptual misadventure of monumental proportions. Even so, the economists themselves have managed somehow to remain totally unconcerned with the nature of the misperception. In fact, they seem hardly to be aware of a wasteland of thought thus produced. Much less could they be expected to be concerned with its arid and intractable expanses.

Evidently, the kind of Gaian critique of the prevailing order can be rooted only in classical *not* statistical thermodynamics. Indeed, the latter may well lead to certain fairy tale and therefore scientifically naive formulations like the late Isaac Asimov's (1979: 43) to the effect that if we wait long enough, even an overwhelmingly unlikely marvel like the reversal of the Arrow of Time may come to pass. 'In fact, if we wait long enough, it must come to pass.' But how long would be long enough? Five billion years or would some fifty million do or perhaps just ten? There would also be the absurdity of the Arrow of Time for the observing Subject moving in one direction and that for the observed Object moving in the one opposite. Incidentally, Professor Samuelson's point about science helping us turn the hourglass over seems to have been inspired by this fairy tale version of thermodynamics.

But, then, our life spans are too short for us to continue to wait long enough in the hope of seeing some corpses spring back to life and then begin to move gradually towards infancy, too (Georgescu-Roegen 1974: 6–7, 165). Should that be possible, then our own reversal towards infancy should at least be probable, no matter how low the probability. Which, however, happens to be not just low, but zero. This absolute irreversibility of disorder explains why no one has ever tried to boil water by burning ash. Or, why the dense forest of conifers which used to surround the Chernobyl complex and has now been uprooted and buried (Gale 1990: 20) will never come out of its radioactive grave. Indeed, any instance of such a thing taking place would be enough to destroy Einstein's claim cited a little earlier that classical thermodynamics will never be overthrown. Besides, as Stephen Hawking (1988: 145–51) has argued, it is only because of the absolute irreversibility of the thermodynamic Arrow of Time that we remember the past but not the future and can thus operate as intelligent beings.

Let us remember that classical thermodynamics is a product of the nineteenth century. It began with Sadi Carnot in 1824, was enriched by William Thomson better known as Lord Kelvin in 1852, and was perfected by Rudolf Clausius in 1865; that is, the year in which Stanley Jevons published *The Coal Question*. Therefore, even Karl Marx perhaps could hardly say a thing to justify his unconcern with the stark economic implications of the entropy law. Much less could the leading economists of the present century, as also all the throngs of their uncritical followers, excuse away their sleepy indifference towards such implications. But then, a full-blooded concern with the logic of entropy proper would have obliged the economists to focus on all the impossibilities which it imposes. And that would be no mean gain even if it would signify a rejection of a great deal of contemporary economics. For by respecting existential impossibilities, we come only to avoid wasting resources on projects which cannot possibly succeed. Impossibility statements, therefore, should, as Herman Daly (1990: 45) has written, be of particular interest to the economists.

But it seems not a little odd to find that by and large unconcerned with entropy that they are, Samuelson and Nordhaus (1989: 881–82) have still taken up an analysis of environmental degradation in the last but one edition of *Economics*. For it is not clear how anyone can comprehend environmental degradation without first comprehending the nature of the entropy process. But that exactly is what Samuelson and Nordhaus are trying to do. So, as they put it, many observers of the global environment have become alarmed by potential resource depletion and environmental degradation, by the abatement of ozone in the stratosphere, by acid rain and by dying forests. 'Are they', they ask, 'the early warning signs of the end of the industrial era and the beginning of an inevitable economic decline?'

But they dismiss all such worries as mere manifestations of Neo-Malthusianism which is nothing but 'warmed-over Malthus'. And, then, Samuelson's 1980 assertion about science beating entropy by turning the hourglass over is revived in the form of a claim about 'the possibility of technological change outpacing resource scarcity'. This is an illusion. For the problem is not one of mere physical scarcity but also of an overall physical degradation of the life-support systems of the planet. Besides, technofixes cannot possibly outpace resource scarcity in a situation which is defined by a frenzied and artificial inflation of civil and military demand—defined, that is, by what Schumpeter said about satiety becoming a flying goal.

In the light of all this, the Samuelson–Nordhaus dismissal of even the limits-to-growth thesis as one evoked by 'the computer that cried wolf' is rather unavailing. To cry wolf is to give a false alarm when there is no danger so that one would not be believed when there actually is one. Samuelson and Nordhaus who have taken note of such critical problems as ozone depletion and acid rain have not dismissed them as figments of a fevered imagination. So they can be taken to have presumed that the ecological alarm is anything but false. So, it can be anything but crying wolf. More important, we would do well to remember that the wolves in the fable as Aesop told it *did* at the end appear after all. Indeed, the Penguin Classics version of it reads, in part, as follows: 'Eventually, however, some wolves really came. They got between the shepherd and his flock and he called the neighbours to aid him. But they thought he was up to his usual trick and did not bother their heads about him. So he lost his sheep.' A few pages later, *The Fables of Aesop* has another tale which has the following title: NONE SO DEAF AS THOSE THAT WON'T HEAR. In the present case, the deafness or rather blindness is only made much worse by a peculiar habit of the ecological wolves: they prefer to remain completely hidden for long, long after they have started wreaking havoc.

Besides, even when their existence comes to be fairly well recognized by ordinary mortals, the economists, unable to question the legitimacy of unbridled money-making, refuse to take any note of them. Little wonder that mercury poisoning which has already assumed catastrophic proportions in the Amazon region has yet to find its way to the economystic psyches.

Talking to Alexander Cockburn (1989: 36), Sussana Hecht, for instance, has ascribed the problem to the extensive use of mercury in the recovery of gold from the slurry collected in the Amazonian Basin. As against some 400 victims of mercury poisoning at Minamata in Japan, about half a *million* people in Brazil are now under threat. It follows that one cannot even cry ecological wolf early enough and loud enough.

This the economists cannot be in a position even to see. Instead, they tend normally *to forget* that the Earth is but one ecological entity so that, contrary to what Samuelson and Nordhaus say, the ecological wolves cannot possibly threaten only 'some' countries and leave the so-called 'advanced countries' largely unthreatened. We would therefore do well to keep Ezra Mishan's (1986: 169) reminder in mind and try not to forget that the wolves would not fail to become ever more visible even in these 'advanced countries'.

In fact, already, and in the United States itself, some 17 per cent of all urban children and two-thirds of black inner-city children have been affected by excessive levels of lead in their surroundings (Sivard 1991: 38). Repeated exposure to this heavy metal can cause grave long-term damage. It builds up in the bones and soft tissues, and impinges upon the blood-forming organs, the kidneys and the nervous system. Only naturally, then, has lead poisoning been singled out as the most serious environmental health problem for the American children, lead paint being the main culprit. Lead is harmful at *any* level and can impair neurological development and thus reduce the ability to learn. But as far as the economists are concerned, warnings such as these can only be mere exercises in crying wolf.

The reason is not far to seek. As ideologues of the status quo they cannot but be afflicted with the all-is-for-the-best-in-the-best-of-all-possible-worlds syndrome. Indeed, Pangloss himself could have a thing or two to learn from them. Far would it be from them, therefore, to experience anything like 'the essential tension'. Which Thomas Kuhn (1973: 79) thinks is implicit in scientific research and which those not willing to give up science altogether must learn occasionally to live with till such times as a new paradigm emerges to dislodge the old, to resolve the crisis caused by fundamental novelty and thus to put things back in shape again.

But the economists have long found a way to render all intellectual tension non-essential and therefore redundant: just ignore the recalcitrant reality and all will continue to be for the best in the best of all possible worlds. For them there never would be 'a world out of joint'. Veritable throngs of indifferents that they are, they simply don't let their sleep be disturbed by mere novelty, even fundamental novelty.

That explains why the mainline economists must remain by and large unconcerned with the damage-potential of heavy metals like lead, mercury and several others which have been introduced into the market by those who can see only their profit-potential. Which also explains the relentless proliferation of chemicals for reasons purely of profit-making. As noted already, some 70,000 of these are now in regular use in the US and little is known about the health effects of most of them.

What we have to question, then, is the validity of unbridled profit-making. A concern instead with any limits to growth, for instance, can only be a red herring. It follows that the Samuelson–Nordhaus (1989: 882) designation of even the limits-to-growth argument as PIPO—pessimism in, pessimism out—can hardly be taken seriously. Indeed, the economics profession itself happens to be guilty of PIPO—purblindness in, purblindness out. Or, of HIHO—hubris in, hubris out. [Let me indulge myself here with a bit of parenthetical hubris. For, Samuelson and Nordhaus, possibly responding to my letter in this connection, have let their 1989 claim about PIPO and 'the computer that cried wolf' disappear from the *Economics* of 1992.]

Conceivably the only antidote to such recklessness as informs the economystic thinking of our time lies in reversing the Cartesian procedure and *to treat as certain all that is grim and possible but may still be doubtful* (Jonas 1984: 37). What this calls for is a self-consciously sustained cultivation *not* of Panglossian smugness but of restless vigilance—of sensitivity to existential hazards both overt and covert. For as Thomas Hardy would have said, 'If way to the Better there be, it exacts a full look at the worst.'

References

Ackland, Len (1990) 'Human Guinea Pigs.' *The Bulletin of the Atomic Scientists*, September.

Adams, Stanley (1985) 'World Drugs and the Profit Addiction.' *New Scientist*, 23 May.

Aldhous, Peter (1990) 'Leukaemia Cases Linked to Fathers' Radiation Dose.' *Nature*, 12 February.

Alter, Jonathan (1984) 'Homeless in America.' *Newsweek*, 2 January.

Amron, Ken (1992) Letter to *The New York Times*, 24 June.

Anderson, Christopher (1991) 'US Challenge to AZT Patent.' *Nature*, 10 January.

Arkin, William M. and **Norris, Robert S.** (1992) 'Tiny Nukes for Mini Minds.' *The Bulletin of the Atomic Scientists*, April.

Asimov, Isaac (1979) *Choice of Catastrophes*. New York: Simon and Schuster.

Augustine, Norman R. (1986) 'Land Warfare.' *IEEE Transactions on Aerospace and Electronic Systems*, September.

Bacon, Francis (1952) *Advancement of Learning, Novum Organum, New Atlantis*. Chicago: Encyclopaedia Britannica.

Baran, Paul A. (1969) *The Longer View*. New York: Monthly Review Press.

Baran, Paul A. and **Sweezy, Paul M.** (1968) *Monopoly Capital*. New York: Monthly Review Press.

—————— (1969) 'Theses on Advertising' *In* Paul A. Baran: *The Longer View*. New York: Monthly Review Press.

Barrett, Todd et al. (1989) 'Has Sneaker Madness Gone Too Far?' *Newsweek*, 18 December.

Bator, Francis M. and **Solow, Robert M.** (1992) 'Useful Investment in a Hurry.' *The New York Times*, 10 July.

Beckerman, Wilfred (1972) 'Economists, Scientists, and Environmental Catastrophe.' *Oxford Economic Papers*, November.

Begley, Sharon (1984) 'The Fallout From Fallout.' *Newsweek*, 21 May.

Bernstein, Aaron (1994) 'The US is Still Cranking Out Lousy Jobs.'*Business Week*, 10 October.

Besharov, Douglas J. (1993) 'The End of Welfare as We Know.' *The Public Interest*, Spring.

Beschloss, Michael R. and **Talbott, Strobe** (1993) *At the Highest Levels*. Boston: Little, Brown and Company.

Blumberg, Louis and **Gottlieb, Robert** (1989) *War on Waste*. Washington DC.: Island Press.

Born, Max (1971) *The Born–Einstein Letters*. New York: Walker & Co.

Borosage, Robert L. (1992a) 'Defensive about Defence Cuts.' *The Nation*, 9 March.

——— (1992b) 'Mugged Again.' *The Nation*, 11 May.

——— (1993) 'Disinvesting in America.' *The Nation*, 4 October.

Boulding, Kenneth E. (1965) 'Is Economics Obsolete?' *Scientific American*, May.

——— (1969) *Economic Analysis: Microeconomics*. New York: Harper & Row.

Boulton, David (1978) *The Grease Machine*. New York: Harper & Row.

Brands, H.W. (1993) *The Devil We Knew*. New York: Oxford University Press.

Brodeur, Paul (1985) *Outrageous Misconduct*. New York: Pantheon Books.

——— (1989) *Currents of Death*. New York: Simon and Schuster.

——— (1990) 'The Magnetic-Field Menace.' *Macworld*, July.

Bullock, Alan (1992) *Hitler and Stalin: Parallel Lives*. New York: Alfred A. Knopf.

Burke, Edmund (1884) *Speeches* Vol. I London: George Bell and Sons.

Bush, Douglas (ed) (1983) *Milton: Poetical Works* Oxford: Oxford University Press.

Cannan, Edwin (1932) 'Review.' *The Economic Journal*, September.

Caufield, Catherine (1981) 'Can Britain Find Room for Nuclear Power?' *New Scientist*, 19 February.

Chakravarty, Subrata N. (1989) 'Acceptably Sexy.' *Forbes*, 13 November.

Chetley, Andrew (1990) *A Healthy Business?* London: Zed Books.

Chomsky, Noam (1984) *The Manufacture of Consent.* Boston: The Community Church.

——— (1991) *Deterring Democracy*. London: Verso.

——— (1992) *Chronicles of Dissent*. Monroe: Common Courage Press.

——— (1993) *Year 501*. Boston: South End Press.

Clarke, Arthur C. (1986) *Star Wars and Star Peace*. Delhi: Government of India.

Cloward, Richard A. and **Piven, Frances Fox** (1993) 'The Fraud of Workfare.' *The Nation*, 24 May .

Cockburn, Alexander (1989) 'Trees, Cows and Cocaine.' *New Left Review*, January/February.

——— (1994) 'Beat the Devil.' *The Nation*, 31 January.

Cohen, Morris R. and **Nagel, Ernest** (1968) *An Introduction to Logic and Scientific Method*. New Delhi: Allied Publishers.

Colchester, Marcus (1994) 'The New Sultans.' *The Ecologist*, March/April.

Coletti, Louis, J. (1992) Letter to *The New York Times*, 24 June.

Commoner, Barry (1976) *The Poverty of Power*. London: Jonathan Cape.

——— (1990) *Making Peace with the Planet*. New York: Pantheon Books.

Constanza, Robert (ed) (1991) *Ecological Economics: The Science and Management of Sustainability*. New York: Columbia University Press.

Corn, David (1993) 'Beltway Bandits.' *The Nation*, 1 November.

Cowley, Geoffrey (1992a) 'Halcion Takes Another Hit.' *Newsweek*, 17 February.

——— (1992b) 'A Deadly Return.' *Newsweek*, 16 March.

Cranston, Maurice (1972) 'Francis Bacon.' *The Encyclopedia of Philosophy*.

Daly, Herman E. (1968) 'On Economics as a Life Science.' *Journal of Political Economy*, July.

——— (1990) 'Sustainable Growth: An Impossibility Theorem.' *Development*, SID, 3/4.

Day, Kathleen (1993) *The S&L Hell*. New York: W.W. Norton.

Delong, James V. (1994) 'Of Mountains and Molehills.' *Brookings Review*, Spring.

Descartes, Rene (1985) *The Philosophical Writings of Descartes*, Vol. I. Cambridge: Cambridge University Press.

Dostoyevsky, Fyodor (1989) *Notes from the Dead House*. Moscow: Raduga Publishers.

Dowd, Douglas (1989) *The Waste of Nations*. Boulder: Westview Press.

Easlea, Brian (1983) *Fathering the Unthinkable*. London: Pluto Press.

Economist, The (1990) 'Hippocrates Meets Mammon.' 22 September.

—————— (1992) 'Pollution and the Poor.' 15 February.

—————— (1993) 'Brazil: Hungry.' 10 July.

Eddington, Arthur (1929) *The Nature of the Physical World*. New York: The Macmillan Company.

Edelson, Edward (1989) 'The Man Who Knew Too Much.' *Popular Science*, January.

Ehrlich, Paul R. (1986) 'Extinction—What is Happening Now and What Needs to be Done.' *In* D.K. Elliott (ed): *Dynamics of Extinction*. New York: John Wiley.

—————— (1989) 'The Limits to Substitution.' *Ecological Economics*, February.

—————— (1991) 'Biodiversity and Humanity: Science and Public Policy.' *Environmental Awareness*, No. 1.

Ehrlich, Paul R. and **Ehrlich, Anne H.** (1970) *Population, Resources, Environment* San Francisco: W.H. Freeman.

—————— (1989) 'Too Many Rich Folks.' *Populi*, No. 3.

—————— (1991) 'Population Growth and Environmental Security.' *The Georgia Review*, Summer.

Einstein, Albert (1949) 'Autobiographical Notes.' *In* Paul Arthur Schilpp. (ed): *Albert Einstein: Philosopher-Scientist*. Evanston: The Library of Living Philosophers.

—————— (1960) *Einstein on Peace*. New York: Simon and Schuster.

—————— (1973) *Ideas and Opinions*. London: Souvenir Press.

Eisenhower, Dwight D. (1988a) 'A Chance for Peace.' *In* Janet Podell and Steven Anzovin (eds): *Speeches of the American Presidents*. New York: H.W. Wilson.

—————— (1988b) 'Farewell Address.' *In* Janet Podell and Steven Anzovin (eds): *Speeches of the American Presidents*. New York: H.W. Wilson.

Elmer-Dewitt, Philip (1992) 'How Do You Patch a Hole in the Sky That Could Be as Big as Alaska?.' *Time*, 17 February.

Elson, John (1990) 'Dumping on the Poor.' *Time*, 13 August.

Evans, Richard (1989) 'Merchants of Death.' *Geographical Magazine*, January.

Farrington, Benjamin (1973) *Francis Bacon: The Prophet of Industrial Science*. London: Macmillan.

Firth, Raymond (1971) *Elements of Social Organization*. London: Tavistock.

Fischetti, Mark A. (1986) 'When Reactors Reach Old Age.' *IEEE Spectrum*, February.

Fitch, Robert (1995) 'Spread the Pain? Tax the Gain.' *The Nation*, 8 May.

France, Anatole (1917) *The Red Lily*. New York: Boni and Liveright.

Freire, Paulo (1976) *Education: The Practice of Freedom*. London: Writers and Readers Publishing Cooperative.

Galbraith, John Kenneth (1990) 'The Rush to Capitalism.' *The New York Review of Books*, 25 October.

—————— (1992) *The Culture of Contentment*. Boston: Houghton Mifflin.

—————— (1993) 'Foreword' *To* Ruth L. Sivard: *World Miliary and Social Expenditures 1993*.

—————— (1994) *A Journey through Economic Time*. Boston: Houghton Mifflin.

Gale, Robert Peter (1990) 'Chernobyl: Answers Slipping Away.' *The Bulletin of the Atomic Scientists*, September.

Gardner, Martin (ed) (1977) *The Annotated Alice*. Harmondsworth: Penguin Books.

Garrison, Jim (1980) *From Hiroshima to Harrisburg*. London: SCM Press.

George, Susan (1990) 'Managing the Global House: Redefining Economics in a Greenhouse World.' *In* Jeremy Leggett (ed): *Global Warming*. Oxford: Oxford University Press.

Georgescu-Roegen, Nicholas (1974) *The Entropy Law and the Economic Process*. Cambridge Mass.: Harvard University Press.

—— (1976) *Energy and Economic Myths*. New York: Pergamon Press.

—— (1983) 'The Promethean Condition of Viable Technologies.' *Materials and Society*, Nos. 3/4.

—— (1986) 'Man and Production.' *In* Mauro Baranzini and Roberto Scazzieri (eds): *Foundations of Economics*. Oxford: Basil Blackwell.

Gibbon, Edward (1977) *The Decline and Fall of the Roman Empire*. New York: The Modern library.

Gibbs, Nancy (1990) 'Homeless, USA.' *Time*, 17 December.

Gibson, Daniel (1991) 'Can Alchemy Solve the Nuclear Waste Problem? *The Bulletin of the Atomic Scientists*, July/August.

Gillispie, Charles Coulston (1973) *The Edge of Objectivity*. Princeton: Princeton University Press.

Glassman, James K. (1993) 'The Great Bank Robbery.' *In* Robert Emmet Long (ed): *Banking Scandals: S&L's and the BCCI*. New York: H.W. Wilson.

Glynn, Lenny (1993) 'Who Really Made the S&L Mess?' *In* Robert Emmet Long (ed): *Banking Scandals: S&L's and the BCCI*. New York: H.W. Wilson.

Goodgame, Dan (1993) 'Welfare for the Well-off.' *Time*, 22 February.

Gore, Senator Al (1992) *Earth in the Balance*. Boston: Houghton Mifflin.

Grier, Peter (1992) 'Cold War Over, But US Continues Designing New Nuclear Weapons.' *The Christian Science Monitor*, 23 July.

Griffiths, Dave (1990) 'Business as Usual at the Pentagon.' *Business Week*, April 16.

Grossman, Dan and **Shulman, Seth** (1990) 'Down in the Dumps.' *Discover*, April.

Guppy, Nicholas (1984) 'Tropical Doforestation: A Global View.' *Foreign Affairs*, Spring.

Hackworth, David H. (1992a) 'When No One Wanted to Fight.' *Newsweek*, 24 February.

—— (1992b) 'You in Congress, Listen Up.' *Newsweek*, 8 June.

Haq, Mehbub ul (1993) *Human Development Report 1993*. Delhi: Oxford University Press.

Hardin, Garrett (1993) *Living Within Limits*. New York: Oxford University Press.

Harrod, Roy F. (1951) *The Life of John Maynard Keynes*. London: Macmillan.

—— (1983) 'John Maynard Keynes.' *In* John Cunningham Wood (ed): *John Maynard Keynes: Critical Assessments*, Vol. I. London: Croom Helm.

Hartung, William D. (1995) 'The Speaker from Lockheed?' *The Nation*, 30 January.

Hawking, Stephen (1988) *A Brief History of Time*. Toronto: Bantam Books.

Heilbroner, Robert (1993) *21st Century Capitalism*. New York: W.W. Norton.

—— (1994) 'Acts of an Apostle.' *The New York Review of Books*, 3 March.

Heisenberg, Werner (1972) 'Rationality in Science and Society.' *In* G.R. Urban (ed): *Can We Survive Our Future?* London: The Bodley Head.

Henry, Jules (1963) *Culture Against Man*. New York: Vintage Books.

Hicks, John R. (1972) *Value and Capital*. London: Oxford University Press.

—— (1983) *Classics and Moderns*. Oxford: Basil Blackwell.

Hightower, Jim (1989) 'Foreword.' *To* Blumberg, Louis and Gottlieb, Robert: *War on Waste*. Washington DC.: Island Press.

Holroyd, Michael (1971) *Lytton Strachey: A Biography*. London: Heinemann.

Horan, Jack (1988) 'Savannah Reactors: On Line and in Trouble.' *The Bulletin of the Atomic Scientists*, January/February.

Howe, Neil and **Longman, Phillip** (1992) 'The Next New Deal.' *The Atlantic Monthly*, April.

Hubbert, M. King (1987) 'Exponential Growth as a Transient Phenomenon in Human History.' *In* Margaret A. Strom (ed): *Societal Issues: Scientific Viewpoints*. New York: American Institute of Physics.

Huxley, Julian (1959) 'Introduction ' *To* Pierre Teilhard de Chardin: *The Phenomenon of Man*. London: Collins.

Illich, Ivan (1974) *Energy and Equity*. London: Calder & Boyars.

—————— (1976) *Limits to Medicine*. Harmondsworth: Penguin Books.

Isaacs, John (1993) 'Bottoms Up.' *The Bulletin of Atomic Scientists*, November.

—————— (1994) 'Not in My District.' *The Bulletin of the Atomic Scientists*, September/October.

Jensen, Bernard and **Anderson, Mark** (1990) *Empty Harvest*. Garden City Park: Avery.

Jevons, W. Stanley (1957) *The Theory of Political Economy*. New York: Kelley and Millman.

Johnson, Elizabeth (1973) 'John Maynard Keynes: Scientist or Politician?' *In* Joan Robinson (ed): *After Keynes*. Oxford: Basil Blackwell.

Johnson, Paul (1990) *Intellectuals*. New York: Harper & Row.

Jonas, Hans (1984) *The Imperative of Responsibility*. Chicago: The University of Chicago Press.

Jones, Philip D. and **Wigley, Tom M.L.** (1990) 'Global Warming Trends.' *Scientific American*, August.

Kaldor, Mary (1984) 'Flourishing, Worldwide, Deadly.' *Britannica Book of the Year 1984*.

Keepin, Bill (1990) 'Nuclear Power and Global Warming.' *In* Jeremy Leggett (ed): *Global Warming*. Oxford: Oxford University Press.

Keju-Johnson, Darlene (1983) 'Marshall Islands, Mon Amour.' *In* The World Council of Churches: *Marshall Islands: 37 Years After*. Geneva: WCC Press.

Kerr, Richard A. (1988) 'No Longer Wilful, Gaia Becomes Respectable.' *Science*, 22 April.

—————— (1992) 'New Assaults Seen on Earth's Ozone Shield.' *Science*, 14 February.

Kirkpatrick, David (1990) 'Can Power Lines Give You Cancer?' *Fortune*, 31 December.

Knight, Frank (1951) *The Ethics of Competition*. London: Allen & Unwin.

Koestler, Arthur (1980) *Bricks to Babel*. London: Hutchinson.

—————— (1981) *Kaleidoscope*. London: Hutchinson.

Kozol, Jonathan (1993) 'Let's "Throw" Money at the Pentagon and Allocate it to Education.' *The Education Digest*, January.

Kramer, Aaron (1984) 'Hiroshima.' *In* Jim Schley (ed): *Writing in a Nuclear Age*. Hanover: University Press of New England.

Kuhn, Thomas S. (1973) *The Structure of Scientific Revolutions*. Chicago: The University of Chicago Press.

—————— (1981) *The Copernican Revolution.* Cambridge Mass.: Harvard University Press.

Leggett, Jeremy (1992) 'Global Warming: The Worst Case.' *The Bulletin of the Atomic Scientists*, June.

Lekachman, Robert (1967) *The Age of Keynes*. Harmondsworth: Penguin Books.

Lemonick, Michael D. (1992) 'The Ozone Vanishes.' *Time*, 17 February.

Leo, John (1989) 'The Proper Place for Commercials.' *U.S. New & World Report*, 30 October.

Leonard, John (1993) 'Listen to the Dispossessed.' *The Nation*, 1 February.

Leontief, Wassily (1981) 'Big Boosts in Defence Risk Economic Calamity.' *U.S. News & World Report*, 16 March.

—— (1982) 'The Distribution of Work and Income.' *Scientific American*, September.

—— (1983) 'Technological Advance, Economic Growth, and the Distribution of Income.' *Population and Development Review*, September.

Levine, Art and **Silverstein, Ken** (1993) 'How the Drug Lobby Cut Cost Controls.' *The Nation*, 13 December.

Lewis, James (1992) 'Iraqi Arms Scandal.' *The Guardian Weekly*, 22 November.

Lifton, Robert Jay (1993) 'Beware the Realists.' *The Nation*, 1 February.

Lovelock, James E. (1987) *Gaia: A New Look at Life on Earth*. Oxford: Oxford University Press.

—— (1989) *The Ages of Gaia*. Oxford: Oxford University Press.

Lown, Bernard (1993) *A Physician's Perspective on Global Priorities*. New Delhi: Association of Indian Diplomats.

Lumpe, Lora (1994) 'Sweet Deals, Stolen Jobs.' *The Bulletin of the Atomic Scientists*, September/October.

Macaulay T.B. (Lord) (1937) *Literary Essays*. London: Oxford University Press.

Machlup, Fritz (1974) 'Proxies and Dummies.' *Journal of Political Economy*, July/August.

Macpherson, C.B. (1988) *The Political Theory of Possessive Individualism*. Oxford: Oxford University Press.

Magnuson, (ed) (1990) 'A Cover-Up on Agent Orange?' *Time*, 23 July.

Mann, Paul (1991) 'Unisys Admits Bribery and Fraud.' *Aviation Week & Space Technology*, 16 September.

Mannoni, O. (1968) *Prospero and Caliban*. New York: Praeger.

Marmor, Theodore R. and **Godfrey, John** (1992) 'Canada's Medical System is a Model.' *The New York Times*, 23 July.

Marshall, Alfred (1974) *Principles of Economics*. London: Macmillan.

Mathews, Jay (1992) 'Rethinking Homeless Myths.' *Newsweek*, 6 April.

Matthews, Ron (1991) 'The Neutrals as Gunrunners.' *Orbis*, Winter.

McCuen, Gary E. (1993) 'The Vanishing Forest.' *In* Garry E. McCuen (ed): *Ecocide and Genocide in the Vanishing Forest*. Hudson: GEM Publications.

McDermott, John (1994) 'And the Poor get Poorer.' *The Nation*, 14 November

McKenzie, Aline (1992) 'Nuclear Arms Labs See More Tasks Ahead.' *San Ramon Valley Times*, 31 May.

McNamee, Mike (1992) 'Can't Live with 'Em, Can't Live without 'Em.' *Business Week*, 7 September.

Medawar, Charles (1979) *Insult or Injury?* London: Social Audit.

Medoff, James (1994) 'Why Business is Axing Older Workers.' *U.S. News & World Report*, 31 October.

Mills, C. Wright (1959) *The Causes of World War Three*. London: Secker & Warburg.

Mills, C. Wright (1972) *The Power Elite*. New York: Oxford University Press.

Milton, John (1958) *Prose Writings*. London: J.M. Dent.

Mintz, Morton (1991) 'Tobacco Roads.' *The Progressive*, May.

Mishan, E. J. (1981) *Economic Efficiency and Social Welfare*. London: Allen and Unwin.

────── (1986) *Economic Myths and the Mythology of Economics*. Brighton: Wheatsheaf Books.

Morgenstern, Oskar (1972) 'Thirteen Critical Point in Contemporary Economic Theory.' *The Journal of Economic Literature*, December.

Morowitz, Harold J. (1979) *The Wine of Life*. New York: St. Martin's Press.

Muir, Kenneth (1967) *King Lear*. London: Methuen.

Myers, Norman (1985) *The Gaia Atlas of Planet Management*. London: Pan Books.

Newman, Penny (1992) 'Killing Legally with Toxic Waste.' *Development Dialogue*, 1-2.

Norris, Floyd (1992) 'Paradox of '92: Weak Economy, Strong Profits.' *The New York Times*, 30 August.

O'Connor, Colleen (1993) 'The Waste Goes On—& On & On.' *The Nation*, 4 October.

O'Connor, Richard D. (1989) 'The Future of Advertising.' *Vital Speeches of the Day*, 9 May.

Ornstein, Robert and Ehrlich, Paul (1989) *New World New Mind*. New York: Doubleday.

Orwell, George (1968) *In Front of Your Nose*. London: Secker & Warburg.

Packard, Vance (1951) *The Waste Makers*. Harmondsworth: Penguin Books.

Paddock, William and Paul (1968) *Famine—1975!* London: Weidenfeld and Nicholson.

Palme, Olof et al. (1982) *Common Security*. London: Pan Books.

Palmer, Edward L. (1988) *Television and America's Children*. New York: Oxford University Press.

Perkovich George (1992) 'Weapons Complexes v. Democracy.' *The Bulletin of the Atomic Scientists*, June.

Peterson, Peter (1984) 'Introduction' *To* James L. Clayton: *On the Brink*. New York: Ramapo Press.

────── (1988) 'Get the Rich off the Dole.' *Time*, 31 October.

Pigou, A.C. (ed) (1966) *Memorials of Alfred Marshall*. New York: Augustus M. Kelly.

Polanyi, Karl (1968) *The Great Transformation*. Boston: Beacon Press.

Pollock, Cynthia (1986) 'Decommissioning Nuclear Power Plants.' *State of the World 1986*.

Pomice, Eva (1989) 'Putting Their Best Face Forward.' *U.S. News & World Report*, 12 June.

Postel, Sandra (1992) 'Denial in the Decisive Decade.' *State of the World 1992*.

Press, Aric (1984) 'A Fast Deal on Agent Orange.' *Newsweek*, 21 May.

Press, Eyal (1994) 'Prez Pampers Peddlers of Pain.' *The Nation*, 3 October.

Prigogine, Ilya (1984) 'Only an Illusion.' *In* Sterling M. McMurrin (ed): *The Tanner Lectures on Human Values 1984*. Salt Lake City: The University of Utah Press.

Puckett, Jim (1994) 'Disposing of the Waste Trade.' *The Ecologist*, March/April.

Rauschning, Hermann (1939) *Hitler Speaks*. London: Thornton Butterworth.

Redfield, Robert (1959) 'Talk with a Stranger.' *In* Morton H. Fried (ed):*Readings in Cultural Anthropology*. New York: Thomas Crowell.

Renner, Michael (1991) 'Assessing the Military's War on the Environment.' *State of the World 1991*.

Renner, Michael (1994) 'Cleaning Up After the Arms Race.' *State of the World 1994.*

Ritchie-Calder, Lord (1970) 'The Atomic Age Environment.' *In* Grants S. McClellan (ed): *Protecting Our Environment.* New York: H.W. Wilson Company.

Robbins, Lionel (1949) *An Essay on the Nature and Significance of Economic Science.* London: Macmillan.

Robinson, Joan (1966) *Economic Philosophy.* Harmondsworth: Penguin Books.

—— (1973) *Collected Economic Papers,* Vol. I. Oxford: Basil Blackwell.

—— (1979) *Collected Economic Papers,* Vol. II. Oxford: Basil Blackwell.

—— (1983) 'The Economics of Destruction.' *Monthly Review,* October.

Robinson, Richard (1970) *Definition.* London: Oxford University Press.

Romm, Joseph J. (1992) 'Laid Waste by Weapons Lust.' *The Bulletin of the Atomic Scientists,* October.

Rossolimo, Alexander N. (1993) 'The Post-Soviet Nuclear Threats are even Bigger.' *International Herald Tribune,* 15-16 May.

Rothstein, Linda (1992) 'No Party for Star Wars.' *The Bulletin of the Atomic Scientists,* June.

Ruff, Tilman (1990) 'Bomb Tests Attack the Food Chain.' *The Bulletin of the Atomic Scientists,* March.

Russell, Bertrand (1956) *Portraits from Memory and Other Essays.* London: Allen & Unwin.

—— (1967) *War Crimes in Vietnam.* London: Allen & Unwin.

—— (1979) *History of Western Philosophy.* London: Allen & Unwin.

Sagan, Carl (1985) 'Star Wars Won't Work.' *Discover,* September.

—— (1992) 'Between Enemies.' *The Bulletin of the Atomic Scientists,* May.

Sampson, Anthony (1992) 'Iraq Export Trial.' *The Times,* 11 November.

Samuelson, Paul A. (1948) *Economics.* New York: McGraw-Hill.

—— (1951) *Economics.* New York: McGraw-Hill.

—— (1961) *Economics.* New York: McGraw-Hill.

—— (1966a) 'The Economics of War.' *Newsweek,* 21 November.

—— (1966b) *The Collected Scientific Papers of Paul A. Samuelson,* Vol. II. Cambridge Mass.: The MIT Press.

—— (1967a) 'Social Security.' *Newsweek,* 13 February.

—— (1967b) 'Keeping the Score.' *Newsweek,* 1 May.

—— (1967c) 'Population.' *Newsweek,* 12 June.

—— (1972) *The Collected Scientific Papers of Paul A. Samuelson,* Vol. III. Cambridge Mass.: The MIT Press.

—— (1973) *Economics.* New York: McGraw-Hill.

—— (1976) *Economics.* New York: McGraw-Hill.

—— (1979) *The Collected Scientific Papers of Paul A. Samuelson,* Vol. IV. Cambridge Mass.: The MIT Press.

—— (1980) *Economics.* New York: McGraw-Hill.

—— (1983) *Economics from the Heart.* New York: Harcourt Brace.

—— (1986) *The Collected Scientific Papers of Paul A. Samuelson,* Vol. V. Cambridge Mass.: The MIT Press.

Samuelson, Paul A. and **Nordhaus, William D.** (1989) *Economics.* New York: McGraw-Hill.

—— (1992) *Economics.* New York: McGraw-Hill.

Samuelson, Paul A. et al. (1966) 'Panel Discussion.' *Newsweek,* 10 January.

Satchell, Michael (1992) 'The Rape of the Oceans.' *U.S. News & World Report*, 22 June.

Schefold, Bertram (1983) 'The General Theory for a Totalitarian State?' *In* John Cunningham Wood (ed): *John Maynard Keynes: Critical Assessments*, Vol. I. London: Croom Helm.

Schine, Eric (1991) 'The $75 Billion Question.' *Business Week*, 8 April.

Schmalensee, Richard (1987) 'Advertising.' *The New Palgrave*.

Schobel, Bruce D. (1992) 'Sooner Than You Think.' *Policy Review*, Fall.

Schrödinger, Erwin (1984) *Collected Papers*, Vol. I. Vienna: The Austrian Academy of Sciences.

Schumacher, Diana (1985) *Energy: Crisis or Opportunity?* London: Macmillan.

Schumacher, E.F. (1976) *Small is Beautiful*. London: Blond & Briggs.

Schumpeter, Joseph A. (1961) *Capitalism, Socialism and Democracy*. London: Allen & Unwin.

Schwartz, John (1991) 'The $93 Billion Dogfight.' *Business Week*, 6 May.

Schwarz, John E. and **Volgy, Thomas J.** (1993) 'Above the Poverty Line—But Poor.' *The Nation*, 15 February.

Schwarz, Walter (1989) 'Economic Growth as a Cancer Destroying the Planet.' *The Guardian Weekly*, 3 September.

Shackleton, Lord (1977) 'Introduction.' *To* Rachel Carson: *Silent Spring*. Harmondsworth: Penguin Books.

Shaw, George Bernard (1962a) *Complete Plays with Prefaces*, Vol. I. New York: Dodd, Mead & Company.

——— (1962b) *Complete Plays with Prefaces*, Vol. III. New York: Dodd, Mead & Company.

Shirer, William L. (1990) *The Rise and Fall of the Third Reich: A History of Nazi Germany*. New York: Simon and Schuster.

Sidel, Ruth (1994) 'The Welfare Scam.' *The Nation*, 12 December.

Singer, Daniel (1995) 'The Stench of Corruption.' *The Nation*, 2 January.

Singh, Narindar (1989) *Economics and the Crisis of Ecology*. London: Bellew Publishing.

Sivard, Ruth Leger (1991) *World Military and Social Expenditures 1991*.

——— (1993) *World Military and Social Expenditures 1993*.

Skidelsky, Robert (1992) 'If Keynes Ruled Our World.' *The Guardian Weekly*, 15 November.

Smith, Jeffrey R. (1993) 'Aspin Takes "Star Wars" Down to Earth.' *International Herald Tribune*, 15–16 May.

Soddy, Frederick (1922) *Cartesian Economics*. London: Henderson.

——— (1924) *The Inversion of Science*. London: Henderson.

——— (1953) *Memoirs of Frederick Soddy*. Muriel Howorth (ed): London: New World Publications.

Solow, Robert M. (1974) 'The Economics of Resources or the Resources of Economics.' *The American Economic Review*, May.

Specter, Michael (1992) 'New York Ending Ocean Dumping, But Not Problems.' *The New York Times*, 29 June.

Sperry, Roger (1982) 'Some Effects of Disconnecting the Cerebral Hemispheres.' *Science*, 24 September.

——— (1983) *Science and Moral Priority*. Oxford: Basil Blackwell.

Steingraber, Sandra and **Hurley, Judith** (1993) 'Foreign Interests Threaten the Forest.' In Gary E. McCuen (ed): *Ecocide and Genocide*. Hudson: GEM Publications.

Steinhart, John S. and **Steinhart, Carol E.** (1974) 'Energy Use in the US Food System.' *Science*, 19 April.

Stengel, Richard (1987) 'Khashoggi's High-Flying Realm.' *Time*, 19 January.

Stiehm, Janie (1993) 'If You're Clever—And Very Rich.' *The Nation*, 18 October.

Stone, Richard (1992) 'Swimming Against the PCB Tide.' *Science*, 14 February.

Subramaniam, Chitra (1993) *Bofors: The Story Behind the News*. New Delhi: Penguin Books.

Summers, Lawrence (1992) Letter to *The Economist*, 15 February.

Sweezy, Paul (1983) 'John Maynard Keynes.' In John Cunningham Wood (ed): *John Maynard Keynes: Critical Assessments*, Vol. I. London: Croom Helm.

—— (1991) 'What's New in the New World Order?' *Monthly Review*, June.

Swift, Jonathan (1978) *Gulliver's Travels*. Harmondsworth: Penguin Books.

Taylor, Steven T. and **Mintz, Morton** (1991) 'A Word From Your Friendly Drug Co.' *The Nation*, 21 October.

Tedder, Lord (1975) 'Foreword.' To H.R. Trevor-Roper: *The Last Days of Hitler*. New York: Collier Books.

Teilhard de Chardin, Pierre (1959) *The Phenomenon of Man*. London: Collins.

—— (1969) *The Future of Man*. New York: Harper & Row.

Terris, Milton (1990) 'A Wasteful System that Doesn't Work.' *The Progressive*, October.

Thompson, William Irwin (1987) 'Gaia and the Politics of Life.' In William Irwin Thompson (ed): *Gaia: A Way of Knowing*. Great Barrington: Lindisfarne Press.

Tinbergen, Jan and **Fischer, Dietrich** (1987) *Warfare and Welfare*. Sussex: Wheatsheaf Books.

Toffler, Alvin (1984) 'Foreword.' To Ilya Prigogine and Isabelle Stengers: *Order out of Chaos*. Toronto: Bantam Books.

Trenn, Thaddeus J. (1979) 'The Central Role of Energy in Soddy's Holistic and Critical Approach to Nuclear Science, Economic and Social Responsibility.' *The British Journal for the History of Science*, November.

Trevor-Roper, H.R. (1975) *The Last Days of Hitler*. New York: Collier Books.

Van der Vat, Dan (1987) 'How the West Recruited Nazis for the Post-War Effort.' *The Guardian Weekly*, 8 March.

Vidal, John (1993) 'Drawing the Poison out of Russia.' *The Guardian Weekly*, 16 May.

Voltaire (1969) *Candide and Other Tales*. Geneva: Edito-Service.

Walsh, Michael P. (1990) 'Motor Vehicles and Global Warming.' In Jeremy Leggett (ed): *Global Warming*. Oxford: Oxford University Press.

Wasserman, Harvey and **Solomon, Norman** (1982) *Killing Our Own*. New York: Delacorte Press.

Weiner, Tim (1992), 'The Pentagon's Secret Stash.' *Mother Jones*, March/April.

Weir, David and **Schapiro, Mark** (1981) 'The Circle of Poison.' *The Ecologist*, May/June.

Weir, David and **Porterfield, Andrew** (1989) 'US Exports Hazardous Wastes to the Third World.' In, *Toxic Terror*. Penang: Third World Network.

Weisskopf, Victor F. (1972) *Physics in the Twentieth Century*. Cambridge, Mass.: The MIT Press.

Whitaker, J.K. (1987) 'Ceteris Paribus.' *The New Palgrave*.

Whitehead, Alfred North (1964) *The Concept of Nature*. Cambridge: Cambridge University Press.

——— (1968) *Modes of Thought*. New York: The Free Press.

——— (1975) *Science and the Modern World*. Glasgow: Fontana.

Wilde, Oscar (1970) *Plays*. Harmondsworth: Penguin Books.

Wilkes, Michael S. et al. (1992) 'Pharmaceutical Advertisements in Leading Medical Journals: Experts' Assessments.' *Annals of Internal Medicine*, 1 June.

Williams, Raymond (1985) *Towards 2000*. Harmondsworth: Penguin Books.

Wilson, Douglas C. and **Rathje, William L.** (1990) 'Modern Middens.' *Natural History*, May.

Worster, Donald (1985) *Nature's Economy*. Cambridge: Cambridge University Press.

Wright, James D. (1989) 'Address Unknown: Homelessness in Contemporary America.' *Society*, September/October.

Young, Hugo (1989) 'Reaching for the Moon at an Unearthly Price.' *The Guardian Weekly*, 23 July.

Young, John E. (1992) 'It's Time to Toss Out the Throwaway Habit.' *USA Today*, September.